ARMED

THE ESSENTIAL GUIDE
TO CONCEALED CARRY

Bruce N. Eimer, Ph.D

FOREWORD BY MASSAD AYOOB

Published by

Gun Digest® Books, an imprint of F+W Media, Inc.
Krause Publications • 700 East State Street • Iola, WI 54990-0001
715-445-2214 • 888-457-2873
www.krausebooks.com

To order books or other products call toll-free 1-800-258-0929
or visit us online at www.gundigeststore.com

ISBN-13: 978-1-4402-3000-4
ISBN-10: 1-4402-3000-5

683.43

Designed by Al West
Edited by Jennifer L.S. Pearsall

Printed in USA

Acknowledgements

Many thanks go to the United States Concealed Carry Association (USCCA; www.USConcealedCarry.com) and Delta Media, the publisher of *Concealed Carry Magazine*, for whom I have been a regular column contributor since its inception eight years ago. Much of the material in this book is adapted from my column that appears there, "The Armed Senior Citizen." Special thanks and my sincere gratitude go to USCCA Founder and CEO, Tim Schmidt, and my Editor at *Concealed Carry Magazine*, Kathy Jackson, for their support and for gifting me with the opportunity of writing and publishing my ideas in their publications.

My sincere and special thanks and gratitude also go to my friend and teacher, Massad Ayoob (www.MassadAyoobGroup.com), for a lot more than just agreeing to write the foreword to this book. Mas has taught me a lot about guns, tactics, and a whole lot of essential skills. He is responsible for educating me and so many other "good guys" about how to stay "good guys." His contributions to my knowledge, as well as to the entire field of citizens' lawful and judicious self-defense, have been gigantic.

I wish to gratefully acknowledge the folks at www.HumanEvents.com and www.GunsandPatriots.com for giving me the privilege of writing for them on a regular basis about armed personal-defense.

I also wish to express my appreciation and gratitude to my friends at Gun Digest/Krause Publications and F+W Media without whose faith in my work and help this book would not have been put together. First, I wish to acknowledge the late Dan Shideler, who was enthused about my project from the outset, when we met at the 2011 SHOT Show in Las Vegas. Second, I wish to give my heartfelt thanks to the Publisher, Jim Schlender, who has also been enthusiastic and supportive of me about this project from the outset and made it happen. Last but not least, I want to thank my Editor at Gun Digest, Jennifer L.S. Pearsall, for her incisive advice, editing, guidance, and coaching.

Many thanks go to my friend and colleague Roger Mullins, master electrician, photographer, and professional gun operator, for his help in taking and providing some of the photographs in this book.

Last but not least, I owe much of the material in this book to my defensive firearms students, those who have trained with me individually, as well as those who have taken my concealed carry permit classes. There is no better way to learn than to teach. I love teaching, and I always learn something new from my students. To all of the folks who have chosen to train with me, I thank you.

About the Author

Bruce N. Eimer, Ph.D. is a clinical psychologist, NRA Certified Law Enforcement Firearms Instructor, Certified Utah Concealed Firearms Instructor, and a professional writer. His daily work includes practicing clinical psychology, conducting forensic evaluations, writing, and training people in the defensive use of firearms through his company, Personal Defense Solutions, LLC (www.PersonalDefenseSolutions.net). Doctor. Eimer has testified as an expert witness in civil, criminal, gun rights, and self-defense cases. He is the owner of the popular online forum, www.DefensiveHandguns.com and writes the monthly "Armed Senior Citizen" column for *Concealed Carry Magazine* (www.USConcealedCarry.com). Doctor Eimer is the co-author of the *Essential Guide To Handguns* (Looseleaf Law Publications, 2005) and has contributed articles to various gun magazines such as *Combat Handguns* and www.GunsAndPatriots.com. He has also authored psychology textbooks and self-help books such as, *Hypnotize Yourself Out Of Pain Now!* (2008) and *Coping With Uncertainty: 10 Simple Solutions* (2011).

Contents

Preface

The first law of nature is self preservation. Most animals, and even plants, are born with protective physical mechanisms to ward off natural predators. Human beings are born with a highly developed brain, at once our most dangerous and formidable weapon. Our ability to use symbols, tools, to delay gratification, and to think abstractly has allowed us to evolve as much as we have. It is because of our mental complexity and our abilities to solve most problems that we are the top predator in the animal kingdom.

Yet, from a physical standpoint, human beings are inferior to many predatory animals. Our strength and place at the top of the food chain come from our intellect or mental intelligence. We can devise and use all manner of tools, readily adapt to different circumstances and environments, and hunt and defeat larger and stronger beasts through a combination of both. But ,our greatest enemy as a species is ourselves. Any given individual's survival can be hampered by other predatory humans (i.e., violent criminals) and by predatory governments that are for themselves, rather than for their citizens.

It has been said that, "God created men, but that Sam Colt made them equal." Nowhere is that more evident than in the history of peoples who rose up against and overthrew their oppressors. Look at some examples in history. There is the classic Bible story in of the armed Judean Maccabees, who rebelled against King Antiochus, who had outlawed the practice of the Jewish religion. There is the unforgettable story of the armed Polish Jew's uprising against the German Nazis in the Warsaw ghetto during World War II. And there is our own country's valiant story of the American Revolution for independence from the British, during Colonial times. These stories and many others tell the tale of peoples who were disarmed by their oppressors and who found a way to become armed and fight back against tyranny.

Firearms are the great equalizer. They allow mankind to hunt larger and stronger animals, they are the means through which outnumbered rebels have managed to overthrow oppressive, tyrannical regimes, and, for those who have the disadvantage of suffering a physical infirmity that limits you in a bare-knuckled fight against an opponent, owning and having been trained to employ a firearm can be an effective means of personal-defense.

I am physically challenged. I suffer from a number of conditions, such as rheumatoid and degenerative arthritis, chronic pain, and spinal deformities. These conditions impair my physical strength, flexibility, endurance, and speed of motion. They also have limited my muscular development and the extent to which I can roll around on the floor and grapple with an opponent in a fight. Therefore, for me, the gun is an essential tool for personal defense.

Of course, the gun is not my only personal-defense tool. It's not even my best. That charge falls to my mind. My judgment, awareness, and efforts to stay out of harm's way are paramount to my safety. I have also studied less-than-lethal personal defense methods and tactics. Some of these are addressed in the chapters here, and while I'm no martial artist, the point is that, no matter how skilled you are at fighting, there are times when only a firearm will give you a chance to prevail and survive.

One is well advised, especially if one carries a firearm, to go to all lengths possible to avoid social confrontations. However, if a conflict cannot be avoided, and you are in a place where you have a right to be and you cannot safely retreat, you will have no other choice but to defend yourself with a level of necessary force. It is a matter of survival.

We shall address the judicious use of deadly force, and appropriate rules for engagement and disengagement, extensively in this book. However, the point I am making here is this: If you are accosted by someone who is bigger, stronger or more skilled at fighting than you, such that your life or limb are in imminent danger unless you go to a greater degree of force than you are capable of mustering with your own two hands and feet, you have the right to step up to the use of deadly force. As I said before, the gun is the great equalizer, as it has been throughout history, and unless you have initiated the fight or caused it to escalate out of control, you are justified in using the gun to defend your innocent life or the innocent lives of those who are under your mantle of protection. Keep in mind the key word here is "innocent." You, as the defender, must be the innocent party, and so must be the people you are defending.

This is why I have written this book. When you make the choice to carry a gun, you are taking on a serious responsibility. There are multitude considerations you need to think though and come to terms with. You must obtain necessary and appropriate mental and physical training with the equipment and gear you choose to carry. You must learn the rules of engagement and disengagement in social confrontations. You must become familiar with the laws as they apply to the use of force and self-defense. You must understand your rights, your lawful roles, your duties and obligations, your capabilities, and your limitations. This book will address these essential considerations. That is why I have chosen to title this book, *Armed—The Essential Guide to Concealed Carry*.

I wish to take responsibility at the outset for being very opinionated. My devotion to effective personal-defense solutions will come through sharply in the pages that follow. I am no politician. I am also not shy about expressing my beliefs when it comes to self-protection. I do not accept the idea that we should sit idly by and accept when others exercise their First Amendment rights to attack our Second Amendment rights.

Given my own physical limitations, I understand firsthand the importance of having the freedom to keep and bear arms. For me, the Second Amendment is all about personal and self-defense, something each individual must take responsibility for. We cannot afford to rely on the police or the government to protect us.

—Bruce N. Eimer, Ph.D.

Foreword

It's an honor to be asked to write the foreword for Bruce Eimer's book, because *Armed* isn't merely one more of the plethora of CCW (carry concealed weapons) books now on the market. While all his information is solid, Bruce brings two particular strengths to the topic.

First, of course, he's a practicing clinical psychologist, with extensive experience in areas related to armed self-defense. It shows in his approach. He understands what has to be going on in the defender's mind before, during, and after an encounter—and he prepares his readers to understand that long before any steel clears leather or any triggers need to be pulled.

The use of lethal force in self-defense is, by definition, a near-death experience. It triggers body alarm reaction, the most intense form of which is known as the "fight or flight" response. Ancient survival instincts kick in, causing us to focus on the threat in a way that tunnels vision, interferes with hearing, and otherwise alters our perceptions. It doesn't happen to everyone, but it happens more often than not, and the potential defender needs to be aware of it beforehand. Doctor Eimer understands these things—things I've been researching and explaining for some 40 years now—and does an excellent job of getting them across to his students and readers.

To prevail in a savage gun battle with a violent criminal, an encounter that may last only three seconds or so, one must have prepared well ahead with mental and emotional conditioning. That three-second street fight may trigger a criminal justice system response that might not be concluded for more than a year, and a civil court lawsuit that will seldom be resolved in less than a year. The "Mark of Cain syndrome"—people seeing you differently because at one time in your life you killed a man—is something you'll probably have to deal with until you take your last breath, and, even then, you can bet someone will mention the long-ago shooting at your funeral. Psychologist and firearms instructor Bruce Eimer wisely prepares you for that, too.

Having seen Dr. Eimer as a student and as a lecturer, I can tell you he's good at both. As a student, he absorbs, analyzes, and incorporates. As a speaker and instructor, he relates to his audience and knows how to powerfully communicate the things they need to know.

Another of Bruce's long-term specialties has been adapting defensive doctrine, including shooting, to those who are physically challenged, whether by illness, injury, or age. He has much sound advice in this book that covers this area.

As a psychologist who understands the gun, and as a committed "advanced student" of the art and science of armed self-defense and the management of its aftermath, Bruce Eimer brings much to the table that is lacking in some other quarters of self-defense training. This, his newest book, is a most worthwhile read, and one I encourage you to take seriously.

—Massad Ayoob, November 23, 2011

CHAPTER 1

Your Safety—Own It

The world is a dangerous place, and, ultimately, you can rely only on yourself to keep safe. It is a myth that the police are in business to protect you and your loved ones. The police are outnumbered by the criminal elements in society, those bad people just waiting to take advantage of a disaster. As we witnessed in New Orleans after Hurricane Katrina, bad characters are ready to capitalize on other people's misfortunes. When the police and firefighters are overwhelmed, such people come out of their holes to loot, rob, rape, pillage, and vandalize. It's worse than a Capitol One commercial.

If you wait until disaster strikes, it will be too late. Now is the time to get the education, training, and equipment that can save your life and the lives of those you love if and when our world turns into a Mel Gibson *Road Warrior* movie. Of course the inner cities are racked with crime, but, even if you live in the suburbs or in the country, you can be targeted by violent criminals. It happens everyday. Crime is rampant. We are totally safe nowhere.

Violent criminals are opportunists. They look for easy prey, people who have not prepared themselves to be hard targets, people who think that, if their alarm goes off in the middle of the night, somehow the police will magically show up in time to save them, and, of course, people who don't even give this stuff a first or second thought. But, the fact is, we are all responsible for protecting ourselves.

A Weighty Responsibility

You hear many clichés in the gun community. Some examples: "An armed society is a polite society;" "Better to be judged by 12 than carried by six;" "A gun should be comforting, not comfortable;" "Don't draw your gun unless you are going to use it," and so on. What's important to remember is that clichés are just generalizations, and generalizations are oversimplifications. Reality is seldom simple, and if you carry a gun, it could be hazardous to your health and your freedom to be simple-minded or ignorant.

The gun is analogous to the fire extinguisher. It is an emergency rescue tool. If you really need one, you really need it badly, because you've found yourself in a violent, life-threatening emergency. Since no one's capable of predicting the future, it makes sense to play it safe and purchase insurance. Carrying a defensive handgun is one form of that insurance.

With that said, how many of us fully read our insurance policies? How many of us understand the language in one? Not being a glutton for punishment, I have fallen asleep more than once after reading beyond my homeowner's policy declarations page.

It is essential to recognize that having a license to carry firearms does not make you a cop or a lawyer. However, it is wise to know something about the law as it pertains to self-defense. Carrying the great power of deadly force on you gives you great responsibility, but it is *not* the same degree of responsibility as that of a police officer sworn to preserve and protect. The responsibility I am talking about is the responsibility to stay away from trouble as best as you can, and to avoid instigating or escalating social conflicts that can turn bad on a dime.

Sworn police officers are mandated to employ *necessary force* to fulfill their duties under the law. As a private citizen, you are limited to using *equal force*, better defined as the same or a little more force than that employed by your opponent. But, real life just isn't simple. If another adult physically attacks you, how can you be certain that he or she doesn't have a deadly weapon? The fact is you cannot. If you value your life and limb, you must be prepared to escalate your level of force up the continuum to that which will counter the bad guy's actions.

Clearly, when you carry a gun, the power of potential deadly force goes with you into every social conflict you encounter. With greater power comes greater responsibility, and this calls for different rules of conduct than when you go unarmed.

Since we all have our moments, reminding ourselves that we are carrying can serve as a sobering thought. I can recall a recent embarrassing moment, when I lost control of my tongue. I was, at least from my point of view, being treated rudely. It was one minute after last call to the register at a bookstore that was going out of business and selling everything at twenty-five cents on the dollar. I had been there for more than an hour accumulating a stack of books to purchase. The sales clerk refused to ring me out and told me to leave. I protested politely, at first. She smirked and said, "Leave *now!*" I became angry and called her a bastard. She called her manager. The manager told me to leave. I protested that I just wanted to purchase the books I had spent over an hour finding. She threatened to call the police. I was carrying a gun, so I left without the books.

Do you think that situation would have gone downhill fast if I'd persisted in insisting she ring my order out? She'd already rung me out! Was there any way to know what a police officer would do if the manager had called the police and I'd waited around to protest? The irate store manager would have claimed I was harassing her employee, and I would have tried to explain my side of the story—but I'd let my tongue slip, and I was armed! It was too bad for me. I had not remained polite. I did not want to wait around to find out what some young police officer's position was on the license to carry!

When we carry a firearm on our bodies, we need to keep a low profile and avoid social conflicts. If a social conflict finds you and you are carrying, it is wise to avoid saying or doing anything that might be construed as escalating the conflict. Back off. Nothing good can come from continuing an argument.

This is the sacrifice we make when we go armed, because, as I said earlier, the power of potential deadly force goes with us into every social conflict we encounter. Carrying a gun is a sobering reminder that *we must be responsible for all of our actions at all times*. We must leave our pent-up anger, hyper-sensitivities, and resentments at home. Perhaps the old saying should be re-phrased as "A society with *responsibly* armed citizens is a polite society."

That being said, power is the first thing a criminal intends to take away from you. But, remember that knowledge is power, too. The purpose of this book is to provide you with the knowledge you need to become prepared to assume the serious responsibility of armed self-protection. It is not enough to simply buy a gun. You need to learn how to use it, and you need to learn when and when not to use it. The responsibility for acquiring the knowledge of defensive measures lies strictly where it belongs, and that is with you.

Statistically, urban dwellers are at much greater jeopardy of criminal assault than are suburban or rural dwellers. Senior citizens and women are more

Training in techniques and tactics for concealed carry is essential, whether you're a beginning handgunner or a practiced marksman. There are many good schools across the country that offer training in a variety of skills, but do your homework, researching which ones offer the tactics you wish to learn, your instructor's resumé, and reviews from past students.

likely to be victims of violent crime than are young and middle-aged men. It is as in the animal kingdom—the sheep and herds have a false sense of security. The proverbial wolf always eyes the weakest herd members, and, if you look like food, you are more likely to be eaten. I'm here to tell you, don't be "sheeple."

Without adequate preparation, your chances of survival are markedly reduced, but there are myriad and essential considerations you must address before you strap on a gun and walk out the door. If you live in a pro-gun rights state and are not a convicted felon, no one will require you have some training before you purchase a gun. For those residing in states that do require a modicum of training as a pre-requisite for obtaining a license to carry or to buy firearms, you can take the required course without much ado or any follow-up. Either approach is foolish. Carrying a handgun and not being educated about the ins and outs of this tremendous responsibility is a poor decision. The issues are complex, and you cannot afford to be ignorant about them. You need to *think* about your decision to go armed.

CHAPTER 2

Everyone Can Learn to Protect Themselves!

People choose to own and carry a handgun for many different reasons. Some simply want to exercise their Second Amendment rights. Others want to feel a sense of empowerment. Many shoot competitively, as a hobby, or to get practice using their handgun in IDPA, IPSC, and other tactical speed-shooting matches. Then there are people who have no experience with firearms and decide that purchasing a handgun and learning to use it safely constitutes a survival necessity. Some folks, like me, believe and feel strongly that over some spilled beer over some spilled beer owning firearms and carrying a gun just make plain sense in today's unpredictable and dangerous world.

As an NRA Certified Firearms Instructor in several disciplines, I get to talk with and provide basic instruction to many folks with little or no experience with firearms. Training folks for whom firearms are foreign and frightening can be hard work. It requires lots of flexibility and the willingness and patience to go over the basics repeatedly. This type of training is certainly not as cool or hip as running a fast-paced defensive handgun training course during which hundreds or even thousands of rounds are fired over a two-day weekend, but it is still very rewarding.

New handgunners often visit a gun shop with the idea of purchasing a handgun, and when faced with all of the choices and unfamiliar terminology, realize that they are not ready to do so. An ethical and experienced firearms salesperson often at this point will recommend that the customer hold off on making a purchase until they have received some basic instruction. It is after this point that I often get a call from the "newbie." (I receive referrals from a number of local gun shops, through word of mouth, and through our website on the Internet, www.PersonalDefenseS-olutions.net.) Many times these calls are from those who have physical and emotional challenges (i.e., lots of anxiety) relative to learning to handle and operate a handgun for personal defense. Not a problem. I was in the same place once myself. I didn't grow up with firearms or hunting. I also have ongoing physical challenges that interfere with the intensity with which I can train tactically, something that also influences what I choose to carry every day.

If you are new to firearms, it is important to realize that there are many choices available. You also need to know that you *can* overcome your anxiety and trepidation. Remember that knowledge is power. This book will provide you with some of the knowledge you need so that you are empowered to make those choices that are right for you.

I am repeatedly gratified to share with my clients/students their joy when they succeed in learning to handle the right handgun for them. However, many of these folks need a kind and gentle hand to guide them to the point where they realize that they are not powerless, that they can handle a serious defensive handgun that had at first intimidated them (and that they didn't have to begin with a .22!) Let me give you an example with the story of just one of my students, "Louise."

Louise was referred to me by the owner of a local gun shop. She called requesting basic handgun instruction to help her acquire the knowledge and comfort level necessary for purchasing a defensive handgun. She had no prior gun ownership or shooting experience and told me that she had severe back problems that limited how long she could stand. We made an appointment for an initial two hour lesson at the local gun club. My plan was to spend the first hour in the classroom going over safety fundamentals and the basic operation and handling of a revolver and a semi-automatic pistol. The second hour was to be devoted to her first experience shooting on the range.

Louise appeared to be a quick learner. She listened attentively and absorbed my preliminary classroom instruction smoothly. With no prior experience, she seemed to pick up, conceptually at least, the fundamentals as we went over them. These included: picking up a handgun safely, performing appropriate safety and status checks, acquiring a proper grip, assuming a proper shooting stance, understanding how to obtain proper sight alignment and sight picture, and trigger press. However, her arthritis and loss of some strength and dexterity in her hands presented a challenge when it came to physically operating the cylinder release latch, opening the cylinder, and applying a smooth trigger press on a snubby revolver. Her ability to operate the slide of the Glock 17 training pistol we used was also restricted.

In each case, I had to work with Louise to devise ways to get around her limitations, and we were able to do so. Based on just the dry handling of the training guns in the classroom, Louise thought that the snubby revolver was going to be the gun for her. However, her opinions changed markedly during the second hour of her instruction on the range!

Louise found that the snubby revolver had far too much recoil for her comfort level, even with light .38 Special target loads, and she also had difficulty controlling the long and heavy revolver trigger pull. When we moved on to shooting the 9mm mid-sized Glock 19, Louise found the recoil and the trigger control much easier to master.

Given her arthritic hands, she initially had a problem racking the Glock's slide. With some experimentation, we were able to design a viable method of doing this that she could perform safely. The same applied to teaching her how to operate the release catch to eject the pistol's magazine.

Obviously, we could only accomplish so much in one hour on the range. However, one hour was all she could tolerate, with breaks, given her back pain and the weakness in her arms and hands. Nevertheless, she was able to pick up the basics of grip, stance, sight alignment, sight picture and trigger control.

Several weeks later, at our second lesson, Louise demonstrated less anxiety and more self-confidence. The noise and recoil of both the Glock and revolver were now less unnerving to her.

During this second session, we also fired a subcompact 9mm Glock 26, as this was the gun she felt might be her best choice for home-defense and concealed carry. She'd actually handled it better than she handled the bigger Glock 19!

As I write this, I know that Louise has purchased several handguns, including a Glock 26, Springfield XD 9mm subcompact, and a Ruger LCR .38 Special snubby revolver. What follows, is Louise's account that she wrote at the time of her training with me.

I have thought about your request (to write up my experience), and I don't think I can write my story without mentioning the impact of my personal abuse. I do have my girls to think of, and even though they are grown, I would not want to put my name out there (Author's note: her confidentiality was assured).

My name is "Louise," and I am 57 years old. I am disabled due to many years of being abused by my ex-husband, abuse that eventually led to two spinal surgeries. While the surgeries did help somewhat, I am still unable to stand or sit for more than an hour without having excruciating pain.

During my years of abuse, which included having guns held to my head, I

Many folks need a gentle hand to guide them to a realization that they are not powerless, that they can handle a defensive handgun—and that they didn't have to start with a .22-caliber!

was scared to death of guns. I got the help I needed regarding the abuse, but still had a fear of guns. I then found myself in the position of having to move from my house where I had been living, basically without fear, and into an apartment. Now, some fear for my personal safety kicked in, and I decided I needed to purchase a gun for my personal protection.

I went and obtained a permit to carry, and, without any knowledge of guns, I went to a gun store. The shop owner could see I was nervous and asked if I had ever fired a gun. When I said I had not, he readily requested that I contact the person on the business card he gave me in order to become familiar and comfortable with guns before I make a purchase.

With many thanks to that gun shop owner, I called the person, who turned out to be Bruce Eimer. We spoke and set up a time to meet at a local gun range for my first class. I let Bruce know up front that I may not last two hours, due to my disability (I also walk with a cane).

When we met for the first time, Bruce put me at ease and went over all the things I needed to know about revolvers and Glocks, since those were the two types of guns I was looking to purchase.

Though my hands were shaking so much I could barely handle the guns, he was patient with me and went over all the marksmanship fundamentals, as well as the correct grip and stance. After leaving the classroom and moving to the actual firing range, my nerves kicked in, but I fired my first gun, a revolver. My heart went crazy, but I hung in there and, with Bruce's help, I went on to firing the Glock a number of times before my back went out and it became too hard for me to carry on.

Training isn't just a good idea in and of itself, it is your responsibility to be well-trained if you're going to be a legally armed citizen. Good training should include classroom work on basic principles and concealed carry laws, as well as dry- and live-fire work on the range.

Even with just this first lesson behind me, I felt that I had accomplished my expectations for myself, as well as the class, and that was to learn about the guns, how they function, proper handling and stance, and the actual 'kick-back' from firing. And, with just that first class and firing of the guns, I felt that I could have walked into a gun shop and purchased a gun if I'd needed to, since Bruce had taken great pains to make sure I'd understood everything I'd needed to learn and that he'd needed to teach me, even with my physical limitations.

With our second shooting session on the range, I was surprised that I had retained a lot of what Bruce had taught me. I found that the smaller Glock 26 seemed to be easier to fire than either the revolver or the bigger Glock. I actually almost liked it! However, I chose not to purchase yet, as I feel I still need more knowledge and confidence before I do so. But I know I will get there very soon, with the proper training I am getting and the self-confidence I have in myself that I can do this. I can learn to protect myself! After two sessions, that was a great feeling from a great teacher, and I am confident that I will master any lingering fears I may have of guns and keep moving in the right direction and learn the proper use and handing of firearms. For that I am immensely happy and proud of myself for facing my fears and seeking out a professional in this journey of proper handling of any weapons.

Anyone, no matter your age or physical limitations, can and should learn to protect themselves, and with the proper weapons training, anyone can do it. I am living proof. I am very happy with what I have learned and look forward to gaining a greater knowledge of weapons. Neither age nor physical impairment should stop anyone from seeking out a good trainer and learning all they can, so that they can begin to feel as confident as I am beginning to feel.

Where Does Your Training Start?

Before you acquired your first motor vehicle, you needed to learn how to drive. Since states issue drivers licenses, this makes driving a privilege, and passing a driver's test administered by your state's department of motor vehicles is mandatory. In contrast, the individual's rights to keep and bear arms are Constitutional rights. Nevertheless, if you choose to exercise these rights, it is of paramount importance that you get educated. Just as Louise did, when you decide to carry a firearm, you must learn firearms safety, shooting fundamentals, firearm maintenance, the principles of self-defense, the law, and more.

I am not an advocate of state-mandated training for obtaining a concealed permit or owning a gun. However, I *am* a strong advocate of training and education by choice. If you own or carry a gun, you should *want* to get training. It just makes sense. If you don't get educated and you handle firearms, you will be a hazard to yourself and others, and if your ignorance and negligence result in an accident, you will lose your rights to your firearms—and, in my opinion, in such a case you should.

You should carry a gun only with the mind-set that you are going armed in case you need to be armed. And, since you can never know when that fateful moment will arrive, you should *always* go armed. You should also appreciate the necessity of training with the firearms you carry, such that, if you are forced to use those weapons in self-defense in a public place, you will hit what you are aiming at and not hit anything you are not aiming at! To accomplish this, you must train. As much as it is your right to carry firearms for self-defense, it is also *my* right to not be put in jeopardy by your poor judgment or lack of training.

> **You should carry a gun with the mind-set that you do so in case you'll need it. And, since you can never know when that fateful moment will arrive, you should *always* go armed.**

It is essential that, in addition to reading books such as this one, you seek competent firearms training. However, buyer beware! Instructors can be great communicators, but they cannot share your own personal-risk profile, i.e., they cannot know the optimal protective measures for you and your family. Therefore, you must have your own diligence and perform your own research in choosing the best gun schools and firearms instructors for you.

If you are new to all of this, a good place to start your odyssey is the National Rifle Association's (NRA) website (www.nra.org). The NRA has supplied academic support materials for firearms instructors for years that help guide students through the various phases of competent firearms training.

The NRA, of course, is also the most prominent and legitimate organization dedicated to the preservation of your gun rights in the United States. It is also truly dedicated to firearms safety education and awareness programs. This may sound like propaganda, but, to the NRA, and to those who understand the organization's missions, firearm safety and competence is all about education, not legislation.

Two other valid organizations whose goals are to preserve our gun rights and disseminate educational information about armed personal-defense are The United States Concealed Carry

Association (www.USConcealedCarry.com) and Gun Owners of America (www.Gunowners.org).

Today it is certainly possible to find a plethora of information about firearms and firearms training on the Internet. However, source material is not always reliable and can often be biased. The savvy student will check out the reliability and validity of their sources on the web before betting their life on the information. Research is a valuable tool, but blindly giving yourself over to and taking as gospel the words of someone whose qualifications you do not know is idiotic. Research the credentials of the instructor or web author. Would you really want an instructor from Nome, Alaska, teaching you self-defense tactical training for use in the inner city of Chicago? Likewise, would you want an instructor from the inner city of Chicago training you on survival in the Alaskan outback?

Research more than the credentials of an instructor before you choose one. Would you really want a tutor from Nome, Alaska, teaching you self-defense tactics for your use in the inner city of Chicago? Probably not.

Books such as this one can, of course, be a useful information source. However, it is important to check out the timeliness of the material, as well as the qualifications of the authors in light of current advances in the field. There are numerous books written about firearms and their use in personal-defense and combat. Ask yourself such questions as: Is this book up to date? Is this book written for civilians or law enforcement or both? Has it been prepared by someone living in the Nevada desert for the last 20 years, or someone actively involved in present day security measures and the intelligence community?

Who Should You Go to for Training?

Qualified instructors should have certain qualities. Here are eight that I consider essential:

1. Tactical experience gained through years of service in bringing an unprepared populace up to speed.

2. Authoring and presenting pertinent literature so that the student can be equipped to evaluate the instructor.

3. Providing personalized training, as opposed to militaristic training.

4. An attitude that the student is the instructor's equal. This facilitates the possibility that the student can eventually become as good as or better than the instructor.

5. An ego that is not swelled. Serious training for civilians demands that egos be put to the side, so that the focus can be placed where it belongs—on training for survival.

6. A thorough working knowledge of firearms, their components, and operation.

7. The ability to demonstrate non-lethal, as well as lethal, personal-defense measures so that students have alternatives. We're not at the O.K. Corral. Therefore, it is not okay to mentally dwell there.

8. A genuine concern for the students, rather than a paycheck. It should not be your instructor's first or even second priority to make money by selling you products. In fact, your instructor should recommend that you shop around, if he or she is legitimate. Think about it for a second. Are you going to place your life or the lives of those you treasure in the custody of someone who lacks integrity and only thinks about making a buck by selling stuff?

In choosing an instructor or school, you should evaluate the quality, attitudes, and behavior of the students who have previously studied there. These are your references, so ask them how the instructors conducted themselves. Are they a model for how you want to act in the area of personal defense and the use of firearms? Do they project the image you wish to project? In a nutshell, are they good role models and are they professional? If they are, then proceed to step two. How did these students evaluate the quality of their instructor's instruction? Also, investigate whether the training is provided in an atmosphere of fun in addition to education, a setting that can help you relax and absorb the information fully. Finally, remember that more expensive training does not equal better training.

How Do You Avoid Bad Information?

Keep an eye out for training you *don't* want. Swelled egos are your first tip-off. Know-it-alls will make themselves apparent within the first two minutes of a conversation. If you hear a lot of "Is," it's time to say goodbye. If an instructor is pretentious or insulting, then, too, it's time to put on your hat and leave. If you are asked to accept information on faith alone, you are bound to come up short, so fly out of there. If you sense any degree of condescension or, worse yet, intimidation, you know you enlisted in the wrong army. And, finally, if the information being provided is based on experiences in the Civil War, my suggestion is that you have a good time by watching *Gone With The Wind* one more time, but don't waste your instructional time.

Competent training requires at least 20 hours over a period of time in order to comprehend and maintain the information in one's "muscle memory" or "motor memory" (the most important muscle, or motor, being your brain). A one- or two-day class firing about 500 rounds will *not* facilitate long-term retention of the important information for most trainees. Good training requires building blocks, not shock.

Honor above profits are our first consideration, when it comes to finding reliable training. An instructor you can go to on a continual basis for updates, clarity, and genuine interest reflects best on your selection of attributes. Facilities that hawk a particular firearm or some other tool to complete their program just might make their main agenda profiteering. Everyone's defensive needs are different and, as such, an honest instructor will always seek to fit the tool to the individual, rather than all individuals to the same tool.

CHAPTER 3

Gun Therapy

As a practicing clinical psychologist, firearms instructor, gun owner, and concealed carry practitioner, I believe that responsible gun ownership is healthy and adaptive behavior. In this chapter, I shall discuss how learning to be a responsible gun owner is both therapeutic and survival-oriented.

I am a "gun therapist" and I practice "gun therapy." No, gun therapy isn't about teaching people how to use firearms to threaten or intimidate others. Those behaviors are both illegal and immoral and will cause you to lose your gun rights. Gun therapy, then, is the art and science of teaching people how to take responsibility for their own personal protection. It is about teaching the principles of personal-defense and how to be self-reliant, responsible gun owners. It is about teaching people how to communicate, negotiate, move, employ less-than-lethal force, and shoot as necessary. It is also about teaching people good manners. To borrow a phrase from Robert Heinlein, "An armed society is a polite society. Manners are good when one may have to back up his acts with his life."

Power Tools are Dangerous

Other power tools that aren't designed to kill, but which nevertheless are very dangerous if not used safely, include saws, drills, lawn mowers, meat slicers, and motor vehicles. Clearly, none of these aforementioned power tools can cause death or severe bodily injury by themselves, as they have no independent agency. Their lethality lies in how they are employed. Firearms, on the other hand, *are* designed to be deadly weapons and would be quite useless if they *weren't* dangerous. Yet they can also be conceptualized as emergency rescue tools designed to kill, when killing is necessary to save innocent lives. Therefore, their proper use and ownership demands requisite knowledge, skills, and attitude to ensure safe handling.

Firearm Ownership—It's Not for Everyone

As I discuss in my book, *Essential Guide to Handguns* (Rementer & Eimer, 2005), there are certain types of people who are strongly advised not to own firearms. Pathologically fearful, depressed, hotheaded, careless, and reckless people, and even sometimes stupid, aggressive, arrogant, rude, impulsive, and irresponsible people, should not own guns. Sociopaths, psychopaths, and violent criminals should not be allowed to own firearms.

People who shouldn't own firearms cannot be counted upon to follow safe firearm handling practices. They cannot be trusted to act smartly, morally, righteously, courteously, considerately, or responsibly, because their brains are just not wired to do so. Our mind is our most powerful weapon and, therefore, also our most dangerous. An unhealthy, misdirected, or runaway mind is destructive. As a practicing psychologist, I help people overcome mental disturbance, build a healthier mind, and make their behavior more adaptive. As a practicing firearms instructor, I advise folks who own firearms to invest in good training and good equipment. As both a psychologist and firearms instructor, I urge people to be responsible gun owners, and I teach them how to do that.

Becoming a Responsible Gun Owner

To become a responsible gun owner, you must acquire a necessary body of knowledge, develop an appropriate set of skills, and adopt a positive attitude. You must cultivate a strong mind, behave in a socially appropriate and adaptive manner, practice safe gun-handling procedures, and know the law. I developed a serious interest in firearms, armed and unarmed self-defense, and training rather late in life. My journey has broadened my horizons and helped me build better morals, develop greater self-reliance, and learn greater restraint and self-control. I have discovered, as have many of my students and clients, that it is never too late to remedy one's deficiencies. Even old dogs can learn new tricks and improved behavioral habits, if they have good intentions and a modicum of intelligence, social and otherwise. The best remedy for ignorance and fear is attitude readjustment through knowledge.

Hoplophobia, the Flight from Personal Responsibility

"Hoplophobia" is defined as the morbid fear of firearms. The term is derived from the Greek word, *hoplon*, which refers to weapons. The late Colonel Jeff Cooper, firearms instructor, author, father of "the modern technique of the pistol," and founder of Gunsite Firearms Academy, attributed anti-gun zealotry to hoplophobia, which he defined as an irrational aversion to and fear of firearms and other forms of weaponry. Cooper opined that anti-gun hoplophobes held the idea that firearms and other deadly weapons have a will of their own. Of course, we know that firearms do not because they are not living things and ,thus, have no independent agency.

As a clinical psychologist and psychotherapist, I know that the reality of hoplophobia is much more complex. A common theme underlying the psycho dynamics of hoplophobes and "gun haters" is the unconscious or semi-conscious fear of their *own* aggressive impulses running wild if they had the means (and the ownership of firearms would give them those means). It is similar to what people with a severe fear of heights (acrophobia) often describe, when they are looking over the edge of a precipice. They fear the irrational impulse to jump. If their fear extends to being in a closed-in high-up place, such as inside a high-rise office or airplane, they typically describe a fear of the irrational impulse to break the window glass or wish the plane to fall out of the sky.

While both the impulse and the fear are irrational, psychological analysis reveals that both are real and understandable. They both are psychologically related to repressed, suppressed, and sublimated aggression and the flight from personal responsibility. This is one source of the "gun-grabbing" mentality. Many of these folks fear their own hostility and know that firearms are not for impulsive, hot-headed people who cannot control their rage—interestingly, many of these folks will often use expressions such as, "I feel like shooting myself." The problem is even more vexing because, instead of taking personal responsibility for their own feelings and looking to develop insight into the source of their own fears, these folks deny their own nature. They attribute their own worst fears and unsociable impulses onto others. In psychological parlance, this defense mechanism is called "projection." So, instead of their deeming themselves as being dangerous with guns in their own hands and working to improve themselves, they attribute dangerousness and recklessness to others, in this case all gun owners.

Hoplophobics tend to overreact. They often believe that people who own handguns would display one to gain leverage in an argument—yet they don't recognize that impulse in themselves. They claim that gun owners are more likely to overreact in heated situations. This is the wanton "blood in the streets" syndrome that many hoplophobes carry on, typically ignoring or not understanding that, in most jurisdictions, threatening someone verbally while possessing a handgun (legally or illegally possessed), will typically result in stiff penalties.

According to the American Psychiatric Association, the medical and psychiatric definition of a true phobia requires that the afflicted or phobic person be aware that his or her fear is irrational and that the phobia causes some kind of functional impairment. Of course, most hoplophobics, especially gun grabbers, do *not* acknowledge these facts. I call this lacking insight.

Firearm Ownership Demands a Higher Standard

Anyone who legally carries a concealed handgun or who is trained in the martial fighting arts is held to a higher standard of conduct both morally and legally. That means the legally armed citizen must think about the use of force continuum. The amount of force that you use to defend yourself must not be excessive under the circumstances. It must, rather, be proportionate to the degree of force with which you are confronted.

There must be an overt act by a person that indicates he immediately intends to carry out a threat, in order for deadly force to be justified. Verbal threats don't begin to come close to constituting this kind of justification. You must reasonably believe that you will be killed or suffer serious bodily harm if you do not immediately take the life of your attacker. And, when it comes to employing deadly force in the defense of another person, the circumstances must justify that person's use of deadly force in his or her own defense. In other words, you must "stand in the shoes" of the person being threatened or attacked.

The actual use of a firearm for self-defense is the highest level on this force continuum and the last resort. When you carry a concealed firearm, you must use extra discretion. You must consider what might happen if you become engaged in a tussle, because every confrontation in which you the armed citizen are involved includes the presence of a deadly weapon. Thus, you must always think about how you can *avoid* confrontation, because, if you instigate or escalate an event and it turns bad to the point you have to use deadly force, you will be held accountable.

The Good Person's Code

R ecently, at a Phillies baseball game in Philadelphia, an argument over some spilled beer began between two groups of men. The argument grew into a melee, and security guards threw everyone out. Afterwards, in the parking lot, three men from one of the groups jumped one man from the other group who was trying to leave the angry and violent scene. The three men beat, kicked, and stomped the other man. By the time the police arrived, it was too late. The victim had suffered severe head trauma and was pronounced dead by medics.

All I could think of after reading this news story in the *Philadelphia Inquirer* was that, had the victim had a gun on him, he might have been able to save his life. This would have been a clear case of the justifiable use of deadly force in self-defense. The three murderers started the violence, escalated it, and had a marked disparity of force in numbers and size over their victim.

Carrying a gun regularly is a big commitment and responsibility. It's not always convenient, nor is it always comfortable. However, as noted firearms trainer and gun writer Clint Smith of Thunder Ranch is fond of repeating, "The concealed firearm is not meant to be comfortable; it is meant to be comforting."

In our increasingly menacing society, staying relatively safe and staying armed seem to be synonymous. As you grow older, when you lose some or many of your physical powers, such as size, strength, flexibility, stamina, endurance, prowess, stealth, and reaction time, you become more vulnerable to predators. This is how it works in the animal kingdom, and it's the same in the human kingdom. Fortunately, the gun can serve as an equalizer of sorts, allowing you to even the odds or tilt them in your favor. God, in his infinite wisdom, may not have created all people physically equal, but old Sam Colt saw to evening the odds.

Few violent criminals fear the gun or other deadly weapons. However, jailhouse interviews reveal that many violent criminals *do* fear the person holding the gun.

When you've been alive for five to six decades or more, you've seen a lot and have had numerous experiences and scrapes. At this point in life, you either have the instinct for survival or you don't, and you wouldn't have lived this long if you didn't. So, whether or not you've consciously thought about it, you have, in fact, internalized a code of rules that guide your life, and they work! If you believe in armed self-defense and have chosen to live the armed lifestyle, there is a code of rules that guide this lifestyle choice. This code is not very complicated.

At this point in my life, the code of the prepared good person has become crystal clear. It's something to live with, and it's all about following the Golden Rule we learned in kindergarten: do unto others as you would want them to do unto you. In addition to the Golden Rule, the code of the good person is largely common sense, but its tenets form the groundwork for effective, armed self-defense for anyone who is committed to living their life. Permit me to elaborate on its five tenets.

Own at Least One Defensive Handgun

Two is better than one, and three or four are even better, but one is a basic minimum. However, it is not enough to just own a gun. There are a number of corollaries to this tenet.

The first and primary corollary is that you must know how to use and maintain your defensive emergency rescue equipment. Therefore, you should read your gun's owner's manual and, if you are new to guns, you should get competent hands-on instruction. The time arising where and when you really need to use your handgun is *not* the time to be figuring out how to most efficiently work its manual safety or decock the hammer! You also need to keep your guns clean. Your guns, as emergency rescue equipment, should be kept in good condition. That requires regular cleaning, adequate lubrication, and periodic inspections and function checks.

A second corollary is that you should join a gun club and attempt to make like-minded friends. One of the secrets of success and happiness, as well as personal safety and security, is building a support network of human resources. This can be done by making friends with available individuals whose talents and abilities complement your own. Not only will you have fun, you will benefit from the camaraderie. If you have a computer, check out several quality online discussion forums where you can make friends and share knowledge. Some recommen-

If one gun is good, two are better. And if two are good, three are better. This picture is a sample of the author's pocket guns, a spectrum of styles, sizes, and actions that he can use in a variety of circumstances and with different clothing.

28

dations would include www.DefensiveHandguns.com, www.USConcealedCarry.com, and www.-WarriorTalk.com.

A third corollary is that you need to go to the range and shoot regularly, so that you become comfortable and accurate with your defensive handguns. You must make shooting them a basic reflex. So join a gun club or range. You'll meet nice people, and it's cheaper than paying by the hour for range time.

Finally, you should also practice handling your unloaded defensive handguns at home. This is called dry practice, and it can build and strengthen your muscle memory for gun presentation and handling. Dry practice develops your unconscious competence in gun handling.

Keep at Least One Handgun Loaded at All Times

An emergency is not the time to be fumbling around loading a handgun. Your self-defense arms should always be loaded and available, and loaded means a round in the chamber and either a fully charged magazine in a semi-automatic pistol, or all chambers of the cylinder loaded in a revolver. This is also called "condition one," and it's the only way you should carry a defensive handgun—at the ready.

The Gun as a Necessity

So often I hear people remark that it is unnecessary to carry a gun. I hear it from cops who don't carry off duty and should know better, from students who take my concealed carry weapons permit course, and even from the owners of gun stores! What in the world are these people thinking?

Without being smug, I can safely say I know the answer. They are thinking two things, *It won't happen to me* and *The police will protect me.*

I also hear people say, "It's too much of a hassle to carry all the time," or "It's not easy carrying a gun." To them I answer, "Hey, it's a lot easier than if you need it and it isn't there!"

There is no valid reason for laziness, when it comes to your own self-protection and survival. We carry our driver's license, car registrations, and insurance cards in case we are stopped or have an accident. That is a real possibility every time we get behind the wheel of our motor vehicles. We also buy insurance in case we need it, hoping that we won't. Such should be the case with a firearm concealed on our person.

Doctor Clara Thompson, a psychiatrist, has argued cogently that "anti-gun people" are really subconsciously afraid of their own aggressive impulses. That technically means they are neurotic and could benefit from therapy, for a neurosis is a psychological disorder that causes one to spend too much energy on unconsciously manufacturing and then defending against dangers that don't really exist. (See, even anti-gunners spend their energies on self-defense!)

Anti-gunners are really unconsciously afraid that *they* would commit murder if they had a gun, a realization that is unacceptable and threatening and so is repressed. That energy and the fear of the unacceptable impulse is projected onto others, so that now it is everyone else who would commit murder if *they* are permitted to own a gun. This same illogic leads anti-gunners to claim it's dangerous to carry a gun because, should you need one to defend yourself, it's likely to be taken away from you by the criminal and used on you. Psychologically, what's really going on is that they fear *they* would give it up.

Neuroses, by their very nature, are illogical and self-defeating. Forget about all the sociopathic, psychopathic criminals who possess illegal guns and weapons—they need to be put away. Neurotic, hoplophobic (having an illogical fear of guns), anti-self-defense, anti-gun people truly need psychological treatment.

Keep at Least One Handgun on You

Let's play the "what if" game. What if I'm attacked? What if someone tries to carjack me? Rape me? Rob me? Kidnap me? What if I'm followed home by two thugs? What if my home is invaded at two in the morning?" If you're going to answer those questions, you must consider having the necessary emergency equipment on hand, at the ready, to respond in a way that will promote your survival.

What good is your .45 in your bedroom drawer, when you are out and about? What good is it if it's unloaded, disassembled, or locked in a safe, if your home is invaded? When your duty defensive handgun is not physically on you, keep it loaded, secured, and *immediately* available. When you are carrying, your gun should be hidden, but instantly accessible.

Be Prepared to Use the Gun You're Carrying

What does "prepared" mean? It means having the right mind-set, the right equipment for you, the training to use your equipment competently, and the commitment to employ deadly force if you are facing imminent deadly peril. When a bad situation starts going down and adrenaline is being dumped into your bloodstream as a part of your body's alarm reaction, good training prepares you to go into reflexive mode.

In the spirit of preparedness, it is also important that, when you carry, you do so legally and with a permit where mandated. I know some people say it is not necessary or even desirable to obtain a license to carry firearms, since concealed means out of sight, so behave yourself and stay under the radar. However, there is a major flaw in this argument. Here's the scenario.

You are attacked and resort to the use of deadly force to defend your life. Your legal defense is that you shot in self-defense, and that may be true. However, the problem is that you are going to be charged and, in all likelihood, convicted of the felony of carrying an illegal handgun. This will make you a felon and you will lose your rights to own and carry firearms. It is not worth it to play Russian roulette with you gun rights. So, get a license to carry! (As an aside, and from a tactical standpoint, I am not an advocate of open carry, because it compromises the valuable element of surprise. For example, if you are sitting at the counter of your favorite breakfast place openly carrying a sidearm and some armed nut enters the joint to plug the cook because he had a bad meal, whom do you think he'll target first? Carry concealed.)

You're Prepared, But Are You Ready?

"Ready" means being willing to do whatever is necessary, including using deadly force, to prevail. It means being willing to fight for your life. It means refusing to lose. It means committing

Chapter 4 THE GOOD PERSON'S CODE

to the principle that, if it's your life versus the life of a violent criminal, you will not hesitate to take the criminal's life.

It would be good at this point to ponder a key word in that last paragraph, "necessary." For deadly force to be necessary, and, more importantly, justified, the person threatening you must have the immediate means, the immediate opportunity, and the demonstrated intent to cause you grievous bodily harm or death right then and there. It's either your life or your attacker's, and, if you did nothing to bring the situation about or cause the situation to escalate to a life and death confrontation, you are justified in using deadly force.*

If You Have to Use Deadly Force, Don't Hesitate

Hesitating in a deadly force encounter can get you killed. Fractions of a second will count. Time may seem to slow down. You will have tunnel vision upon realizing the threat. Only training and the will to prevail (a good dose of luck won't hurt either) will enable you to break your tunnel vision, maintain a cool head, and save yourself. In most gunfights, the person who scores the first shots gains the winning advantage.

Note: I would recommend reading Massad Ayoob's classic book, In the Gravest Extreme *(or anything by Massad, for that matter), to learn more about the issues involved. Massad writes a regular column on the law and self-defense for the monthly magazine,* Combat Handguns, *also highly recommended.*

Also, in his Massad Ayoob Group (MAG) training (see www.MassadAyoobGroup.com), Ayoob talks about a jurisprudence concept called the "Doctrine of Competing Harms," which is pertinent to the topic of this chapter. This refers to the fact that the law (and most reasonable and prudent law abiding citizens) will typically excuse the breaking of a law (i.e., killing another human being) to prevent the commission of an even greater harm (i.e., getting killed yourself or with your innocent loved ones). Ayoob further talks about when there is a "disparity of force" that favors a stronger, more dangerous, unlawful aggressor over a weaker would-be victim. In this case, the victim is justified in employing a force multiplier, including deadly force (such as a firearm), if that's what is necessary to save his or her life. This would apply if a man attacks a woman, a younger, stronger, or bigger man attacks an older, weaker, or smaller man, or a number of men attack one man.

CHAPTER 5

Don't Be A Hero

We all have limitations, no matter what our age. Limitations can be inherited physical traits, fundamental personality traits, cognitive and physical talents or abilities, age, gender, and cultural background. These are factors that cannot be changed, and, therefore, these limitations need to be acknowledged and accepted. Acceptance is the first step in personal improvement. Once we accept our limitations, we can compensate for the restrictions they impose. For example, physical conditioning can be improved by working out, knowledge can be acquired by becoming educated, and attitudes can be changed.

In addition, regardless of our economic and professional positions, we all have limitations imposed by situational circumstances. Some things, such as clearing a house as a SWAT team would do, typically should not be done even if one has the skills. Likewise, taken to a public street level, if you are with your family in a public place and you hear gun shots, your immediate goal should be to get your family to safety, not take out the shooter.

The Reason To Carry A Gun

If you carry a gun, you need to recognize that the reason you do so is for personal protection, *not* to transform yourself into a would-be super hero. Carrying a gun does not give you a license to get involved in situations that are none of your business. Nor does it give you the authority of a police officer. Your job is to stay safe and keep your loved ones safe. It makes good sense, as a general principle, to avoid becoming inextricably involved in confrontations where you are not directly affected in the first place. It's a risk to involve yourself in other people's arguments. This is not to say that there will never be a situation that is worth the risk, but that is a personal decision.

My friend and teacher, noted firearms trainer John Farnam of Defense Training International, recently sent an e-mail to his students that drove home why discretion is the better part of valor. Here, in summary, is what he related.

Somewhere in the conservative West, a super-sized young man was physically beating his girlfriend in line at a movie theater, as people looked on. A middle-aged gentleman stepped forward and commanded the offender, whom I'll call Biff, to stop, at which point Biff instantly turned on him. According to witnesses, the good Samaritan repeatedly told the offender to stop beating him, with no results, and while he was still able to make sense, the Samaritan informed Biff that he had a gun and that he would use it if Biff did not stop beating him up. To no one's surprise, Biff responded with something like "Take your gun and shove it where the sun doesn't shine!" The Samaritan, now a victim himself, then produced a .22 LR North American Arms mini-revolver and fired two rounds into Biff at close range, striking him in the groin. The result was that Biff stopped his attack and backed off.

Biff survived, and, within a few days, the local prosecutor cleared the good Samaritan shooter of any wrongdoing. Nevertheless, local newspapers started receiving angry letters calling for the immediate recall of the prosecutor, referring to his decision to clear the Samaritan as "vigilante justice," with the argument that, no matter what the circumstances, no one should be able to take the law into their own hands. Farnam points out that this case is a prime example of the phenomenon known in Latin as *nemo curat*

Being a responsible, legally armed citizen does not mean you can chase someone out of your yard with your gun pointing at them. You must use your head and keep calm. If your attacker is fleeing you, then he's no longer an attacker.

which, translated into English, comes out to "nobody cares."

As you can see, social reality is itself a limitation. Farnam points out that the moral of the story is that we should avoid becoming a victim of unrealistic expectations. It is foolish to ignore reality. Getting involved voluntarily in any situation that has the potential of requiring the use of lethal force on your part carries enormous risks, and one should never expect to be thanked or hailed as a hero. The fact is, it is foolish to expect that people, even friends and family, will understand or sympathize with you. Getting involved carries the very probable risk of plummeting yourself into a desperate, life-threatening position in which Farnam notes you will be "criticized, ridiculed, and denigrated in the media and by others who weren't there, indicted by an over-zealous prosecutor who hates guns and everyone who owns one, and sued by the shootee/decedent, or his 'estate'/family, for 'wrongful death,' et al." Unfortunately, reality is a limitation that must be heeded if you want to survive. Real life is not a Marvel comic.

Children and teens growing up in our media-driven society are fed useless and often harmful information, while overstressed, disconnected, and preoccupied parents frequently have little knowledge of what their children are learning. The result is an anything-goes culture.

Money, materialism, deception, lies, narcissism, sound bites, sensationalism, and greed rule the mainstream media, governmental bureaucracies, and corporate boardrooms, while street crime, white collar crime, and political and corporate corruption are rampant. Those who profit from such a morally bankrupt society naturally cringe at the idea of thoughtful, self-reliant people with guns.

Today, Americans who believe in honor, traditional values, definitive moral standards, and a polite society constitute the largest sector of legally armed citizens and concealed carry practitioners.

Honor Still Lives

Fortunately, honor does still live. Inspired by a week I spent at a writers' conference at Blackhawk Corporation in Norfolk, Virginia, where I became more aware of my own fallibility and limitations, I formulated the H.O.N.O.R. model

> Getting involved in any situation that ends with you using lethal force, however justifiably, carries enormous social risks. It is foolish to expect even friends and family to understand or even sympathize with you.

for striving for personal integrity and excellence. I believe that this model is applicable to every legally armed citizen and concealed carry practitioner. In this context, I define excellence as possessing and using the highest level of necessary skills and qualities to live one's life to its fullest and with the utmost in moral and ethical integrity. When it comes to armed personal-defense, mediocrity and a lack of integrity just won't do.

"Honor" is defined in the Oxford English Dictionary as "personal integrity; allegiance to moral principles; and holding a clear sense of what is morally right." Living honorably is a formula for success in many walks of life. For the legally armed citizen and for the professional warrior, as I see it, living honorably requires the cultivation of five essential habits. As a mnemonic, the first letters of each of these habits spell the word "honor."

H = Honesty

Being honest means having integrity and being reliable, trustworthy, consistent, dependable, and incorruptible. This also lays the basis for loyalty. In the firearms industry, companies that are not honest do not last long. Honest companies that are loyal to their customers build customer loyalty in return. Just witness the comeback that a company such as Smith & Wesson made as a result of providing reliable customer service and flexible lifetime warranties.

Likewise, in the real world, people who are dishonest have to expend lots of energy covering up their lies. Massad Ayoob is known for saying that, in the aftermath of a defensive shooting, lies will in all likelihood condemn you to prison, but the truth can set you free—as long as you know when to talk and when to keep your mouth shut!

O = Observant

Being observant means staying alert, attentive, aware, perceptive, and mindful of what is going on around you. It enables you to be quick to notice and perceive things—a necessity for surviving on the street, in the jungle, in the corporate boardroom, or in the sandbox. The legally armed citizen, law enforcement officer, soldier, or operator who is not observant will be unable to bridge the reactionary gap if attacked.

N = No-Nonsense

Being no-nonsense means being ready and willing to take whatever action is necessary. It demands decisiveness, as opposed to dithering. If you are attacked, you *must* do something, preferably something explosive that startles your attacker. You cannot afford to freeze in deliberation, for that is pretty sure to get you killed. Being no-nonsense also refers to having the ability to act purposefully and non-emotionally. Whining about how unfortunate you are will not save your derriere.

Defending yourself doesn't mean you should go about clearing a room and investigating what's behind door No. 1. Those types of tactics are best left to highly trained law enforcement agents. If you entered your home to discover open doors you knew you'd left closed, you should never investigate. Show restraint. Leave the house (watching your 360), find safe haven, and then call the police and let them deal with the situation. Being armed means avoiding potentially deadly situations whenever possible.

O = Organized

In order to survive a violent confrontation, in addition to being decisive, you must also be efficient and methodical. Being organized and prepared means being unconsciously competent in your ability to launch into effective action at a moment's notice. You do not have to stop and think about how you are going to run your gun, or access your blade, or parry a strike, or run away. You are well trained and have trained well. It also says that you have trained with and have with you the right equipment to get the job done. Do not settle for cheap and iffy equipment on which to bet your life. Your life is worth more than that. Remember, you get what you pay for, and you pay later for what you didn't pay earlier.

R= Restrained

In the jungle, those who survive generally blend in. You would probably be wise to do the same, especially if you are carrying a gun. This means that your clothes shouldn't mark you as someone who is carrying a gun. What you wear should be discreet and fit in with your environment. Also, your concealment holsters should not print through your clothing.

Equally important, your actions should be reserved and judicious. Avoid loud and injudicious people, and don't become one. Don't brag. Cultivate humility. Keep yourself in check and under control at all times, especially when you are carrying. Train yourself to think before you act. Use your knowledge to avoid problems before they develop. Train so that you do not need to use your training. Find ways to avoid confrontations, and, if a confrontation is unavoidable, try to de-escalate it. As wisely pointed out by Massad Ayoob, with the greater power that carrying a deadly weapon bestows upon you, there is also a greater responsibility to meet a higher standard of care. Discretion is always the better part of valor.

CHAPTER 6

Trust Only Yourself

The elderly woman had just been telling her daughter the day before how much she trusted her cleaning lady, how nice she was. Nevertheless, her daughter advised her not to leave the cleaning lady her keys. She did anyway. Two days later, when the elderly woman came home from an evening movie, she was assaulted in her apartment by an intruder, who had let himself in with those keys.

The police picked up the woman's assailant, after questioning the cleaning lady. It turned out that he was the cleaning lady's old boyfriend, and he admitted to the crimes. He had been recently released from prison, where he had served three years for a string of similar crimes, all of which involved elderly victims.

The moral of this story is don't take anything or anyone for granted. Be suspicious. Don't give away your trust. Never give out your keys! You might end up in shock and awe, and that's not a good thing! As the famed defensive firearms trainer Clint Smith says, "Don't be a deer caught in the headlights of the Kenworth of life!"

Stay Aware and Conscious

Trust no one. Apathy and unawareness can lead to unconsciousness—permanently! If you look vulnerable, especially due to physical disabilities or limitations as a result of aging or illness, expect people to try to take advantage of you. But, if you are trained and licensed to safely use and carry a firearm, capitalize on the important variable of the "surprise factor."

For example, an acquaintance, who is in her sixties and challenged by lifelong orthopedic problems associated with childhood polio, surprised me one day, when she shared that she was a shooter and a concealed carry permit holder. Her outward appearance is of an alert, situationally aware, confident, mature woman. She also has a notable postural list and limp and walks with a cane. I would have never guessed she packs heat. In all likelihood, neither would a predatory criminal, and that spells survival for my acquaintance (and a real bad day for anyone who would attack her!).

Go Armed

Carry a gun, knife, and flashlight on you as much as you can. This also means having your gun in an instantly accessible place in your home should you need it. Think of it as a security blanket.

Develop safe gun handling and good marksmanship skills so that they are reflexive if you should ever need to use them for real. Go to the range regularly and practice, practice, practice your shooting skills. The lead won't kill you, but if you are unprepared, a predator might!

At the same time, the knife can be a wonderful addition to your gun. A sharp blade—either a one-handed opening folder or a fixed blade—is the ultimate close-quarter fighting tool. In a close-up, sudden attack, you may not have a chance to draw your gun.

Carry a flashlight. Before you open your car door, check under and in your car. Before you enter your home, have your flashlight ready. When you answer your door, use your peephole and have a flashlight ready to shine into the eyes of a potential miscreant if you choose to open your door. A bright light will temporarily blind an unwelcome caller and give you time to slam the door shut. If he has his foot in the door, slam the light into his noggin!

Vary Your Routines

Keep your shades drawn at night. Don't let uninvited eyes in on your party. Vary your daily routines. As we get older, we tend to become more set in our ways. This is not good. It makes us too complacent. By varying our routines, we counter complacency and add stimulation to our lives. Furthermore, predators and stalkers don't feel comfortable if they have to track an erratic target. They like to prey on nice and predictable victims.

Senior citizens are typically thought of as being predictable, because they typically are! While you can get your social security check by mail, you don't have to check your mail at the same time every day. Don't go shopping on the same day and same hour of the day each week. Shop on different days, and preferably at more than one market.

Stand Firm

Say "No" to overly persuasive attempts to get your attention and compliance. For example, when approached by people who persist in trying to get you to help them, let them in your house so they can use the telephone, check your gas meter, etc., stand firm, saying something like, "No! Go away now or I'll call the police." Don't be afraid of insulting people or being rude. Your life is worth more than that. It's better to be thought of as rude than to be found dead. I want you to enjoy your life and work and live your life to its fullest. Don't let some dirt bag retire you!

If you are attacked by a predator, fight aggressively in every way. Your attacker has no heart, thus, he deserves no quarter. Convince yourself beforehand that, if you are attacked, you will win the fight. Convince yourself that no dirt bag is ever going to take your life before your time.

Disparity of Force

As a peaceful and law abiding person who does not try to cause trouble, there will exist an obvious disparity of force between you and an attacker. An attacker will not expect you to fight back. This will give you the advantageous element of surprise. Additionally, if you have to shoot an attacker to stop him from killing you or causing you grievous bodily harm, a jury of your peers will understand that, were it not for your gun, you would have been food.

If attacked, expect to get hurt—maybe badly—but you must fight to prevail. Tell yourself, no matter what, *you will survive*. Getting hurt is better than the alternative. This is not to say that you shouldn't escape or run away if you can, because you should. But if you can't, do what you have to in order to survive.

There is no such thing as fighting fairly on the street. Predators and criminals will never give you any quarter. So, bluff if you have to. Fake a heart attack. It will momentarily disorient your attacker and might buy you time. Also, recognize that how you carry yourself may determine whether a predator picks you or the next person. If you look like food, you will be eaten.

Most criminal predators hunt for easy prey. Criminal assaults against the elderly, for example, are on the rise, and unprepared and unarmed victims are often hurt, disabled, and murdered. Yet, wherever the citizen's right to keep and bear arms is honored, the effects and reach of criminal predators are reduced. This is because most criminal predators are street smart and realize they are more likely to get shot by a threatened armed citizen than they are by the police. Thus, guns save lives—two-fold.

If you look physically weak to a predatory criminal, you probably look like food to him. If you are a senior citizen, a woman, or a person with physical challenges, you may not be as strong or fit as a bad-to-the bone, 18-, 20-, or 30-something-year-old criminal in his prime. Additionally, if you suffer from physical maladies, you really *are* vulnerable—unless you can balance or reduce that vulnerability with fighting tools and the skills to use them.

This is why you should consider carrying a concealed firearm (or two) and consider keeping one (or several) firearms accessible for home-defense. Both of these measures are forms of preparation should you encounter a problem, just as carrying a spare tire in your car and having smoke detectors and a fire extinguisher in your home are forms of preparation.

Refusing to be a victim is an active, ongoing process that involves taking responsibility—or, rather, *response*-ability—for your own safety. It means developing the ability to respond decisively and aggressively to any dirtbag who presents an immediate threat to your continued well-being and existence.

Knowledge is power, and now you know that you must take appropriately realistic steps to strengthen your personal security. In fact, you're probably reading this book because you realize that your first step is learning about defensive firearms, the great equalizer. Our nation's founding fathers wrote the Second Amendment into our Bill of Rights to guarantee our right to keep and bear arms, because they understood that those who were armed were equal.

As a law-abiding citizen, you deserve to live your life free from the fear of threats from violent criminals. This book has been put together to give you some of the essential knowledge you'll need to safely and effectively exercise your constitutionally guaranteed right to keep and bear arms at home and on the dangerous streets. I want you to stay healthy and safe so that you can continue enjoying your life. So, read on and learn how to not let yourself become food, and how to stay within the boundaries of the law when it comes to defending yourself against uninvited violence. Remember that no one has the right to take away your right to life, liberty, and the pursuit of happiness. Nobody has the right to cut your life short.

CHAPTER 7

Confrontation Psychology

Most in-your-face confrontations do not need to escalate into violence, if they are managed appropriately. In order to preclude violence, it is necessary to take control by using some tried and true psychology.

The fact is that everyone uses psychology whether they are consciously aware of it or not—but it's better to be consciously aware and have a plan. That's why we carry a gun. Remember President Teddy Roosevelt's words, "Speak softly, and carry a big stick." If you have that proverbial big stick, you can feel confident that you have the strength to back up your politely stated position on the matter at hand.

As I've hammered away earlier in this book, and as I will continue to preach in later chapters, if you do choose to carry a gun, you had better be mentally and physically prepared to confront an aggressor who is intent on doing you bodily harm. To that point, you must understand that physical fights are almost always quick and ugly. Successfully resolving and winning an ugly, violent, social confrontation involves more than just fighting skills. To be a winner or survivor, you need:

1. situational awareness and preparedness
2. the ability to read peoples' behaviors
3. the ability to communicate, move, and fight
4. the ability to control fear
5. the ability to quickly take whatever actions are appropriate to the situation
6. the willingness to do whatever it takes to survive and the means to do so

You also need to have the right ethics—yes, ethics. When you have justification on your side, you have a lot more power than when you do not, and sometimes the right thing to do is to just back off. You have to use your head, always.

Post-Hoc Analysis

When an incident occurs and you make it through it, it's important to analyze what you did right and wrong. For example, my wife and I once were at the movies, and two apparent gang-bangers in their late teens or early twenties sat down next to us. Their behavior was rude and obnoxious. I was in the aisle seat, with my wife seated to my right. The kid who sat next to my wife started fidgeting, taking cell phone calls, playing with his Game Boy, and flipping around what looked like a butterfly knife and a small flashlight. In the space of a half-hour, he was in and out of our row three or four times. I traded seats with my wife, and we softly discussed our options, including:

1. Say something to the restless, crazy kid seated next to me. I chose not to say anything, as I felt anything I said would fall on deaf ears.

2. Report his behavior to the management. I ruled that out, since no one around fit that role.

3. Find another pair of seats. Not viable, all seats were taken.

4. Leave. We chose not to do that.

Post-hoc analysis? We made two major mistakes. First, we should have made an effort to find someone in management and report the kids' behavior to them. By doing so, we would have created a record of what was going on to protect us legally, had things had escalated. It also would have given the manager the option of talking to the kids, asking them to behave or leave the theater, or calling the police. Second, we should have left and gotten a rain check from the theater, taken in another movie, or gone for coffee or a drink.

When my wife and I left the theater, I watched our backs. I watched where the punks walked to in the parking lot, and I also watched my rear view mirror on our ride home. I was armed with my .40-caliber Glock 27 in a strong-side inside-the-waistband (IWB) holster; an extra magazine; a SureFire E2D Executive Defender flashlight; an Emerson pocket karambit; my keys, which are attached to a kubotan; and my back-up gun, an L.W. Seecamp .380, in my off-side front pants pocket. My wife carried her pepper spray.

I was prepared if the situation had turned ugly, but I could have made some better decisions when I was in the theater. I felt foolish when we got home, and this telling of the story probably is my *mea culpa*.

As prepared as I was for a conflict that night in the theater, I must say that being armed wasn't then and never is a mandate to act with bravado. Quite to the contrary, it carries with it an obligation to behave conservatively and avoid confrontations when at all possible. If a confrontation is unavoidable, then the armed citizen has an ethical obligation to do whatever is reasonable to try to de-escalate the situation. But, when given no other choice but to choose aggressive action, be swift, decisive, and utterly relentless so as to get the job done. Referring to something Jeff Cooper calls his color codes, you should live in Code Yellow (maximum situational awareness), and be prepared to transition to Code Orange (something doesn't feel right) at a moment's notice. Code Red, means you're ready to take action, and Code Black, the next and final step, means you're in action.

Observe, Orient, Decide, and Act

This is what is called the "OODA" loop. We all go through this perceptual motor loop when we are confronted or surprised, or when we encounter novel or discrepant stimuli.

First we *observe* something out of the ordinary. That triggers the reflex to automatically *orient* to the discrepant stimulus. We must then *decide* what to do to handle it, then *act* on our decision. Most of the time, this OODA cycle takes seconds, and we OODA hundreds of times a day.

In a confrontation, the goal is to make our adversary OODA, so that we can buy time to react and gain the upper hand. We want to throw our adversary off balance. This gives us time to OODA outta there, or finish the fight before it gets started. What this often translates into is distracting and disorienting our adversary, all while keeping your cool. Let's look at some examples.

Say a guy is tailgating you. You keep your cool and keep driving. He passes you and flips you the bird. But you don't flip it back. Instead, you gesture with your hands and eyes that he has the right of way.

How about a common big-city situation? A guy approaches you on the street and asks for money in an aggressive manner. You keep your distance, and you don't take out your wallet. You have a couple dollar bills in your pocket folded in a paper clip just for such an occasion. You tell him "Sure, no problem, here you go," as you toss the bills onto the ground and move away quickly, watching your back and 360.

Want something more dire? You're rushed at gunpoint by a guy who wants you to come with him. There is no distance between you; it's a close-in situation. You redirect his attention to "the big guy behind him," relieve him of his gun, and render him inoperable or beat feet.

Be assertive. As a trained clinical psychologist, I have had quite a bit of experience with assertiveness training. "Assertiveness" means standing up for your rights, verbally stating your preferences and needs, making your personal boundaries clear, not being afraid, and knowing how to say "No."

Being assertive is *not* the same thing as being aggressive; to be aggressive is to be belligerent or antagonistic. It's important to mentally rehearse being assertive in different situations in which you may find yourself. Predators like easy prey, so when you give off assertiveness vibes, it tends to send them away.

Practice speaking up for yourself without overt anger, and practice good eye contact. Keep your head up or level—a bowed head is a sign of submission. Work on perceiving what's going on around you with all five senses. You have two ears, two eyes, and two nostrils, but only one mouth, because it is more adaptive to listen, look, and even smell than it is to speak before we have enough information.

Rehearse paying attention in different situations and asking yourself questions such as, "What's happening here?" "What's going on?" "What's the best course of action?" "What do I need to do?" Finally, practice exercising a sense of humor when appropriate. It's often a good way to defuse tense situations.

Bluff and deceive, as you might do by claiming you're late for your shift in the scenario above. Stay calm. Act as if you feel confident, that you can remain in charge. Communicate through words and body language that you have the upper hand and that it would be a mistake for your adversary to resort to violence. Mentally rehearse these behaviors, responses, and feelings. Practice with a partner. Practice talking to a mirror. Flexibility and the ability to control fear come from having a range of adequate response options.

At the same time, don't waste words. Don't be overly talkative. Be clear in what you say. Say what you mean, and don't threaten unless you're prepared to back up the threat with real action. If your bluff is tested and you come up empty, you'll have more of a problem.

45

CHAPTER 8

Managing Uncertainty: Ten Simple Solutions

W ho knows what the world will be like five years from now, let alone in 20? The only thing we know for sure is that change and uncertainty—a condition in which you lack knowledge or confidence about what will happen to you in your daily life—will always continue. Those who know how to adjust will live more comfortably and successfully.

The Key to Coping with Uncertainty

The key to coping successfully with uncertainty is to stay calm and apply logical and effective solutions. Staying calm means controlling the intensity of your negative emotions—anxiety, fear, anger, grief, sadness, rage, helplessness, alienation, cynicism, and the feeling that you have no future. When these emotions are not controlled, they impede your ability to think clearly and process the information and facts around you in an effective and organized fashion.

Staying calm is a way of taming your emotional brain so that your executive logical brain can rationally assess and plan. The payoff for staying calm in the face of uncertainty is that you are able to see your options and choices more clearly and, thus, make the right choices. Staying calm also enables you to ignore matters that could hinder achieving your goals.

The costs of not staying calm in the face of generalized uncertainty include damage to your health, family life, effectiveness on the job, and the possibility of ending up feeling miserable and hopeless (all of which can lead to bothersome physical symptoms). In addition, the ineffective management of ongoing generalized uncertainty can lead to a chronic sense of feeling alienated from society. This can manifest in the form of cynicism, rejection of all moral and religious principles, and the feeling that life has no meaning, causing you to feel lost, dejected, and adrift, without purpose or direction. When you feel alienated like this, you become internally distracted and unable to stay abreast and aware of what is really going on in the immediate world around you—this is not conducive to maintaining personal security and assuring survival.

During this first decade of the 21st century, many people, with good reason, have become less trusting in general, given the increased media exposure of ever-evolving scams and a wide range of ways in which innocent people have been criminally victimized. Threats of violence, wars around the world, unstable and oppressive governments, and the use of terror also have contributed to instability. This has been reflected in a major change in the stability of the world economy. In addition, technology is changing at a pace that can be described conservatively as warp speed. All of this change has made people feel more vulnerable.

Given all the instability and uncertainty in our world today, I want to empower you by giving you 10 simple and practical solutions for coping with daily uncertainty. These solutions can help you to counter your feelings of vulnerability, fear, and alienation and aid you in mastering your fears of the future. (For a more detailed exposition of these concepts, see my book, *Coping With Uncertainty: 10 Simple Solutions*.)

Accept Uncertainty as Part of Life

Let's face it. When we leave the house in the morning, we don't know for sure what is going to happen to us. We can get hit by a dump truck, accosted by criminals, come home to a burglarized house, and so on. So, it is necessary for us to accept uncertainty as a fact of life. We must follow the Boy Scout motto to be prepared for the worst and expect the best.

Learn to Think Tactically

Prepare yourself mentally for tactical situations. Use mental rehearsal to go over different scenarios in your mind and rehearse mastery of them. Learning to think tactically means learning to think about how you can apply various self-defense and personal security techniques to accomplish survival tasks. These can be as simple and as commonplace as entering and exiting your vehicle with awareness—with your eyes, ears, and nose open and your mouth shut.

Which of these two photos of the author arriving at his gym demonstrates situational awareness? Hint: it's sure not the one on the left. On his cell phone, his attention directed toward the vehicle's interior, he's a prime candidate for a carjacking, a gun grab, or worse. This is not how you want to behave if you're carrying concealed.

Stay Present and Aware

Awareness refers to self-awareness, as well as environmental awareness. This means avoiding distractions. You want to nurture a developing, ever-present awareness of how you appear and employ your personality in different situations. And you want to develop a continual 360-degree awareness and attention to the world around you. You do not want to let people sneak up on you.

Manage Your Negative Moods

Managing negative moods is imperative for maintaining your personal safety. When you are depressed, angry, or afraid, you are often focused inward and not paying attention to the world around you. You then become a prime target for victimization. Additionally, if you suffer from chronic feelings of fear, which can often turn into depression and anger turned inward—it's not a frame of mind conducive to carrying concealed. Your focus is on how you feel, rather than what you can do. Don't languish in regret. Focus on what you have to accomplish.

Improve Your Tolerance for Frustration

Frustration results from not getting what you want—and sometimes getting what you *don't* want. It refers to being hindered or restrained, and it's a fact of life. To live a healthy life, you must improve the coping skills that enable you to deal with frustration.

How well you handle frustration forms the basis for how well you cope with uncertainty. Chronically facing uncertainty with no resolute strategy for handling it can lead to a state of chronic stress. This is because we have a basic biological need to resolve uncertainty. This need is what motivates new learning experiences. In fact, there is an optimal level of uncertainty. Too much may provoke excessive anxiety and tension, while too little may lead to boredom and indifference.

Unbound, continuing anxiety exacts a toll on your body. It triggers the stress response, also called the "fight-or-flight" response. This set of physical and mental reactions to uncertainty, to excessive demands, and to perceived or real threats is an adaptive response. It motivates you to reorient yourself in a reflex-like way, so that you can better cope with the stress.

The fight-or-flight response was bred into our species through Darwinian natural selection, because it was necessary for survival in prehistoric times, when humans lived in the wild with regular exposure to danger and life-threatening uncertainties. It continues to be basic to our survival today. We still live in a jungle of sorts.

The downside of the fight-or-flight stress response is that, when it continuously activates and re-activates, cascading hormonal and biochemical changes in your body even after the reasons for your stress are gone, then you don't get any rest. Eventually you and your body become exhausted from the strain.

Your brain and body work in harmony together, because there is a feedback system of chemical messenger molecules and hormones called "neurotransmitters." Chronic stress triggers this system to work in overdrive. Eventually, it gets worn down and you get worn down with it. Again, this is not conducive to effective personal-defense and your safety and security.

Always Carry a Gun

I've said this before and I'll say it again now. Let's face it. When we leave the house in the morning, we don't know for sure what is going to happen to us. Chances are that, while in your home, when you leave your home, at the mall, in school, and so on, nothing hair-raising is going to happen. However, tell that to the survivors of the Luby's Cafeteria massacre in Killeen, Texas, or to the survivors of the Columbine High School tragedy!

Say you're just taking a ride to the convenience store—a.k.a., the local stop-and rob. It's too inconvenient to pack your piece, right? Think again.

I recently trained a beginning female student who had never shot a handgun before. She was receiving threats from a local gang, which wanted a piece of her successful neighborhood business. She decided to buy a handgun and get her license to carry. She purchased a Ruger SP-101 .357 magnum snubby revolver and called me for lessons.

After one two-hour session, that gun became her constant companion and best friend. After a second lesson, she became a natural at shooting that gun. She became, as they say, "one with her gun." Good thing. One day, she was cornered in an alleyway by two gang members. They thought she was a helpless female. This femme fatale made them realize otherwise (and, thankfully, no one was hurt).

Release Tension Regularly—With a Gun

Thomas Jefferson, from age 19, had a tendency to develop prolonged, incapacitating headaches, usually correlated with stress. He was very fond of shooting, as a form of exercise and stress release. He stated, "A strong body makes the mind strong. As to the species of exercises, I advise the gun. While this gives moderate exercise to the body, it gives boldness, enterprise and independence to the mind. Games played with the ball and others of that nature, are too violent for the body and stamp no character on the mind. Let your gun, therefore, be the constant companion of your walks."

Can there be any doubt that this founding father believed in the individual's right to keep and bear arms?

Evaluate Your Real Risks

In different situations that create anxiety, you must evaluate your actual risks in order to prepare yourself to deal with any eventuality, thus managing your anxiety and preventing yourself from becoming paranoid. When you feel afraid, you tend to believe that your worst fears are just around the corner. Most of the time, this is not the case. Most of the time, fight or flight is unnecessary. However, in those rare circumstances when your worst fears really are just around the corner, your odds of survival increase greatly when you are prepared with knowledge, the necessary coping skills, and the necessary tools to get the job done.

Don't Waste Time Worrying

When you worry, you overestimate the threats or risks associated with uncertainty, and you underestimate your resources for handling it. The bigger you perceive the threat to be and the smaller you perceive your resources to be, the more anxiety you tend to have. When fear escalates out of control, it can paralyze you and cause you to avoid everything associated with the object of your fear. It then can lead to inaction or a rash action that is maladaptive and self-defeating. "The only thing we have to fear is fear itself." Sound familiar?

Change Obsessive Thoughts

It is quite common to deal with uncertainty about the future by thinking repetitive thoughts and worrying about what could possibly happen to you. Sometimes these thoughts take on a life of their own, becoming obsessions.

Having obsessions is like paying interest on trouble before it falls due. This is because obsessions not only fail to control the underlying anxiety, they make us *more* uncomfortable, because we experience them as intrusive and alien to our sense of self. However, it is very important to view obsessions not as your enemies, but as your brain's unsuccessful attempts to control your underlying fear and anxiety about the unknown. Viewing obsessions in this new way allows you to change the way you think about this problem. Instead of fighting the obsessions by telling yourself to *Stop thinking this way. This is crazy!* you can re-educate your brain to control the underlying anxiety in a new and more functional way. This process involves the following four steps:

1. Redefine the problem as a thinking habit that needs to be changed.

2. Re-educate your brain to believe that repeatedly thinking about the worst possible disaster is dysfunctional and ineffective. In fact, it becomes a problem of its own. Re-educating yourself helps you to recognize that this circular, repetitive way of thinking must be changed into a more functional and effective way of managing your anxiety.

3. Refocus your thoughts. This entails an active shift into thinking, feeling, and doing something different. One of the most successful ways to do this is to change what you are doing at the moment you become aware you are obsessing. For example, imagine walking down the street in a seedy section of town and becoming aware of your obsessive thoughts about possible disasters on the street ahead. An effective way to refocus would be to shift your awareness to what is going on around you. Be aware of your 360—watch your back, front, and sides. Keep moving. Remember the verbal tape loops you have rehearsed, should you run into a potential problem. Keep your hands ready to access your personal-defense tools wherever you carry them. This solution shifts your brain's awareness into a new focus, one associated with a feeling of control, perception, preparedness, and mastery.

4. Change the way you think about a problem. This is best accomplished when you are in a calm state and in a safe place where you can think about the problem and possible solutions without getting anxious.

CHAPTER 9

Psychological Preparedness for Combat Survival

Winning a fight for your life and surviving depends on both psychological preparedness and well-practiced fighting skills. In this chapter, I shall focus on four key elements of psychological preparedness: situational awareness, positive self-talk, fear control, and mental rehearsal.

When you are psychologically prepared for survival, you are tuned into reality. In the real world, unawareness of an imminent threat, lack of preparedness to effectively deal with it, or denial of its presence mean not surviving. History often provides memorable lessons. For example, Wild Bill Hickok certainly knew how to fight. Yet, he was shot in the back of the head and murdered during a moment of unawareness, while playing a poker game. He had let his guard down.

Good guys and gals like us normally don't go out looking for a fight. That means we have to be psychologically and physically prepared for worst-case scenarios, and that attitude should be taken just as seriously by the non-sworn law abiding armed citizen as it is by any sworn law enforcement officer.

In an emergency, I'll call 9-1-1 just as fast as I can—*after* I've dealt with any immediate threat. The fact is the police (God bless them) cannot be counted on to get there on time to save you if you are attacked. We must all must be prepared to deal with a criminal aggressor before the cavalry arrives.

Many years ago, the brother of a friend of mine was murdered in a home invasion. In more recent years, a physician in my neighborhood was similarly done in. Despite my rage at these tragic events, I am ashamed to admit that there had always been a part of me that felt that if my "moment of truth" ever came, I'd turn yellow! Then came September 11, 2001, and my outlook underwent major changes.

The events of 9/11 were our nation's wake-up call. Today, we are better prepared to preempt and defend against an attack on our borders. Truly, to my post-9/11 way of thinking, every law-abiding citizen has a stake in maintaining our "homeland security" and a responsibility to do their part. That means being psychologically prepared to use lethal force in defense of one's own life and limb.

Just so you know, I have never served in the military, I'm not a cop, and I have never been in a gunfight. However, given my professional background as a clinical psychologist, and my personal background as the son of a Holocaust survivor, the psychological keys to combat survival are of special interest to me.

Disarmed citizens are at the mercy of violent criminals and tyrannical governments. However, having a weapon will do you little good if you are caught unaware and do not have the chance to employ it (like poor Wild Bill Hickok). Worse yet, if you are unaware, and/or untrained in weapon retention techniques, your weapon can be taken away from you and used against you (one of the arguments employed by the anti-gun rights/pro-gun control crowd). So, the first step in survival is situational awareness.

"Situational awareness" means being your own bodyguard. I like to use Colonel Jeff Cooper's color codes for training on this topic. Cooper's color codes are a continuum that ranges from "Condition White" (completely tuned out and unaware) to "Condition Black" (you're in a fight for your life). It is important to point out that the rationale for the continuum is that you cannot shift directly and abruptly from "Condition White" into "Condition Black." Just as you cannot shift from reverse into drive in your car without first going through neutral, you must go through the intermediary states of awareness and readiness. Let's examine each more closely.

"Condition White" is never appropriate when you are outside the safe confines of your castle, and, even then, it may only be wise to settle into this level of unawareness for brief periods. (Certainly when you are in a deep sleep, you're in White.) So, you'd better have reliable door and window locks and a good alarm system.

Next up is "Condition Yellow." This is the level we should train ourselves to be in most of the time. "Condition Yellow" does not mean being paranoid. It means remaining alert and aware of what is going on around us.

Going into "Condition Orange" means there's something that feels not quite right. You've turned up the flame on the burner and are ready if the situation escalates into a real and imminent threat.

In "Condition Red," you are prepared for a fight. You *expect* there's going to be a fight, but you are not fighting just yet. All conditions spell "GO!" yet you remain cool because you are analyzing your tactical options—*If he does that, then, I'll do this*. You are readying yourself to prevail and survive, and you are confident that you will retain the upper hand.

"Condition Black" is the last stage. You are *in* the fight. If you have prepared up to this point, you're ahead of the game. You are employing every advantage at your disposal, and because street fights and gun fights are ugly and unfair, you do not give your attacker any benefit of the doubt or any chance to kill you. You fight dirty and cheat to live another day.

Positive Self-Talk

Self-talk is the voice we have in our head that tells us what's going to happen, and the next thing, and the next. Noted psychologist Albert Ellis has written that we are all born with a biological predisposition to think negatively, pessimistically, and irrationally. If that's true, and I think it is, then we have to work at countering this. The bottom line is that, if you think you're going to lose a fight, then you probably will. But it works the other way, too. Assuming you have the requisite physical skills and training, if you think you're going to win a fight, you have a much better chance of doing just that.

It is a good idea to become more aware of your inner self-talk, or inner voice. First, practice asking yourself, *What am I feeling right now? Scared? Sad? Mad? Glad?* Once you become familiar with identifying your emotional states or feelings, practice asking yourself, *When I feel this way, what am I telling myself?* By doing this, you will become familiar with the types of repetitive thoughts and mental images or pictures your mind generates in response to different situations.

If your inner self-talk is negative and self-defeating, it is necessary to practice countering it with positive (but realistic) self-talk. For example, replace *I can't learn to do this* with *I can learn to do this, and I will learn it.* Replace, too, negative mental images with those that program your subconscious mind for mastery, victory, and survival. For example, if you see

> Having a weapon with you will do little good if you are caught unaware and don't have the chance to deploy it. "Situational awareness," the solution to this, means being your own bodyguard.

or imagine yourself looking like an easy mark to a couple of punks, practice imagining yourself displaying a more confident and self-reliant demeanor.

Fear Control

Author and security consultant Gavin de Becker wrote a book called *The Gift of Fear*. What he was trying to get at with the title is that fear is a feeling that should be acknowledged and then responded to, as a signal that there may be a problem that needs to be dealt with. Fear must be heeded for the information it can provide. It is your body's and mind's automatic responses to a perceived threat, a signal it's time to move from "Condition Yellow" to "Condition Orange" and as far along the color continuum as the situation dictates.

When we are confronted with a threat to our survival, our bodies automatically prepare for fight or flight. The perceived threat triggers what Massad Ayoob, the developer of the Stressfire defensive shooting system, has clearly explained as a physiological "Body Alarm Reaction," or BAR. When the BAR is triggered, there's a massive adrenaline dump into the bloodstream. This stimulant hormone causes our heart to race, our blood pressure to rise, our muscles to tense, our visual and auditory focus to narrow, our visual and auditory acuity to increase, and our breathing to quicken and become shallow. If we are trained to fight, and there is no opportunity to preclude the fight, our body is physiologically prepared to do so reflexively. If we perceive an opportunity to flee and avoid the fight, our body is prepped to do that, also. So, the BAR is adaptive, at least to a point.

If the BAR gets out of hand, or we are not prepared to fight and we perceive no opportunity to flee, then we may freeze. This is definitely *not* a good option in the face of the tiger. Remember, to survive, fear must be controlled. And, for fear to be controlled, it first must be acknowledged. Recognize that fear is a natural response when facing the tiger, and *not* a sign of cowardice.

Now, once fear is acknowledged, the body alarm reaction must be controlled and harnessed to pump our fighting machine.

When fear gets out of hand and the BAR is in overdrive, psychologically, we feel that we are going to die. As a result, physiologically, not only do our muscles tense up (or sometimes go limp), but we tend to hold our breath, feel a tightness in our chest, breathe shallowly (or heavily) from our upper chest, and/or hyperventilate and become light-headed. Our body temperature drops and our hands and feet turn cold (or perhaps sweaty). Our stomach, bladder and bowels also react. We may feel butterflies or pain in our stomach, and we may lose bladder or bowel control. We may feel as if our body is going to explode or implode, or that we are going to jump out of our skin. All of the above result in our feeling more tense, vulnerable, and out of control. There are three remedies for this.

The first is a physiological step. You must become aware of breath holding, erratic or shallow breathing, or hyperventilation and control it. You can begin to learn breath control by taking three to five slow, deep, and controlled breaths when you are by yourself in a safe environment (in Conditions White or Yellow). I teach my clients to inhale deeply through their nose to a count of five, hold it for a count of three, and then to exhale forcefully through their mouth to a count of eight, blowing stress and tension out into the atmosphere. If this is too difficult at first, you can inhale as deeply as you can, hold, and exhale as forcefully as you can to lower counts, and then work up to greater breath depth and higher numbers as you get better at it. At first, you may feel somewhat light-headed, but with continued practice, the light-headedness will disappear and you will notice that you feel more relaxed, alert, and in control.

Faced with a 2 a.m. home invasion, you must control your fear. Part of that control should be positive self-talk, such as *We've planned for this, we're going to follow that plan, and we are NOT going to die tonight!*

Slow, controlled, deep breathing is a switch that turns down the BAR and turns on the relaxation response. It's a good idea to practice this skill often throughout the day and enjoy how much more in charge you feel. It only takes a minute or so. As you retrain yourself to become more aware of your breathing, first in normal situations and then in normal, everyday stressful situations, you will eventually be able to employ your breathing to your advantage in a crisis such as a fight. Of course, in the middle of a fight, you are not going to have time to focus on your breathing. The point is that, if you've practiced, you'll automatically breathe away your unnecessary stress and tension.

The second remedy to runaway BAR is a psychological step and the second key element discussed above, positive self-talk. If you were faced by three gang-banging punks, but you had Steven Seagal and Chuck Norris on your side, you'd probably feel more confident wouldn't you? What would you be telling yourself?

The idea is to talk to yourself in such a way that your body gets the message to turn the BAR down to a level that is optimal to the circumstances at hand, just enough activation to be able to use your training to smartly deal with your attackers and prevail. For example, faced with a home invasion in the middle of the night, you want to be telling yourself things like, *We've planned for this. We are going to follow our plan. Step one is … . Step two is … . We are NOT going to &*%$ing die tonight!*

The third step to reducing BAR is mental rehearsal. Like dry-fire practice with an empty firearm, this enables you to practice employing all of the above techniques and your physical and tactical training in your mind enough times so that, if the real deal ever transpires, you are ready. Competitive shooters use visualization techniques like this, as do other successful athletes. The key is to mentally visualize and go through in your mind (mentally rehearse) how you want to handle a challenging situation.

This exercise works best if you first put yourself into a relaxed state using slow, controlled, deep breathing. When you are relaxed, you cannot also be tense, stressed, or scared, because relaxation and these other states are emotional and physical opposites. So, by first getting relaxed, you calm your mind and, thus, can think more clearly and concentrate better. You are more alert and aware and in tune with reality. Your negative self-talk, which is often exaggerated and unrealistic, gets turned down, and your subconscious mind is more receptive to positive impressions

Use mental rehearsal to run movies in your head of you dealing with a challenging situation, doing what you have to do, and winning. You are the producer and the director, so take full editorial privileges. Explore different scenarios, different variables, different tactics, and different outcomes. Run it forward and backward. Cut and splice segments.

You can also employ mental rehearsal as a means of learning techniques from an expert role model. The first step is to closely observe the expert performing the skill. The second step is to imagine what it would feel like to be that expert as he or she performs the skill. If your fear or distraction level goes up, simply interrupt the imagery rehearsal to get more relaxed with your neutral breathing, and then go back to your mental rehearsal.

You can also employ mental rehearsal (which I cover more fully later on) by triggering a mini BAR and then employing breath control and positive self-talk to turn it down. Purposefully seek out and confront uncomfortable or slightly risky situations that get your level of physiological arousal up. Then practice your neutral breathing and positive self-talk to overcome it.

CHAPTER 10

Common Gun-Control Myths

Guns Kill People?

More often than not, weapons save lives. But, because our media is so often anti-gun, the positive aspects of self-protection often go unreported, despite the literature published by various firearms presses that regularly describes situations where civilians have successfully defended and saved themselves or others with a firearm. (The scholar John Lott wrote a data-based book about this selective news reporting on the part of big media, entitled *More Guns, Less Crime*, a must-read for doubters.) I've even seen firsthand some students I have trained come back and describe situations where their knowledge and unimpeded access to a usable firearm have deflated a situation that could have easily gotten out of hand or become lethal.

Firearms training and knowledge is a proactive, as opposed to reactive, response to your personal defensive needs. No serious trainee ever wants to take a life or use a firearm inappropriately. But, the fact is a firearm used appropriately by a trained individual can level the playing field, when such an individual is confronted with the threat of a physical confrontation neither sought nor expected.

It is important to highlight the fact that a firearm is just a tool that can be used appropriately—or inappropriately—just like any other. Without adequate preparation, any tool is valueless, and sometimes dangerous. But, back to an answer to the original question. A firearm does not have independent agency, because it does not have conscious thought. Therefore a gun cannot shoot anyone or discharge unless there is someone who misuses its capabilities.

Throughout recorded history, society has produced numerous effective and deadly protective tools. Often times, the people with the weapons were the source of power and the people without them their victims. The invention of firearms did not alter human beings' violent propensities. It just somewhat equaled the playing field for the underdog who had access to firearms.

Do More Guns Mean More Crime?

The majority of firearms are legally purchased and owned by responsible, law-abiding citizens. Percentage-wise, the firearms used in crimes are mostly attached to the underground market, though a small number of cases of illegal usage of firearms by registered owners does occur. In reality, the number of firearms produced does not correlate with the number of crimes with them. It is only when an isolated event (e.g., the Virginia Tech University and Columbine

High School mass shootings, the Washington, D.C.-area snipers, etc.), gets reported by the news media and purported to be a sign that firearms are the most destructive element of our society that undue attention is raised about the need for gun control. It is also important to recognize that, in many of these cases (e.g., Columbine), the perpetrators had other lethal weapons as well, such as explosive devices, knives, and so forth—yet few people have gone on record arguing for bomb or knife control.

The majority of statistical and epidemiological studies have shown that the legal availability of guns is actually correlated with a *lowered* incidence of reported violent crimes. These studies have revealed that, in the United States, states with rigid restrictions on citizens' access to firearms have a higher incidence of violent criminal activity than do states that are less restrictive and allow concealed carry. Other studies demonstrate that countries that have taken away citizens' rights to own firearms (e.g., Canada, Great Britain, Australia, Japan) actually have higher rates of violent crime per capita than do countries where such regulation is not legislated.

> A majority of studies, including those statistical, has shown that the legal availability of guns actually correlated with a *lowered* incidence of reported violent crimes.

Totalitarian regimes flourish in countries where only the government, the military, and the police are permitted gun rights (e.g., Cuba, Iran, Iraq, North Korea). In such societies, citizens are at the mercy of the state. For the best example of this, one has only to look at the bureaucratic net that was cast in Nazi Germany during the 1930s, when Hitler was building his power. The end result was the ultimate in fascist governments, mass genocide, and the elimination of a generation.

Statistics compiled by leading criminal justice authorities reveal, in numerous cases, that the showing of a firearm is often a powerful deterrent to a criminal otherwise intent on carrying out an attack. Therefore, carrying a handgun as a viable defense measure makes good sense—so long as you remember that you should never draw a firearm unless absolutely necessary (read ,in a life threatening situation), and you should never draw a gun unless you are ready to use it. The goal should always be to defuse a situation as quickly as possible without violence, before the situation can turn violent.

Carrying a firearm is a responsibility that should not be taken lightly, because it is often the last resort for defusing a situation, rather than escalating it. Responsible gun owners recognize and understand this, thus, they are peacemakers, not the outlaws some would have us believe.

People who legally carry concealed handguns are not cowboys. They value and cherish human life and do not denigrate it. In fact, assuming the responsibility of legal gun ownership highlights how important it is to be in control at all times. One must celebrate human life and detest aggression and violence.

Do Gun-Control Laws Stop Criminals From Getting Firearms?

The underground marketplace is a viable source of goods for criminals. One has only to look at the failure of the United States government to control the distribution, sale, and use of illegal drugs to see why: people who are determined to use any illegal commodity usually find an available source, despite government regulatory restrictions.

The most compelling issue that distinguishes firearms from other regulated or prohibited commodities is that firearms are capable, in the right hands, of repelling criminal attack, violent confrontations, and promoting personal survival. Therefore, in many overly regulated states that discourage firearm ownership and prohibit the right to carry weapons for self-defense, many citizens are faced with a dilemma between carrying illegally to protect themselves and finding themselves criminal violators, or surrendering themselves to opportunistic criminal attack. This then creates a breeding ground for black market enterprise. The fact is that, when legal avenues for obtaining desired products are closed by the state, opportunities for other sources to profit with open up. So, then, the question is, do we want to see criminal organizations control the sale and distribution of firearms?

Of course not. Firearms ownership is a basic right and not a privilege. Therefore, the best way to demonstrate genuine concern for the public good is not to make criminals out of its citizens. At the same time, education and training should be strongly encouraged. Gun safety demands more education, not more legislation.

What's in a Name?

Many organizations purposefully choose names that mislead the public. For example, there are organizations that have the words "public safety" in their name, yet they do nothing to teach people how to live safer lives. They are, in fact, ultimately dedicated to taking away people's rights and property!

On the other hand, organizations such as the National Rifle Association (NRA), are dedicated to running organized educational programs that help people enjoy self-defense safely. As well, there are many firearms manufacturers that have devoted large sums of money to public safety awareness and education, including Ruger, Glock, Smith & Wesson, and many more.

Are Guns Just for Militias?

The founding fathers who designed the Bill of Rights had direct experience with the era's European tactics of oppression. As such, they specifically designed and appropriately positioned the Second Amendment as one of the most important to the Constitution. It specially mandated the right of the individual citizen to keep and bear firearms in order to combat oppression, tyranny, and injustices so often perpetrated in the European theater. The founding fathers realized that a citizenry prohibited by its government from arming itself was at the mercy of that government, and that any government that did so was not "by and for the people."

61

CHAPTER 11

The Judicious Use of Deadly Force

When would the use of deadly force by a private citizen against another human be considered judicious? How can a private citizen be authorized to kill another human under his or her own summary judgment? The very simple answer is that deadly force is recognized as a last resort for use only when you need to save your life.

We are referring to the "doctrine of competing harms" and the "doctrine of necessity." Put very simply, you are allowed to break the law (in this instance, kill), in the rare circumstances where following the law (not killing) would cause more injury to you or other innocent humans.

In reality, the answer is not so simple. Any time you even draw your gun in a social confrontation, you are walking on thin ice. If you are going to keep or carry a gun for self-defense, in addition to being well trained in marksmanship and tactics, you should be well-educated about the circumstances under which the use of deadly force is warranted legally and morally, so that you can be judicious.

There is probably no one who has contributed more to our understanding of the conditions under which the defensive use of deadly force is ethically, morally, and legally justified than has Massad Ayoob. Ayoob is a prolific firearms author, master instructor, legal expert, and the founder and director of the Massad Ayoob Group (www.MassadAyoobGroup.com). In this chapter, we will examine some of the important points taught by this expert.

Deadly or lethal force is that degree of force a reasonable person would consider capable of causing death or grave bodily harm. Those of us who carry a concealed handgun carry the power to use deadly force. This is a tremendous power, and, as Ayoob points out, there comes a tremendous amount of responsibility and a higher standard of care with their power. This higher standard of care *demands* that the armed citizen, senior or otherwise, exercise good judgment and appropriate restraint.

Good judgment includes always effectively concealing your firearm and retaining it. It entails properly securing your firearm at all times so that your weapon does not fall into unauthorized hands. It also means avoiding situations you know beforehand could turn ugly, as well as never provoking (and leaving, if possible), a confrontation when you are armed.

Ayoob teaches that, as civilians, our only obligation and right is to keep ourselves and our families from being unlawfully injured or killed. We may only use equal force in response to the application of force against us. If we are not innocent of provoking a confrontation, or we are not being immediately threatened with deadly force, we cannot use deadly force in response. This is unlike the obligation of a sworn police officer, who may use necessary force to fulfill his or her duties.

Ayoob's formula for determining the circumstances under which we would be justified in employing deadly force is both simple and complex. This formula is based on English Common Law and Dutch/Roman Law, and it applies in all 50 states. It is determined by three criteria that can be remembered by the acronym AOJ (think "Administration of Justice"). The situation must meet all three criteria to justify the use of deadly force.

Here's a guy holding a knife in an aggressive manner. Can you shoot him? Not a chance, with that fence in between you. Though this guy is behaving in a threatening manner, unless he vaults over that fence like Superman, there's no real threat to you.

A = Ability—The person deemed to be a threat must possess the ability or power to kill or maim.

O = Opportunity—The person deemed to be a threat must be capable of immediately employing his power to kill or maim.

J = Jeopardy—The person deemed to be a threat must be acting in such a manner that a reasonable and prudent person would conclude beyond doubt that the intent of that person is to kill or cripple.

All of the above are judged by the doctrine of the reasonable man, that is, your defense of self-defense is affirmative if you knew all of the above at the time you employed deadly force. Now, with that said, I would add a fourth criterion to Ayoob's three, that being preclusion. What this means is that you must have done everything within your power to have *avoided* having to use deadly force in the first place.

Let's now look at some caveats that Ayoob covers in his teaching. One of those he teaches first is that, "If you have warning that a situation is likely to turn bad, you

Same guy, same fence, same knife. But now you're both on the same side of the fence. Can you shoot him? Maybe, maybe not. He's still at a pretty good distance—do you have the time to escape and a direction in which to do so? This would be a really good time to yell, "Stop! Leave right now! I am armed!"

If this isn't too close for comfort, then you're wearing head-to-toe body armor. Can you shoot this knife-wielding attacker, who's now at bad-breath distance and looks like he's about to gut you like a fish? Possibly, probably—but you have lots of other questions to answer first. Do you have a knife and are you physically equal to the attacker? Is there still time to escape? Is there any other less-than-lethal force, such as pepper spray or martial arts skills, that can diffuse this situation? You must, *must*, think through every and all options before you draw your gun and shoot.

should not venture knowingly into it. For example, if someone says that, if you show your face at a particular place (a bar, a street corner, a class, etc.) they will kill you, don't go there! If you do go there, and then you are forced to use deadly force in self-defense and you kill the guy, you may be found culpable. We don't live in the Wild West, although there may be some who beg to differ."

Another caveat has to do with how you size up the criterion of ability. Here we are talking about the concepts of power and disparity of force. Clearly, a person with a gun or a knife and the ability to use it has the power to kill or cripple you. However, you can't shoot that person unless he has the *immediate* opportunity to use that ability on you and he acts in such a manner that leads you to reasonably conclude you are in immediate jeopardy. But, what about if the threat does *not* have a gun, knife, or bludgeon? There are several other factors that would fulfill the criterion for ability.

1. **Force of numbers.** Two or more threatening persons, even without identifiably deadly weapons, against you alone, would constitute a disparity of force. If they attack you and act in such a manner as to lead you to believe that, unless you do something, they are going to kill

> When can you use deadly force? Well, your attacker must possess the ability and opportunity to do you grave harm—but *you* must also have to have done everything in your ability to *avoid* a confrontation.

or cripple you, then you are on solid legal ground. Against a group of attackers, each member of the group shares the same responsibility for the fear the group creates in the intended victim, and also shares the danger from the intended victim's lawful response.

2. **Able-bodied versus the disabled.** If you are old and frail or physically challenged and you are viciously attacked by a younger, more able-bodied man (and the criteria of opportunity

No doubt, the guy in the gray T-shirt appears to be in imminent and deadly danger. If he could draw his gun and discharge it at this point, he would most likely be in the right, when it comes to self-defense and the law.

and jeopardy are in play), you are on solid legal ground.

3. **Greater physical size and strength.** If you are attacked by King Kong Bundy, you are on solid legal ground in using a force multiplier (a weapon) to avoid being killed or crippled.

4. **Training or reputation.** Is the attacker a person known to you to be highly trained in the martial arts? For this criterion to be considered a valid, affirmative defense for the defensive use of deadly force, you must have known about it *before* you resorted to using deadly force. It is not valid if you didn't know it at the time, but learned that it was so after the fact. You will be judged based solely on what you knew at the time.

5. **Male versus female.** Our society assumes that females are more vulnerable and that there is a cultural predisposition for males to be more inclined to violent physical aggression than females. So, if you are female, you are being attacked by a lone male, and the other criteria of opportunity and jeopardy are in play, you are on solid legal ground in terms of using deadly force if you have no other viable choice to avoid being killed or crippled. This would also include self-defense against rape.

Rape is Violence

Ayoob notes that criminal justice statistics show 79 percent of rapists are unarmed, but nevertheless, there is a disparity of force present—rapists are armed with ferocious aggression, greater size or physical strength, or strength of numbers, as in gang rape situations. It also notes that 14 percent of rapists are armed with contact weapons (e.g., an edged weapon, a bludgeon, etc.), while the other seven percent of rapists tend to be armed with a gun.

Edged Weapons as a Lethal Threat

Clearly, a knife or edged weapon is a contact weapon, as opposed to a firearm, which is a remote weapon. So, a man who yells and threatens to kill you with a knife from 100 feet across a busy street is not an immediate threat. You can *not* shoot him. That same man brandishing a firearm is an immediate threat if, by his actions, he places you in imminent jeopardy.

When it comes to knives, opportunity is of special importance and is a component of two things, distance and obstacles. It may not be common knowledge, but a man with a knife or club and who is 21 or fewer feet away from you has the ability and opportunity to place you in imminent jeopardy. Thanks to the pioneering work in the 1980s of Dennis Tueller, a now-retired

Salt Lake City Police Department Lieutenant and an instructor at Gunsite, we now know that it takes around 1.5 seconds for a person with a knife to close a gap of 21 feet and be on top of you. For the average trained person carrying a concealed handgun, it will take *more* than 1.5 seconds to draw from concealment, fire, and hit the target at those same seven yards.

This has been a summary of the key considerations that must be present for the application of deadly force to be justified. Always bear in mind, though, that every situation will be different. Each deadly force situation will be judged based upon the totality of the circumstances. This chapter has just highlighted what Massad Ayoob teaches. I strongly recommend that, at a minimum, you get his DVD and read his book, *In the Gravest Extreme: The Role of the Firearm in Personal Protection*.

CHAPTER 12

The Rules of Engagement

Anyone who would *want* to shoot somebody is either extremely naïve or insane. Once the trigger is pulled, the consequences are grave and irrevocable. Using a gun as a social problem-solving tool in a non-war environment is a very last resort saved for the gravest of extremes. Therefore, because the potential for petty conflict in today's society is high, carrying a firearm for self-defense requires that you adhere to a higher standard of care than if you were to go unarmed. Bullets cannot be taken back.

As an armed citizen, you must exercise good judgment and behave in a responsible manner at all times. "Judgment" refers to your decision-making ability, being able to find and evaluate the essential facts in a situation and come to a conclusion about what to do that is adaptive, smart, and healthy.

Anything that clouds or dampens your judgment does not mix with firearms. This is why alcohol doesn't mix with guns. In fact, anything that is associated with excessive exuberance, the potential for erratic behavior, or unnecessary attention directed at you doesn't mix with carrying a gun. Carrying a gun should not be what gives you courage. Indeed, as an armed citizen, you have *less,* not *more,* latitude to behave in a reckless or brash manner.

In order to justify the use of lethal force, and in order to be able to establish an affirmative defense of self-defense, you must follow certain rules of engagement. I recently came across a little booklet on this topic authored by firearms expert Chuck Klein and entitled *Klein's C.C.W. Handbook: The Requisite for those who Carry Concealed Weapons*. In my opinion, this excellent guidebook should be in the library of everyone who carries. At minimum, I recommend that you commit Klein's "Rules of Engagement" to memory.

Klein states, "In order to justify the use of lethal force, i.e., establishing the defense of self-defense, the discharge of a firearm at another person shall be instituted only when all of the following apply:

1. You were not at fault or did not create the situation that gave rise to the taking of another's life.

2. You believe you were in danger of imminent death or great bodily harm.

3. You must not have violated any opportunity to retreat or avoid the danger.

4. You have exhausted all other means to avoid the use of deadly force.

5. The use of deadly force presents no substantial risk of injury to innocent persons.

Rule No. 1: You were not at fault.

You can't start the fight or egg someone on so that, when they attack you, you then bring out the hardware. Anything you do to escalate a confrontation adds to your responsibility for what ultimately happens.

For example, a driver with road rage thinks I cut him off. He pulls up beside me at the next stop sign and aggressively demands to know why I cut him off. I capitulate by telling him, "I am sorry. I thought I had enough distance. I didn't mean to cut you off. I am really sorry." He drives away. Or maybe he won't accept my apology and gets out of his car, in which case I could drive away. These are the right ways to handle situations like these, for if either had turned really bad and I hadn't backed down, I could be deemed the aggressor in the eyes of the law.

Rule No. 2: You believe you were in danger of imminent death or great bodily harm.

The key is what you *believe* to be the case at the time—do you have reasonable grounds to believe the threat is real?

First, does the attacker appear to have the *ability* to cause you irrevocable harm? Here, again we are talking about disparity of force. Ability can refer to force of numbers (more of them than you), the able-bodied against the disabled, male against female, (men are typically stronger and more aggressive than women), young against old, etc. Ability can even carry to train versus untrained, if your opponent is known to you to be a boxer, special forces, black belt, etc., *prior* to your using your firearm.

Second, does the attacker have the *immediate opportunity* to cause you irrevocable harm? Is he capable of immediately employing his power to seriously hurt you?

Third, is your opponent acting in such a manner (by words and/or deeds) that a reasonable and prudent person would conclude that he harbors intent to kill or cripple you? In other words, are his actions placing you in imminent jeopardy?

Rule No. 3: You have not violated the opportunity to retreat or avoid danger.

John Farnam teaches that you must do what you can to disengage safely at the earliest point in a confrontation (or potential confrontation—the best sort of disengagement is to not be there in the first place.) Avoid confrontations by making an exit at the first hint of trouble.

Farnam also teaches that avoidance has several layers. The first layer is to not be where the confrontation is in the first place. The second is to leave before a potentially bad situation turns worse and goes in the toilet. The third layer is referred to as "functional invisibility." This means you should try not to turn heads; live a stealth existence below the radar. Finally, the fourth layer is to act in a decisive, deliberate, confident, and assertive manner so that you are consistently *de-selected* for victimization.

In keeping with Rule No. 3, it is a good idea to make it a habit of identifying the points of entry and exit every time you enter a place. Look around the room and notice who is noticing you. Parking lots and driveways are places where victims are often selected, and that is where people unwittingly tend to get distracted.

The other day, I was eating in a diner with my wife and daughter, when a man at the next table began to get loud and belligerent with his companions. I told my wife and daughter "Let's get out of here," and we left. Should that problem have escalated, I wanted us to be far away. The kind of witness we want to be is the type who left five minutes before something happened!

Rule No. 4: You have exhausted all other means to avoid the use of deadly force.

You are not justified in shooting a knife-wielding aggressor if you can drive away. You must avail yourself of other options if you safely are able before you resort to using deadly force. Farnam teaches that, if you are walking down the street and approached by a stranger, keep moving. Walk right on through. Do not stop in the spot that the potential predator has chosen, because you are probably being set up. Do not answer his questions. Politely dismiss him with your pre-rehearsed verbal tape loops.

For example, if you are asked for spare change or directions, your response should be something like, "I'm sorry, sir, I can't help you." Indeed, whatever the request is, your response should be the same. And you should keep moving as you respond verbally and while making brief eye contact. Remember that prey behavior excites predators. So, act assertively and confident.

Failing these tactics working, Farnam wisely points out that you want to divide the potential predator's focus and disrupt his plan. So, you can point down at the ground just behind the person, with your support hand and away from your gun side as you verbalize with excitement something to the effect of "Uh-oh! Look out!" Then move around him.

If that fails, escalate the ante. Verbalize something like "Get away from me! Leave me alone!" Then break contact and disengage.

Maybe none of that works. Next, some intermediate, non-lethal form of persuasion may be called for, such as a blast of pepper spray in the predator's face. (If you carry a gun, you should carry pepper spray. It is good to have options!) Remember, your goal is to keep from getting hurt. You work your way up the force continuum if that is safe and possible. If you have no other option than to resort to deadly force, you still want to find a way out of the gravest extreme safely if possible. If you have time and can draw your firearm and not use it, this is infinitely better than the alternative. Just because you draw your gun does not mean you have to shoot. It means you must be *prepared* to shoot. If there's time and it's still safe to do so, drawing your gun and shouting a challenge such as "Please! Don't move! Drop your weapon!" and *then* evaluating your situation is infinitely better than just letting it rip.

Rule No 5: Deadly force presents no substantial risk to innocent persons.

What if deadly force is your only option? The lawfully armed and trained citizen with a moral conscience presents a much safer bet for protecting innocent bystanders than does the amoral criminal predator. But, you still must consider where you are and who is around you.

CHAPTER 13

A Clear View of Your Defensive Needs

Do you have a clear view of your defensive and security needs? Your personal safety depends on it. If you are too paranoid, you may become overly focused on perceived threats to the exclusion of all else. If you are not paranoid enough, you may walk into an ambush. The world is a dangerous place, and you don't want to become some scum bag's lunch, but you do want to be able to enjoy your own lunch. What's the solution? Develop a realistic and clear view of your defensive and security needs.

How Vulnerable are You?

Ask yourself whether you look vulnerable. If the answer is "Yes," there are some things you can do to look less vulnerable. Through appropriate physical exercise and good diet, you can probably improve your health and build physical strength. You can take a self-defense class geared to your level of physical fitness. You can train with your carry firearm and develop skill in its deployment. When you improve your physical conditioning and increase your skill level with your personal defense weapon, you will also develop greater self-confidence, which will be reflected in your outward appearance.

"What If ... ?"

Prior to anything ever taking place, there are several questions you should ask yourself about how you are going to respond in a wide variety of "What if?" scenarios. You should write your answers down for each scenario and review them. You can also prepare by mentally rehearsing your options. Employ relaxation, mental visualization, and mental imagery, along with self-affirmations. Then, if an incident occurs that is similar to what you have mentally prepared for, you will instinctively run through your checklist of responses as the incident unfolds, and you will be prepared.

For each "what if" scenario, ask yourself these seven basic, universally applicable questions. By doing so, you will be preparing yourself to handle most possible scenarios.

1. What options can I choose to avoid being in such a situation?

2. If I can't avoid it, who will I be facing, and what will they be armed with?

3. What are my responsibilities, and what actions must I take to survive and prevail?

4. From where is my best defensive posture taken?

5. How can I prepare myself well ahead of such an incident and what tools will I need?

6. How can I best defend myself in the particular setting in which I'm involved, unfamiliar and uncomfortable as I am, at the worst possible moment?

7. How can I prepare myself to deal with the aftermath once I've survived, and how can I avoid or be better prepared for such an incident should it happen again?

Appropriate Restraint

Appropriate restraint means the ability to exercise good judgment about the threat level you are exposed to and the appropriate level of response to the situation. Your major influences should be time of day, distance from your assailant, ability to get help, and your ability to prevail. In most jurisdictions, a prosecutor or grand jury will not condone the use of a much greater level of force than that with which you were confronted. In other words, you can't pull a gun on someone for rude behavior. If you are threatened, the laws in most jurisdictions state that you have the duty to retreat if possible, except in your own home. (Regarding the home, most jurisdictions call this the "Castle Doctrine.")

> In most jurisdictions, a prosecutor will not condone the use of a much greater level of force than that with which you were confronted. In other words, you can't pull a gun on someone for rude behavior.

Command Presence

In a confrontational situation, it is imperative that you take control and command. "Command presence," a component of this, is an absolute. Police departments base their authority upon it—they give orders to people on a daily basis on how to get out of the line of fire. On a smaller scale, if you are in your residence or in a vehicle on the road and you are threatened with imminent bodily harm, you must give commands to your children, your spouse, or to other companions who may otherwise be panic stricken. Panic will get you killed. Someone must take the responsibility. A weak-kneed person is probably a dead person. Without command and control, the situation will end badly.

The Ability to De-escalate

The ability to de-escalate refers to ceasing your lethal response once you are sure that the threat and aggression have been contained and/or have ceased. This is an important part of your total defense plan. We're *not* the aggressors. We're the defenders. Our right is to survive, not to punish. The latter job is for a judge and jury. We must do whatever it is that we have to do to stop an attacker from doing whatever it is that he is doing that threatens us with imminent death or serious bodily harm. So, for example, we can't shoot someone who is running away and are no longer an immediate or continuing threat. In fact, you have a *duty* to retreat, if this option is available.

The Aftermath

Anyone who carries a gun for self-protection should have a lawyer whom they trust and can call for representation, should they be forced into a lethal encounter. Keep in mind that, after such an encounter, you will have to justify all your actions to the authorities. You will have to articulate and authenticate your actions—but the time to do so is not as the police are arriving. You are well advised to keep your talking to a bare minimum, until you have met with your attorney. Even though right after a deadly force critical incident you will have the urge to talk and get things off of your chest, cease and desist from doing so. You will be so shaken up, there is no way that you can render accurate statements of the details of what just unfolded. Everything you say can and will be used against you, so you need to say nothing beyond something to the effect of, "Officers, thank goodness you're here. He attacked me, I thought my life was in danger, and I had to defend myself. I'd like to press charges." Then tell the officer that you'll be happy to answer any of their questions *after* you've met with your lawyer. Do not talk yourself into a bad situation.

CHAPTER 14

Your Plan for Concealed Carry

What would you do if you saw a stranger dragging your granddaughter or wife into a shed, you were attacked, someone tried to carjack you, someone began to beat you up, or someone broke into your house? People usually answer with, "I really don't know!" or "You really have to be in the situation to know how you'd react" or "I'd probably freeze." Such lack of preparedness is not conducive to survival.

As discussed in the NRA's Basic Pistol and Personal Protection curricula (www.nra.org), your personal-defense plan and security rest on the triad of acquiring the necessary knowledge and equipment, developing the needed skills, and cultivating the right attitude—things we've been talking about in this book all along. Let's expand on that now.

Hardware

The right gun for you is a personal decision, but one that should be influenced by the desire to own quality products you can depend on to help you defend your life. There are many good manufacturers in today's firearms marketplace, but the handguns you choose should not be a function of the latest hype advertised in the gun magazines. You should research what your particular needs are—how you dress, where you travel, what calibers you can handle, your hand size, etc.—and choose accordingly.

How you dress is a top concern. You have to dress differently to carry concealed, and many times this means looser fitting clothing. Your firearm must be under your control at all times. Your handgun must be on or about your person, something that isn't always convenient, but if you are going to carry, it is your responsibility to assure your gun is not taken away from you!

The purpose of a holster is to keep your handgun secure and clean, and your gun should be in a holster when it is on your person. The gun must be hidden from view and be accessible only to you, its rightful owner. As with choosing a gun, your choice of a concealed carry holster is a personal decision that should be based on what your particular needs are.

No matter how you carry, be safety conscious. The primary causes of firearms-related incidents are ignorance and carelessness. So get educated. You must burn into your brain and muscle memory these six basic firearm safety rules:

1. Know how to operate and maintain your firearms. You should thoroughly read and famil-

iarize yourself with the manufacturer's operating manuals of your self-defense firearms. You should know the components of your defensive handguns, how they work, and how to operate and maintain your handguns. Keep your guns clean, and check their operation routinely.

2. Know what the proper ammunitions are for your firearm and when to use certain types. For example, 9mm Parabellum (a.k.a. 9mm Luger or 9mm NATO) is not the same as 9mm Kurtz (a.k.a. 9mm Short or .380 ACP). Although it is a good idea to practice occasionally with the ammunition you carry, conserve your more expensive hollowpoint (HP) ammunition just for that duty. The less expensive, full metal jacket (FMJ) ammunition is what you want for general practice, but not for defense. Especially in calibers smaller than .45 ACP and .40 S&W, they tend to be poor fight stoppers. They also tend to over-penetrate, which can create a safety hazard to innocent bystanders. Hollowpoint ammunition, which is generally more expensive, is what you want to carry for defense. This bullet design is less likely to over penetrate and more likely to create fight-stopping tissue damage due to the expanding, mushrooming effect it has when it penetrates flesh. It is a good idea to run the HP ammunition that you intend to carry for self defense through your self-defense firearms to make sure they like the ammo (no gun is equally accurate with all ammo or, necessarily, reliable). Also, make sure to regularly inspect your personal defense ammunition for imperfections, and recycle ammo yearly. Don't let ammo get wet, and avoid using reloaded ammunition for personal defense and carry!

> **While hollowpoint ammunition is generally more expensive than ball ammo, it is the best choice for your carry gun, as its potential for over-pentration is reduced and the possibiity for tissue damage enhanced.**

3. Handle all firearms as if they are loaded and immediately ready to fire, all the time. "Unloaded" guns are handled no differently than loaded ones.

4. The muzzle of any firearm must not, at any time, be allowed to point in an unsafe direction. Never point a firearm at anything you are not willing to destroy!

5. Always keep your finger off of the trigger until your sights are on a target and you have made the conscious decision to fire at the target at that instant.

6. Before firing, be sure of your target and the area around and beyond it.

Skill Development

Here are several basic skills you'll need to incorporate into your daily life.

1. Rehearse disengagement responses to strange people on the street who approach you. For example, a panhandler asks you, "Hey Mister, can you help me?" Be ready for his come-on. As John Farnam of Defense Training International (www.defense-training.com) teaches, interrupt him half way through his sentence, raise your weak/support hand in a half-wave/half-dismissive chop and say politely, but firmly, and in a clear voice loud enough for everyone nearby to

hear, "Sorry sir. I can't help you." Continue walking without hesitancy. Leave no doubt in the possible predator's mind that he has selected the wrong victim. Farnam points out in his classes that, "Successful disengagement can usually be accomplished via posture and firm verbalizations, but you must be practiced and have your 'tape-loops' ready to go!"

2. Get good training. There are many good shooting schools these days, but, as you would with any school, do your homework and get references. Talk to people who have attended a given school so you don't waste your hard earned money and valuable time. A good way to find a list of shooting schools is to join the organization called the United States Concealed Carry Association (www.usconcealed-carry.com), as well as the NRA (www.nra.org). Both organizations are dedicated to preserving and advancing our gun rights

Training to shoot defensively isn't remotely like target and accuracy training. While both require mastery of trigger control, stance, sight picture, grip, and safety basics, defensive training is about acting on the need to fire a gun in a close-in, fast-moving situation—if you take the time to focus on making one-inch groups, you'll be dead.

and providing life-saving education and information that you can use. The United States Concealed Carry Association's *Concealed Carry Magazine* is a good magazine to subscribe to. It regularly runs articles that review various defensive firearms training courses. Also, when you join the NRA you have your choice of subscriptions to several excellent monthly magazines, such as the *American Rifleman* and *America's First Freedom*. These magazines routinely contain lists of gun schools.

3. Be well grounded in your defensive shooting fundamentals. There is a big difference between static target shooting and defensive shooting. For defensive shooting practice, find the stance or firing position that is most comfortable for you. Recognize that, in a fight for your life, you may have to shoot from an unconventional position. You may have to shoot from a retention position. This should be incorporated into your skills training.

4. Learn to get a good grip on your pistol. Your handgun is an extension of your hand and, on a gun, it should be firm. It is your shooting platform.

5. Learn how to use your sights. The shooter should look through the rear sight notch at the top of the front sight, which is placed on the point of aim on the target. The top of the front sight blade should be level with the top of the rear sight blades and centered in between them (i.e., EHEL: Equal Height Equal Light). The bullet will go where the front sight is pointed.

6. Trigger "press" versus "squeeze." Learn to isolate your trigger finger to press the trigger though its full range to its break point as opposed to squeezing with your whole hand. That's

called "milking the trigger," a bad habit that leads to dropped shots. Learn and practice good trigger control. It's the heart of the beast!

7. Follow-through. Don't move the gun away from the target after you fire. Give the bullet a chance to exit the barrel!

8. Learn how to maintain and clean your handguns. If you want your handguns to take care of you, you must take care of them. It is important to keep them clean and regularly check them for operational problems. You must learn how to field strip them for cleaning. You do not have to clean your guns after every time you shoot, every 250 to 500 rounds will do. Wipe your guns down after you're done shooting at the range. Be sure to follow all safety rules when cleaning your firearms. Do not allow yourself to get distracted.

Know the Law

Just as important as knowing about gun safety is knowing the laws. It's your responsibility to stay aware of changes that occur in the state and federal laws. Understand that the laws are different for every state. If you are going to transport a firearm into any state, it's your responsibility to know the laws and restrictions of that state and abide by them.

In all jurisdictions, "concealed carry" means carrying an approved lethal weapon on or about your person in such a manner as to conceal it from the ordinary sight of another person. (Open carry, while optional in some areas, I view as a bad idea, because it eliminates the advantage of surprise.) Permit holders need to be aware of areas where they cannot have a firearm within the jurisdictions in which they carry, and they should know what the laws of the jurisdiction require them to do if confronted by the police when they are carrying.

Most jurisdictions hold that, if a person is ever justified in the use of deadly force, it is only if they believe such force is necessary to prevent imminent death or great bodily harm to himself or another innocent person. However, jurisdictions vary in their laws regarding the duty to retreat in the face of an imminent threat. Pay close attention to those that have Castle Doctrine and Stand Your Ground laws, which do not require retreat if you are in a place where you have a right to be when you are accosted. Know, too, that deadly force may not be used to protect property or to stop an escaping criminal. A fleeing person may not be shot while running from you.

> Castle Doctrine is not a license to kill. Nor is it a license to protect property or bring down a fleeing criminal. Remember, if your threat is leaving, it's no longer a threat.

Simply put, Castle and Stand Your Ground laws are not a license to kill. If someone breaks in your house and you confront that intruder at gunpoint, thus far, you are on solid ground. But, if the intruder sees you are armed and remembers that he has an engagement he needs to attend elsewhere, you cannot legally detain him at gunpoint or shoot him!

At the time of this writing, the Florida Non-Resident CCW Permit is valid in 32 states. If your state does not issue CCW Permits, you should be eligible to obtain the Florida Nonresident CCW Permit provided you're a U.S. citizen, you're not a convicted felon, and you haven't been convicted of domestic violence. Even if you do obtain your own state's CCW permit, the Florida nonresident permit is a good thing to have, as it will expand the number of states where you can carry. To learn more about obtaining the Florida permit, you can log onto the Florida Division of Licensing website, http://licgweb.doacs.state.fl.us/weapons/index.html.

It is truly foolish to make the mistake of carrying without a license. In fact, in most jurisdictions, carrying without one is a felony! It is a mistake to assume that because you are a quiet law-abiding citizen and you are carrying concealed, that no one will ever know or that it will create no harm and no foul to do so. If you are forced to present or fire your concealed handgun, even if you are totally justified in doing so, you have committed a felony by carrying without a license. This is sure to get you jail time and result in a loss of your gun rights.

CHAPTER 15

Concealed Carry: Five Dos and Don'ts

Concealed carry is not for folks who lack good judgment and restraint. Even a right must be exercised responsibly, and carrying a gun is a grave responsibility. Carrying a gun is not for everyone. If you go armed and act stupidly, you may lose your right to carry. Make intelligent choices and carry responsibly.

Five Dos of Intelligent Concealed Carry

1. Be **AWARE**—Being AWARE entails being Alert, and Willing, having a good Attitude, being Ready, and being Even-tempered.

Be **A**lert. You need to watch your 360, so you can see trouble coming in advance. Action is faster than reaction, so if you see trouble coming, you can stack the deck in your favor. That might mean just leaving.

Be **W**illing. You need to be willing to do whatever you have to do to survive a lethal force confrontation. You need to be willing to use deadly force if you find yourself in the gravest of extremes. This would be when you believe your life or some one's under the mantle of your protection is in imminent danger as a result of your being confronted by a person (or persons) who is presenting an immediate and unavoidable threat of death or grave bodily harm.

Have a Good **A**ttitude. Be thoughtful, willing to learn, humble, and reasonably friendly. Lawful concealed carry is for the good guys and gals.

Be **R**eady. A gun will do you no good if you are not ready. Being in a state of perpetual readiness entails being alert and aware, so you can observe what is going on around you. You have to be observant to a level you notice something out of the ordinary. Once you observe something is out of kilter, then you will orient to it in order to rapidly analyze the situation and decide what to do.

Be **E**ven-Tempered. You mustn't be impulsive, angry, or rash. These qualities do not go together with carrying a gun, nor do they go along with thinking clearly or rationally. Remember that we carry a gun for self-defense, not to intimidate or punish.

2. Be Invisible—You do not want to draw unwanted attention to yourself. It is best to go unnoticed. Be polite. It is better to dress plainly dull and boring than it is to dress spicy and exciting. Good people who go unnoticed are less likely to get in trouble. Also, do your best to avoid

"hot spots." These are places where hot-tempered people butt heads, such as bars late at night and political rallies or confrontations.

3. Know Your Equipment—If you are not intimately acquainted with your gun, holster, and other accessories, how will you be able to operate it all smoothly and efficiently in an emergency? The idea is to drill and practice regularly with your equipment, so that its deployment becomes second nature. If you are a musician, you get to Carnegie Hall through practice. If you carry a gun, you get to survive though practice.

> **Your firearm does not and should not give you "gun courage." In other words, you shouldn't go anywhere with a gun you wouldn't normally go without one.**

4. Practice Safe Gun Handling—Guns are dangerous. Always handle them with a focus on safety. That means you should (a) always handle all guns as if they are loaded, (b) never point a gun at anything you aren't willing to destroy, (c) keep your finger off the trigger in a stable "register" position at all times, unless your gun is on target and you have made the decision to shoot at that moment, and (d) positively know your target and what is around and behind it.

5. Know The Laws—Ignorance is no excuse for the law. Sure, the laws can be confusing, especially in anti-gun-rights, heavily gun-controlled states, such as New Jersey. But you need to know what they are. If you break the law and are caught, you can lose your gun rights.

Five Don'ts of Intelligent Concealed Carry

1. Don't Be Impulsive—Impulsiveness and guns do not mix. It's like mixing drugs and alcohol. If you cannot control your aggressive impulses or your rage, you probably should not carry a gun. Hot heads get in trouble—add a gun, and you have the makings of a news flash. You must learn to stop, think, and act appropriately.

2. Don't Advertise—Don't let people know what kind of gun you're carrying, where you are toting it, or even that you are carrying at all. You don't want anyone to have the drop on you. You want to retain the element of surprise—your trump card. If you want to advertise for your favorite gun manufacturer, become a gun writer or apply for a PR job in the firearms industry.

3. Don't Develop "Gun Courage"—Have you ever heard of "canned courage?" Have you ever heard of anything good coming of it? "Gun courage" is destructive. Never think you should go anywhere with a gun (unless you have no other choice), where you would not dare to go without one. We do not carry to intimidate, except to intimidate a violent criminal into finding something to do other than preying on you.

4. Don't Ever Lose Your Gun!—Practice sound weapon retention. You cannot afford to lose your gun. If anyone other than someone you authorize gets their mitts on your gun, you are in for big trouble! So, carry in a secure retention holster. If you have trouble with this, consider pocket carry. It is the easiest way to securely tote a concealed handgun out of sight.

5. Don't Become Complacent—Complacency is bad for your health. Don't rest on your laurels. Shooting is a perishable skill. So practice regularly. Inspect and clean your guns regularly. Stay vigilant to your surroundings. Survive.

CHAPTER 16

Safety Awareness—
Your First Priority!

Building on several points from the previous chapter, let's talk about safety awareness. It bears keeping in mind that all firearms are dangerous, inanimate objects that do not forgive oversights or mistakes. They are weapons designed to kill two-legged, four-legged, many-legged, and no-legged creatures! Being the dangerous tools they are, firearms, just like poisonous snakes and spiders, are ready to bite the first person who handles them carelessly. Thus, all gun owners must always make firearm safety awareness their first priority.

The Learning Stages

We all go through stages in learning and living the armed lifestyle. Once we became aware of the vast amount of information we *didn't* know, many of us probably felt awkward at the gun shop or shooting range. Perhaps we felt that everyone else knew what they were doing, while we stood out as beginners. So, many of us embarked upon an odyssey of reading, enrolling in basic classes, and taking individual lessons to learn what we needed to know.

As we acquired essential knowledge and skills, we also developed conscious competence in the basics of safe firearm handling and shooting. Safety awareness took center stage, and the four universal firearm safety rules became our mantra:

1. Handle all firearms as if they are loaded.

2. Always be aware of where you are pointing the muzzle of your firearm. You should never point the muzzle of any firearm at anything you are not willing to destroy.

3. Always keep your finger off of the trigger until your gun is on target and you have decided to shoot at that instant.

4. Always be sure of your target and what is around it.

"It Was Unloaded, I Swear!"

Over time, as we became more familiar with firearms and more comfortable around them, conscious competence evolved into unconscious competence. Gun handling and living with guns became second nature. We developed certain gun handling habits—but not all of these habits were good.

The old saying, "Familiarity breeds contempt" may be too extreme. Perhaps it is more accurate to say that familiarity can breed carelessness. The problem is that, as we get used to being around firearms and living the armed lifestyle, there is a natural tendency to grow complacent about safety. This must not be allowed to happen!

Advanced skills in gun handling and shooting are not some new bag of tricks. They are the proficient and reflexive application of the basics. Therefore, as we become more experienced in living the armed lifestyle, we must continue to attend to the fundamentals of safety. Once complacency in gun handling sets in, we are headed down a very dangerous road, one that invariably leads to numerous day-to-day violations of the basic rules of firearm safety. This is a recipe for disaster. Therefore, it is worth discussing a few of the most common safety violations, so we can better guard against committing them.

A local newspaper recently reported the tragic story of a college student who accidentally shot and killed her sister. Police were called to the women's apartment and found a 21-year-old female with a single gunshot wound to the chest. She was taken to the hospital, where she was pronounced dead on arrival. The investigating officer reported that the victim's 23-year-old sister told responding officers that she fired the shot accidentally with a handgun that she thought was unloaded, and which was owned by a male roommate.

In a second incident, a man was preparing to clean his Glock semi-automatic pistol; Glocks require the handler to pull the trigger and decock the gun before they can be field stripped for cleaning. The man removed the charged magazine from the pistol, but, just as he was about to eject the live round from the chamber, the phone rang. He put the gun down and answered the phone. After getting off of the phone, he picked up the pistol again. Forgetting to check the chamber, because he "always" did so right after removing the magazine (if he wasn't interrupted!), he pulled the trigger. Fortunately, he made sure to point the gun in a safe direction, because the gun discharged. All that was damaged was some property and the calm of the evening.

Another fellow, in a similar situation, failed to observe safety rules one and two was not so lucky. The bullet went through the dry wall and into the next room, striking his wife in the neck. She was dead before she hit the ground.

What do these three stories have in common? All three violated the first safety rule, and that is to treat all guns as if they are loaded. Each and every time you pick it up, check it! Unloaded guns must be handled no differently than loaded guns. More people are unintentionally shot by "unloaded" guns than by loaded ones.

Muzzle Your Muzzle

Have you ever observed any of the following violations of this cardinal safety rule?

• Drawing a handgun from the holster and bringing the support hand in front of the muzzle. This is also called "lasering." The problem? You can shoot your support hand. The solution? Never cross or cover any part of your body with the muzzle.

• Positioning your support hand too close to the muzzle or ejection port when checking or clearing a semiautomatic pistol. The problem? If you are startled and your finger is anywhere near the trigger, you could shoot your support hand. Also, it's possible for the live round you are ejecting from the chamber to be detonated while being ejected, also injuring your hand. The solution? Keep your hand away from both the muzzle and the ejection port! Many people check the status of their pistol by grabbing the slide somewhere forward of or over the ejection port as they rack the slide back to expose the chamber. Some folks were taught to use their support hand to reach up from underneath the dust cover to rack the slide, using their fingertips. In fact, some pistols have serrations on the front of the slide just for this purpose. Most pistols also have serrations on the rear of the slide. I strongly suggest using these.

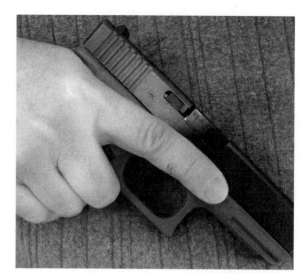

If you are not pointing the gun at something your are completely prepared and ready to shoot, this is where your trigger finger belongs, in register, alongside the gun's frame.

• Holding onto a loaded handgun while doing something that requires two hands. The problem? Do you really want to be holding a loaded gun and not have full control over it? Secure the gun first.

• Catching the live round from a semi-auto's chamber in one's hand after ejecting it. The problem? This may look cool, but it's a foolish thing to do! The ejector can impact the primer and detonate the round in your hand. Let the round eject by itself.

• A loaded gun unsecured on a dresser, under a pillow, under the bed, or in a drawer. The problem should be apparent. The solution? Secure loaded handguns being used for personal protection in a quick-access lock box or handgun safe. Secure loaded long guns that are "on duty" in a quick-access long gun safe.

Where's Your Trigger Finger?

A student caused a negligent discharge while holstering her pistol. What she did wrong was to keep her finger on the trigger as she hurriedly holstered her Glock 17. The lip of her holster forced her trigger finger against the trigger as she pushed the gun into the holster, and the gun subsequently did exactly what it was designed to do. Fortunately, she suffered only minor injury. This student is a competent shooter and competes regularly, but I'm guessing she learned a very valuable lesson from this accident.

You may need to draw rapidly, but you should re-holster your pistol reluctantly. Don't let any body parts, such as your hands or fingers, get in the way, and be sure to keep your finger off the trigger and alongside the frame of your handgun. Then, as you insert your pistol into its holster, your trigger finger moves down along the outside of your holster.

Conversely, when you draw your handgun up out of your holster, you must make sure to keep your finger off the trigger and in the register position alongside the gun's frame until that gun is pointed away from your body and oriented towards your point of aim on the target.

Just What are You Aiming at?

Just as we must always be sure of our target, we must also always remain totally aware of who and what is around our target. This is the reason it is essential to have a good flashlight on you when you carry your handgun. The flashlight enables you to make out the location and identity of your target. It also enables you to determine if there are any innocents around your target. Choose a handgun or flashlight that is small and unobtrusive, as you'll be more likely to carry it all the time. In my opinion, the best concealed carry tactical flashlights on the planet are made by three companies: Surefire (www.Surefire.com), Insight Technology (www.insight-lights.com), and Streamlight (www.Streamlight.com). Give one a try. Remember, collateral damage is not acceptable.

The Element of Surprise

I recall the morning I was eating breakfast at my then-favorite diner, when I observed an exchange that inspired this chapter. A seventyish-year-old man, one I knew to be a retired Philadelphia cop, was putting on his coat, when an elderly couple seated nearby complimented him on his coat. He responded, "Thank you, but you wouldn't like what's in the pocket."

That really drew my attention! Anyone who is into concealed carry (good guys or bad) would have been alerted by that foolish comment. I can only speculate as to the man's motives for making such a statement. Some people get a thrill out of hinting to others that they are armed. Regardless, I can certainly say with confidence that it was a foolish statement to make.

The purpose of carrying a concealed handgun is to be ready to defend yourself without anyone knowing you are armed. This capitalizes on the element of surprise, if you are attacked. The retired cop's comment gave him away. If I had been a bad guy, whether or not I knew he was a retired cop, I would have had the drop on him.

It is important to remember that an attacker capitalizes on the element of surprise. Since action beats reaction, and we good guys and gals are forced to react to a spontaneous action someone else initiates, we are already behind the speed curve or, as we call it, the reactionary gap. Therefore, the majority of our training and preparation should take this reality into account.

First, we want to minimize our visibility as a "target." We must look confident and keep our heads up, as looking down is perceived by the predatory criminal element as a sign of submissiveness. Also, keeping our heads up allows us a wider range of vision and awareness of our 360-degree world. We must make eye contact when approached by strangers, so that we don't look submissive and we can read what's happening, but without appearing unnecessarily aggressive.

As I've said, letting on that you're armed gives potential evil-doers the drop on you. To avoid this, we often must adjust our wardrobe around our chosen concealment weapons, clothes that do not allow the gun to print through. This, of course, is easier to do in colder climates, where there are more clothing options. In warm weather, or in business attire, many of us default to pocket carry of a small five-shot revolver or a small 9mm, .380, or .32-caliber pocket pistol. For these you need a good pocket holster, one that minimizes bulk in your pocket, doesn't "print" the gun, keeps the gun upright, and stays in place in your pocket when you draw the gun.

Now, with these considerations in mind, let's revisit the element of surprise. If we are the target of a spontaneous, vicious attack, our best chance of prevailing and surviving is to fight back aggressively and viciously with an offensive counterattack and make Mr. Monster react to us. We must naturally train for this in the manner of reflecting on the realities of how we are likely to need to use our handgun in self-defense. Likely such a situation will be a vicious close-quarter attack within a three-yard radius with no seconds to spare. This means that we must train to draw our concealed handgun in less than one second, and shoot accurately at the high center of mass of the attacker repeatedly in less than another second. There will be little or no time, in a close-quarter attack, to focus on our front sight and get a sight picture.

The element of surprise is all about speed and accuracy. But accuracy is not defined as getting all of your shots within the small circle or square of a paper target. Combat accuracy with a handgun is defined as hits in the target's high center of mass, the torso. It's all about keeping the dispersion pattern of your shots within an approximately 12-inch-by-18-inch area, which is roughly the size of a human torso.

The victim who doesn't give up, who keeps on fighting until his or her adversary gives up or is neutralized, will win the fight and survive. So, never give up, never give any quarter. If you are attacked by a predator, it is probably because your attacker expects you to give up. So, surprise him!

CHAPTER 17

Post-Shooting Trauma

A traumatic event is a harrowing experience during which you feel like you or someone you care about may be killed or gravely injured. Trauma can occur in the form of a single experience or cumulatively as a result of repeated or ongoing horrors. Some examples of single traumatic events are motor vehicle accidents, physical or psychological assaults, rapes, and molestations. Some examples of ongoing trauma are the aftermath of natural disasters, life-altering physical injuries or diseases, war, genocide, and ongoing sexual, physical, and emotional abuse. Trauma can also result from the loss of loved ones.

As defined on www.MayoClinic.com, "Post-traumatic stress disorder (PTSD) is a type of anxiety disorder that's triggered by a traumatic event. You can develop post-traumatic stress disorder, when you experience or witness an event that causes intense fear, helplessness, or horror." The major symptoms of PTSD include intrusive and upsetting memories, dreams and flashbacks, intense fears and phobias, feelings of numbing, detachment, guilt, depression, shame, and anger, sleeplessness, loss of libido, inability to experience pleasure (known as "anhedonia"), irritability, memory loss, hyper-vigilance, and increased startle reactions.

Often, trauma survivors suffering from PTSD can be helped to recover with competent counseling and psychotherapy. Getting treatment as soon as possible after a traumatic event may prevent the onset of full-blown PTSD. However, a survivor's prognosis also depends on the nature, severity, complexity, and duration of the trauma, the survivor's psychological and physical resilience, the presence of strong social supports, and the reaction of the community.

Primary Prevention

As a clinical psychologist, I have treated hundreds of patients who suffered from the symptoms of PTSD after experiencing discrete or ongoing traumatic events. Keeping in mind the adage that an ounce of prevention can be worth a pound of cure, my work with trauma victims led me to research ways to help people avoid becoming victims of violence. In psychological parlance, this is known as "primary prevention," and it was one of the main motivators that influenced my entry into the personal-defense field. It's better to avoid becoming a victim in the first place than to have to try to fix the traumatic damage afterward.

I think of carrying a defensive firearm and training on a regular basis as primary prevention. Skill breeds confidence. Those who become knowledgeable, skilled, confident, and prepared to fight back also become less attractive targets for violent criminal predators. They are less likely to get into situations where they need to use their fighting skills.

Post-Shooting Trauma

If you are involved in a deadly force incident, which is a traumatic experience, you may experience post-traumatic stress. However, the severity of symptoms will depend on the variables I've enumerated above. If you are forced to employ a firearm to end a deadly attack on yourself or other persons under the mantle of your protection, you may experience a variant of post-traumatic stress called "post-shooting trauma" (PST). This is one of the serious costs associated with having to employ deadly force to defend your life.

Until the current conflicts in the Middle East, PST was most apparent in combat veterans who returned from Vietnam. The soldiers of that latter era fought in a war that was heavily contested on a morality basis at home. When Vietnam War soldiers returned home, there were no organized programs dedicated to healing their psychological wounds. In his book *On Killing*, retired Special Forces soldier Lt. Col. Dave Grossman discusses the trauma the solder who kills in battle faces when he returns to civilian life. Grossman emphasizes how naturally horrifying the act of killing is to non-psychopaths, and how destructive such an act is to one's mental health. His research underscores the fact that non-psychopathic humans harbor a natural reluctance to kill other human beings.

The reaction of normal soldiers to having killed in close combat can be best understood as a series of psychological stages. If this post-violent event trauma is typical for trained soldiers, it is not surprising that it is even more typical for normal, non-psychopathic civilians who have been forced to employ deadly force in life-threatening confrontations.

Massad Ayoob has written and teaches extensively about PST. Most of what I have to say here is based on what I have learned from Ayoob in his seminars and classes, books, DVDs, and from personal communications with him and others (www.massadayoobgroup.com).

The Abyss

A self-defense shooting is a near-death experience. As Ayoob points out, "You have stood on the edge of death and looked down into the abyss." If you survive, it is natural to experience some degree of elation and survival euphoria. After all, you prevailed and you are alive! However, anyone other than a blooming psychopath will likely feel guilty about feeling good after killing someone. Cognitive dissonance may arise as a result of the co-existence of two incompatible feelings, guilt and elation, and this can lead to anxiety and depression.

In this type of situation, the good guy or gal who stood on the edge of death, the abyss, and survived, may develop PST. The eventual resolution of the survivor's intra-psychic conflict and psychological distress will require total emotional and cognitive acceptance of the inexorable fact that the survivor had to kill in order to survive.

However, this is not the only hurdle. The situation after the deadly force incident will involve much more than the survivor's personal feelings. The survivor's inevitable encounters with the legal system, the community, the media, and society will introduce continued trauma.

A Scarlet "K?"

The upshot is that anyone other than a blooming psychopath can suffer from PST, if they are forced to shoot an attacker in defense of their life or another person's. PST is a survivor's reaction to two major factors. The first is our ingrained reluctance and aversion to killing another human being. The second is society's reaction to a person who has killed, and, after the event, this becomes the problem. Society will not let you feel good after you have killed someone, even if the person you killed was a raging madman trying to murder you.

Despite the fact that the person you killed was your potential murderer, from society's standpoint, you will bear the mark of Cain, the reaction of society to the knowledge that you killed. This can plunge you into a deeper abyss. Very soon thereafter, you can develop emotional numbing, clinical depression, and a host of physical stress-related symptoms such as headaches, indigestion, and physical pain.

Recovering

On a basic level, the cognitive dissonance arising as a result of the factors discussed above may be resolved both cognitively and on an emotional level by recognizing that you feel good simply because you have defeated someone who tried to murder you. You have been visited by the devil and you survived! Your recovery from PST depends upon attaining the realization on a feeling level that you did not kill out of malice. You killed to live. That is not murder.

That acknowledgement is the first step, but you also need to know that research shows recovery from PTSD follows the "rule of thirds." One-third of those afflicted are predisposed and weak and are never the same after their traumatic incident. One-third go through a coping period before they recover, although they are changed and left with some residual PST symptoms. For the remaining third, it's a character-building experience. With that in mind, let's examine the other variables associated with PST recovery.

> **Resolving post-shooting trauma requires the total emotional and cognitive acceptance of the inexorable fact that you had to kill in order to maintain your own survival.**

Circumstances of the Incident

In the field of law enforcement, a "clean shoot" refers to a shooting that is legally justified by the facts and circumstances. Such would be the case if the post-shooting investigation determines that the decedent had a deadly weapon (such as greater size, strength, buddies, fighting ability, a gun, a knife, a bat or bludgeon), intended to use it on the defender, and the defender had no other viable choice but to use deadly force to stop the decedent from continuing his murderous behavior. The surviving defender's ability to cogently articulate, with the help of a lawyer, why the use of deadly force was the only option can set the survivor free legally, from the criminal justice system, and socially, from society's criticisms.

Strength and Resilience

People who are psychologically strong tend to recover more rapidly and more thoroughly from trauma. In the case of PST, this would be referred to as having a "defensive mind-set." If you carry a gun for self-protection, you must have this mind-set. It means being mentally and emotionally prepared and ready to use deadly force to save your life or that of someone else if an attacker leaves you with no other option.

Massad Ayoob talks about the "doctrine of competing harms." If you have only two choices of action and both are undesirable (such as either dying or killing the person trying to kill you), you must make a choice. In such a circumstance, it makes sense to choose the least undesirable option and survive. It helps to keep in mind that, when a violent criminal predator buys away somebody else's right to live, he forfeits his own.

> It helps to have contact list and and job assignment detail for each person on that list, in the event you are arrested after a self-defense shooting. The better educated your family members, friends, neighbors, and even your lawyer are about your personal integrity, the more helpful they're likely to be.

People who are physically in good shape also tend to recover more rapidly and thoroughly from trauma. Fit bodies can absorb more physical and mental stress. Too, the better shape you are in, the more strength you will have to fight for your life, and the more you train to use the self-defense weapons you carry, the more prepared you will be to employ them should the need arise. Training regularly in the employment of defensive skills has another desirable outcome: the repetition serves to desensitize you to the employment of your skills, so that if you have to employ them for real, you will be ready.

Knowledge is Power

A key principle of psychological therapy is that if you understand it, you do not need to fear it as much. In fact, 90 percent of curing a neurosis is being able to understand its psychological dynamics. At this point, you should recognize that you may experience some degree of PST if you are involved in a deadly force incident. But the goal is to alleviate the syndrome's severity and duration. Knowing what to expect, that PST is a natural and normal reaction, can prepare you, if it happens, to tell your subconscious something like, *Hey, subconscious, I got the message already, knock it off.*

Social Support

Understanding peer groups helps to mitigate the blow of PST. Typically, civilians do not have that. Cops often do. Cops with group support cope best after being involved in a line-of-duty shooting or being a first responder on a disaster scene. So, to the extent that you can convene support groups, you will be building your psychological strength should the unthinkable occur.

Support groups help you get bonded. Becoming active in local grassroots gun clubs is one route. Another is joining national organizations dedicated to helping law-abiding citizens who have been involved in deadly force incidents. Such groups can help you conclude that you did the right thing and that you are not like the criminal who tried to murder you. One such organization is the Armed Citizens Legal Defense Network (www.armedcitizensnetwork.org). This is a national grassroots educational organization that organizes and disseminates information on attorneys and legal experts who specialize in defending people involved in self-defense shootings. The Network publishes a monthly online newsletter, has an active website, and organizes continuing education conferences. It educates members about the legalities of using deadly force for self-defense and how to interact with the criminal justice system after a shooting.

Another source of psychological and social support may come from faith-based organizations. For many people, their spiritual beliefs and religious faith help them to handle the aftermath of trauma. Most religions distinguish between killing and murder.

It also helps to have a plan in place regarding whom to contact and what their job should be if you are arrested after a self-defense shooting (such as to call your attorney or to arrange bail). The better educated your family members, friends, and neighbors are regarding your personal integrity and the factors that justify the use of deadly force, the more helpful they are likely to be if the balloon goes up. It will help to have a self-defense lawyer (or several) available to call. Cops are instructed not to make any statements to the investigators without their FOP attorney present, and it only makes sense for the average citizen to follow this principle, as well.

One last thing. Your community's reactions to a deadly force incident will vary as a function of where you live. The local news media disseminates information to the community, and the media both influences and is influenced by local politics. It is wise to not make any statements to the media, lest distorted facts turn to burn you in the court of public opinion. Such bad social feedback can fuel the fires of PST.

Post-shooting trauma is nearly inevitable for anyone who is forced to shoot someone in self-defense. To learn more about PST, I encourage you to familiarize yourself with the work of Massad Ayoob. By doing so, you will become a more responsible concealed carry practitioner and gun owner, and, in the event you are attacked and you do what is necessary to survive, you will be more prepared afterward to cope with the pain and with society's reaction.

CHAPTER 18

Choosing a Defensive Handgun for Concealed Carry

When you go to purchase your first defensive handgun for concealed carry, you may find yourself feeling nervous and out of your element at the gun shop. If this sounds familiar, I promise, we've all been there and done that. Know that this is where the value of a truly concerned and dedicated professional can shine through, and that would be the gun shop sales person from whom you decide to buy your first gun.

The salesman's role is to explain to you, in terms you can comprehend and with no condescension, the varieties of handguns available and how they operate. An ethical gun salesperson or firearms instructor wants to see you on a regular basis and keep you as a customer. An ethical professional will also never push you into buying a particular product and should work to keep you, as a first-time buyer, resist being seduced into believing that cute, sleek, shiny, or complicated makes for a better defensive weapon. Rather, a good salesperson will help you make a truly informed choice, and they stay updated on quality products on the market.

Try Before You Buy

I suggest that, when shopping for a defensive handgun, you find a range facility that will let you rent different handguns, as well as offering basic handgun, personal protection, and concealed carry classes taught by qualified, certified instructors. In such a customer-friendly environment, you can best determine which type of handgun will best suit your particular needs.

As you begin to shop, you first need to educate yourself by gathering information about the different handgun types, makes, and models available. Then, compile a list of your objectives based on your own personal attributes and needs, so that you can make an informed and personally appropriate selection. No one handgun is perfect for everyone or every situation.

What Makes a Carry Gun?

Think light and thin, which equates to carrying comfortably. Also, think about how you dress. Will the gun be easy to conceal with your normal, every-day wardrobe? You may want to try before you buy. A customer-friendly gun shop will permit you to hold a handgun you are considering and maybe even try it out in a holster on your hip to see if it is the right type for you to carry.

Reliability

While the above criteria are important, we mustn't sacrifice reliability and durability in a carry gun. Remember, if you are going to carry your handgun everyday and practice with it, it must hold up!

Good Fit

In choosing your carry handgun, you must judge as to whether each option provides a good fit for your hands. Does it point naturally? Is your trigger finger comfortably able to reach the trigger without your having to distort your proper grip? Unless the gun is a point-and-shoot gun, are the sights usable? Can you see the front sight clearly with your corrective lenses on?

Manageable Recoil

Is the gun comfortable to shoot? Is the recoil manageable? Seriously, if you can't answer "Yes" to those questions, you will not shoot it, and you won't get in the necessary practice time. So, choose wisely. It is better to shoot a 9mm pistol accurately than a .40 S&W or a .45 ACP erratically.

Trigger Control

You want a trigger that is neither too heavy of a pull nor too light. Bottom line—does it feel right for you? Can you operate it without getting finger cramps? Conversely, can you feel it when you press it? Too light of a trigger can spell accidental discharge. Can you repeatedly dry fire the gun without making figure eights with the front sight?

> Ease of operation includes a gun that's easy to field strip and clean. Choose one that's difficult to maintain, and you may not keep it in good working order, and that means it may not work when you need it most.

Accuracy

In your hands, the gun needs to be reasonably accurate when you shoot it at 10 yards and closer. Is the gun forgiving of the arc of movement created by your hand tremor? Are you able to place accurate follow-up shots? Bad guys have a nasty habit of not going down after just one shot, so good second-shot recovery is essential.

Ease of Operation

Your defensive handgun should be simple and safe to operate. Do you have the hand strength to pull the slide all the way back on a semi-auto pistol to cycle a round into the chamber or to clear the gun? Can you easily operate the slide stop/release lever to lock the slide back? Can your thumb reach and operate the magazine catch to drop the magazine? If you have a revolver, can your thumb easily reach and operate the cylinder release latch? Under stress, whatever fine motor skills you do have tend to fly away.

Two different Kimber custom shop .45 ACP handguns are shown here, but which one is right for you? The smaller model might be easier to conceal, but it will have more recoil than its bigger brother. If you're particularly recoil sensitive, opt for the bigger one and experiment with different holsters to discover which one conceals it best.

Ease of operation includes choosing a gun that's simple to field strip for routine cleaning and maintenance. Choose one that's difficult, and the end result will be that you won't maintain it, and then it won't work when you need it. Keep in mind, too, that, as we age, many of us develop arthritis, which makes it difficult to disassemble and reassemble mechanical devices with many stubborn little parts. For those of us with weaker hands, it is important to choose a gun that does not require Herculean hand strength to disassemble and reassemble.

Affordability

Your gun should be affordable to purchase and use. If you're on a fixed income, you don't want to have to sell your firstborn grandchild to stay protected! Also, if practice ammunition is too expensive, then you may become reluctant to practice. Choose a handgun in a substantial caliber for which there's plenty of cheap, quality target ammunition and a good supply of affordable, defensive hollowpoint ammunition—9mm would fit the bill.

So What Handguns Fit the Bill?

If you want thin, Kahr Arms is a well-known and respected firearms manufacturer that makes reliable double-action-only (DAO) pistols that are thin and light enough for comfortable concealed carry. The company offers a wide range of models, in both polymer and steel frames, and in substantial calibers (9mm, .40 S&W, and .45 ACP). Its P9/P40 and budget version CW9/CW40 are the lighter weight, compact polymer-framed pistols, and the K9/K40 are the heavier steel-framed pistols. These pistols are also offered in a sub-compact size. Its .45-caliber offerings come in polymer-framed models only and include sub-compact (PM45) and compact models (CW45 and P45).

Walther has also recently come out with its PPS pistols in both 9mm and .40 calibers. These

Small guns are easy to hide, but don't be dissuaded from considering medium and large handguns. As you can see with the full-size Glock .40-caliber (right) and the Browning Hi-Power (below), both lay nice and flat against the body in a well-made and form-fitting, inside-the-waistband holster. Unless you're wearing a skintight shirt over these rigs, neither would "print" to the outside world.

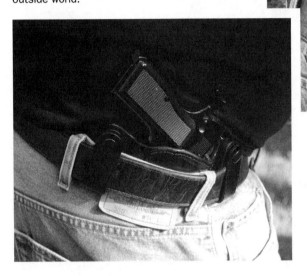

DAO pistols are light and thin and conceal comfortably and effectively. They are also excellent shooters.

Single-action semi-automatic pistols such as .45-caliber Colt 1911 types and the 9mm Browning Hi Power make excellent carry guns, especially the aluminum-framed lightweight versions. However, these types of pistols are not for beginners, nor for anyone who is not comfortable with carrying in "condition one"—cocked and locked—the only viable way to carry these guns. In my experience, Kimber gives you the most bang for your buck, if you are in the market for a 1911 of any size. You can purchase a new Kimber 1911 with numerous custom features bundled together at the factory at a reasonable price, given the towering prices of high-end custom 1911s. I am also partial to Colt, the one and only originator of John Browning's masterpiece. You really cannot go wrong with a Colt 1911.

If thinness is not a necessary criterion for you, your range of choices opens up. Glock, Ruger, SIGarms, Smith & Wesson, and Heckler & Koch make the most reliable defensive pistols on the planet! With the exception of the thin Glock Model 36 .45-caliber compact, these manufacturers all make substantial pistols that are on the thicker side. Springfield Armory's XD line of pistols in 9mm, .40 S&W, and .45 ACP also have an excellent track record of reliability.

When I work with new shooters looking to purchase their first or second pistol, I typically give them the opportunity to handle the above products. Choices vary with each individual's tastes, hand size, and specific requirements or preferences for carry. However, when beginners are given the chance to shoot these different pistols, several keep coming up as top choices.

Many folks choose Glocks for their simplicity of operation and maintenance. Glocks are double-action-only, which means they have one consistent trigger pull from the first shot to the last. For concealed carry, in 9mm or .40-caliber, the compact Glock 19 and Glock 23 tend to be the most popular, offering the owner the best of both worlds—compact size and substantial round capacity. For those who want something sub-compact, the baby Glock 26 in 9mm remains a top choice.

Many who consider Glocks as serious candidates for their initial purchase also like Smith & Wesson's line of M&P pistols. These come in a variety of flavors (9mm, .40 S&W, .357 SIG, .45 ACP) and sizes. They also can be had with or without an external, manually operated, frame-mounted thumb safety. The M&Ps have proven to be good shooters and reliable weapons, with smoother triggers than the Glocks have. They also come

Glocks have always been a popular choice for concealed carry, but Smith & Wesson's M&Ps, Ruger's SR line, and Springfield Armory's XD and XDM series are all strong contenders in the medium- to large-frame category.

with replaceable backstraps, so that the operator can adjust the grip to his or her hand size. It is an intelligent feature that enhances their functional appeal.

Ruger Firearms also offers an excellent DAO polymer-framed pistol in its SR series. The SR9 in 9mm and SR40 in .40 S&W can be had in a full-size or compact version (the SR9C and SR40C). These pistols do have a thinner feel to them. All the Ruger SR pistols also have an adjustable backstrap that is removable and can be turned around to change it from a flat to a curved design.

The SR pistols come with numerous internal safety features, including an external frame-mounted manual thumb safety. These Rugers have proven, in my experience, to be reliable shooters offered at a very affordable price.

Many folks also favor a Springfield Armory XD. The XDs come in various sizes, and although classified by the BATFE as single-action, actually operate as DAO. The XDs have an exceptionally smooth trigger and have proven to be very reliable. The newest versions of the XD, the XDMs, now feature adjustable backstraps.

SIG Sauer and H&K make superb pistols, but their price range is above that of those I've just covered. If price isn't a worry, though, the guns from these manufacturers make great choices. In particular, SIG's sleek, compact

Snub-nosed revolvers are a terrific choice, if you have trouble operating the slide on a semi-automatic. Choosing models that have a bobbed hammer, like this one from Smith & Wesson, also make smart sense for concealed carry, as they're absent an exposed hammer that can snag on clothing.

P239 in either 9mm or .40 S&W is a very popular choice. This gun seems to fit all sizes of hands—men's and women's—and has very little perceived recoil in either caliber. It is also ergonomically designed for comfortable concealed carry. This SIG and similar models come in traditional double-action, better known as double-action/single-action (DA/SA). This means that the first shot is double-action and then all subsequent shots are single-action. To restore the cocked pistol to its neutral, decocked, hammer-down state, the operator must use the manual frame-mounted decocking lever. For those shooters who don't mind the transition from a double-action first shot to single-action shots, the SIG P239 is a superb choice.

Recently, SIG responded to market demand for DAO pistols and released its pistols in a configuration that is proprietarily referred to as the DAK. DAK stands for double-action-Kellerman, after the designer. In my experience, the DAK SIGs have not been as popular as their DA/SAs. People who seek a DAO pistol tend to choose either a Glock, the S&W M&P, or a Springfield Armory XD.

> Revolvers, especially small ones, require more fine-motor dexterity to operate than does a well-selected semi-auto. While they have their place in concealed carry, revolvers are not for everyone, particularly those who are new shooters or who have poor hand strength.

SIG's model P226 in 9mm (and, to a lesser extent, .40 S&W and .357 SIG) and their model P229 in .40 S&W, .357 SIG or 9mm, continue to be popular and excellent choices. However, it is a fact that these models are pretty thick, and people with smallish- to medium-sized hands often find the grips too thick. Additionally, one feels the thickness and the weight of these pistols when carrying them. So, while these are superbly reliable pistols and great shooters, their mass appeal, especially for concealed carry, is limited by their girth.

In my experience training beginners, the SIGs tend to be more popular than the H&Ks, but make no mistake, H&K makes very fine pistols. Its classic USP Compacts in 9mm, .40-caliber and .45 ACP are excellent choices and can be had in a number of versions. The most common are the ones with the frame-mounted manual safety/decocker lever. Similar versions can be had in DAO, featuring what H&K calls their LEM or Law Enforcement Modification. I have found the LEM triggers to be exceptionally smooth and fast, and I like them more than SIG's DAK version, due to the shorter reset.

H&K's newest pistols are the sleeker and more ergonomic 9mm and .40-caliber P-30, and the HK45 full-size and compact .45 ACP pistols. Again, these guns can be had in varying configurations, but unlike the USPs, they feature multiple backstrap options. The P-30s are proving to be quite popular in some circles, and they are all excellent shooters.

This chapter has covered a lot of semi-automatic pistols. In my experience, more beginners come to me for advice on selecting the right semi-auto for them than do those looking for a re-

Many full-size autos, like the M&P Series pistol from Smith & Wesson, now come with features that allow the gun to fit a variety of hand sizes. This gun, for instance, comes with interchangeable backstraps that help provide a customized fit for almost any shooter.

volver for concealed carry. I have worked with many students, more female than male in this regard, who initially think a small-frame snub-nose revolver is the right choice for them. However, once they shoot one and experience the substantial recoil, they often change their mind and head over to the semi-auto department. Additionally, revolvers, especially the small ones, often require more fine-motor dexterity than that to operate a well-selected semi-automatic pistol. Some students have trouble opening and closing the cylinder and loading and unloading the snubby revolver. Further, students with hand and finger strength issues have difficulty with the longer, heavier revolver trigger. Lastly, cocking the double-action revolver with an external hammer for defensive shooting is not recommended, and it can be an ordeal for a person with limited hand strength and dexterity to safely cock and decock the hammer.

Because of this safety issue and the other practical problems that I have mentioned above, a small-framed revolver in .38 Special or .357 Magnum is usually not the best choice for most beginners. Additionally, the small-framed revolver is limited in ammunition capacity (to five rounds typically). This limitation is significant in light of the fact that it takes considerable training, practice, and dexterity to rapidly reload a revolver when compared to reloading a semi-auto. Lastly, I want to mention that, when a revolver jams, malfunctions, or experiences a stoppage in the field, the chances of being able to clear the stoppage rapidly in an emergency situation are poor. This typically makes the semi-auto a more reliable choice, assuming that the operator has the requisite training and know-how.

> **Revolvers are limited in their capacity, and jams and malfunctions tend to be much more difficult to clear quickly than is the case with a semi-auto handgun.**

With all of the above said, I do not wish to downplay the utility, functionality, or beauty of small-framed revolvers or revolvers in general as defensive handguns. I personally love revolvers, and they ride nicely in one's pocket in a good pocket holster, but I do need to underscore their limitations. Keeping these facts in mind, suffice it to say that I have worked with many students whose handgun choice is a snubby revolver, and they do very well with them. On the advantages side of the ledger, revolvers do tend to malfunction less often than semi-autos. A

If you have trouble manipulating the slide on a semi-automatic pistol, consider choosing a small gun like Beretta's .32 ACP Tomcat. The tip-up barrel eliminates racking the slide for loading/unloading purposes, good for hands that are stiff with arthritis or that have otherwise lost dexterity.

quality revolver also tends to be more tolerant of neglect, such as not being cleaned often, lint in the pocket, different types of hollowpoint or reloaded lower power ammunition, and so forth.

In my opinion, S&W, bar none, makes the best revolvers. I am especially fond of the remarkably lightweight Airlite scandium and titanium models and the aluminum Airweight lines of snubbies. These guns can be a bear to shoot full-house .38 or .357 Magnum loads through, but they carry nicely all day. In fact, you hardly know you have one on you. This makes it more likely you will venture out of the house armed. After all, a small .38 in your pocket is superior to that high-capacity 9mm you left at home!

Ruger's recently introduced Light Compact Revolvers (LCRs) in both .38 and .357 have also gained a loyal following. These affordably priced, high-quality snubby revolvers carry nicely in a pocket holster and they shoot very well. They are also ergonomic in the hands, have a very nice trigger, and their felt recoil isn't too bad, considering their light weight. Highly recommended!

Ruger's larger-framed .357 magnum revolvers, such as the five-shot SP-101 and six-shot GP-100 series, and the .44 Magnum Super Redhawk Alaskan, a large-framed six-shot 2.5-inch barreled snubby (with surprisingly tame recoil), are also quality weapons that will last their owner a lifetime.

Smith and Wesson's large-frame .357 Magnum revolvers are highly recommended. I especially like the snubby versions, such as the eight-shot lightweight scandium and titanium 2-inch-barrel Model 327 PD, eight-shot S&W Performance Center Model 2.5-inch 627, and eight-shot Model 327 Night Guard with tritium front dot sight. Last but not least, I have enjoyed owning and carrying my full-steel S&W Model 686 2.5-inch seven-shot .357 Magnum snubby for many years.

If you want to carry one of these large-frame magnums, you are going to need a good leather concealment holster. The best in my mind are manufactured by Rob and Jan Leahy of Simply Rugged Holsters (www.simplyrugged.com). For these revolvers, the couple handcraft a concealment holster called the "Sourdough Pancake" that is made from steer shoulder. It is tightly molded to the gun and does not require a thumbstrap for retention, as the design securely holds the revolver with the opposing tension of the offset belt loops. The hand molding of the holster to the revolver's contours also helps. The company also offers optional inside-the-waistband straps that bolt on to the holster with supplied Chicago screws, allowing you to easily convert this belt-slot pancake holster into an inside-the-waistband holster.

Whether you are going to carry one of these large-frame eight-shot .357 Magnums, or you are going to keep it in the bedroom for home-defense, you should have the ability to rapidly reload your revolver. You can purchase eight-shot speedloaders made by a company called 5 Star Firearms (www.5starfirearms.com). These rugged aluminum loaders fit the mentioned eight-shot large-frame Smiths perfectly. The company also make speedloaders for the large-frame six-shot .44 Magnums, such as the Ruger Alaskan.

For home-defense bedside access, Lynn and Sandy Tompkins of Frontier Leather Works (www.frontierleatherworks.com), handcraft a leather holster called the R7 NS Mid-Night Intruder Sleeper Holster that can be easily hung on a bedpost or chair for instant access to a holstered gun in the middle of the night. Lynn can make your Sleeper Holster to fit several guns. My Sleeper fits my large-frame .357 Magnum revolvers, as well as my large-frame Glock 17 and SIG P226 with accessory rail.

CHAPTER 19

Living With "Mouse Guns"

I can carry any gun I want to carry. However, most times, I carry a small-caliber gun, what some call a "mouse gun," in my pocket. Why is that?

Small-caliber guns are easy to insert into a pocket holster and throw into your pocket. This takes much less time than strapping or clipping on a belt or inside-the-waistband holster, holstering a compact to full-size pistol, and finding and donning an appropriate cover garment to conceal the piece.

Small-caliber guns are also small and light. Yes, I know that small and light means harder to shoot. They do have more recoil and less accuracy beyond bad-breath range. However, small and light also equate to comfortably concealable, and this makes a mouse gun easy to tote around all day.

The harder-to-shoot part is addressed through training and practice. Mouse guns are not guns for beginners. They require good technique to shoot so that they do not malfunction and so the little bullets go where intended. But shouldn't you train with any gun that you are going to stake your life on?

I like my mouse guns because they don't drag me down. They don't pull my pants down or strain my back. Heavy sidearms will do that to you, and, when something hurts, you are less apt to do it again. I am not saying that I never carry substantial side arms concealed—I often carry my Glocks, SIGs, H&Ks, Kimber 1911s, etc. However, I carry these substantial weapons because I enjoy them, and I believe that it is important when being prepared for the worst. That being said, if you are well-trained and can shoot a .32 or a .380 well and it is comfortable to carry, then you are more prepared than if you are walking around with an aching back.

Quiet Confidence

Carrying one or more mouse guns in your pockets can give you quiet confidence. I am not talking about "gun courage." That is silly. I am talking about the peace of mind that comes from knowing that you have protection with you at all times and that no one but you knows it. It is better to have a little gun in your pocket that you can forget about until you need it, than to have a big gun on your hip that you are constantly adjusting, because, in the latter case, you will be self conscious. You will also be noticed.

No Printing

Carrying little guns means I don't worry about printing. There are no tell-tale bulges anywhere except for my big belly.

The Cute Factor

Mouse guns to me are cute and pretty. I admit I have a thing for them. My .32 and .380 ACP Seecamp and North American Arms Guardian pistols are little jewels. My .32 and .380 ACP Kel-Tec pistols are beautiful in their own right, as are my .380 ACP Ruger LCP and .380 ACP Kahr P380.

Myths About Mouse Guns

There are some myths or half truths about mouse guns that need to be dispelled. These myths can kill you. Well, not the myths themselves, of course. What I mean is that, if you take these myths or half truths too seriously, you may end up not carrying.

Myth No. 1—If I get into a gunfight, I'm outgunned. The last thing you want to do is get into a gunfight. And, if shooting does erupt, you want to take cover. Unless you are on a SWAT or HRT team, you want to avoid trading bullets with bad guys. Let's face it. Even if you're carrying a full-size Glock or SIG, if you're attacked by more than one armed and serious bad guy, you still may be outgunned.

Myth No. 2—I will need to take out a shooter from a distance. This is unlikely. Most lethal force confrontations occur within a range of less than nine feet.

Myth No. 3 – Mouse guns are not reliable. Just plain not true. There are plenty of high-quality small guns on the market today.

Myth No. 4—Mouse guns are too hard to shoot and practice with. This is nonsense. While they are not for everyone, many are perfectly handleable, but, as it is with any gun you carry, you need to practice with a mouse gun to master shooting it.

Myth No. 5—Mouse guns come in marginal calibers. Marginal for what, I ask? Nobody wants to be shot by any gun. If you need to deploy your firearm, no bad guy is going to say something like, "Ha! Go ahead and shoot me. That's just a mouse gun!"

Mouse Guns to Love

I love Seecamps, NAA Guardians, Kel-Tecs, Kahrs, and Rugers. They are all reliable and they all keep working like the Energizer Bunny. They are cute and pretty, intrinsically accurate, and are fun to shoot. Also, factory customer service is exemplary.

I shoot these guns at the range in two ways. One is to plink with them. The other way is to shoot them like my life depends on them at the moment. Both modes of practice build and sharpen my skills with these guns.

Small Calibers

Small-caliber handguns are defined as those chambering the .380 ACP or smaller cartridges, such as the .22 LR, .22 Magnum, .25 ACP, or .32 ACP. These smallbore guns are typically also small in size.

Small-caliber handguns are carried when concealment is more important that power. Everything in life is a trade off, but carrying a gun in your pocket offers a number of advantages over other modes of concealed carry.

Concealing a substantial handgun on your person is not easy. While concealed means out of sight, if your piece prints through your clothing, it's a big clue that you are carrying. So, what do you do if it is difficult to effectively conceal a handgun on your hip or inside your waist band?

A bird in the hand is worth two in the bush. Likewise, a gun in your pocket is worth two or more at home. Therefore, a little .22 LR pistol in your pocket is worth more to you from the standpoint of personal-defense on the street than is a big .45 left at home. So, if the only way you can conveniently carry a gun is to carry a small-caliber handgun in your pocket, do so, and go forth armed, even if the little

Some people believe mouse guns come only in marginal calibers. Marginal for what? If you have to draw down, your opponent is highly unlikely to laugh and point and dare you to shoot him with your "itty-bitty" gun.

gun in your pocket is what some folks call a "mouse gun." The good news is there are more quality pocket guns than ever and more pocket holsters for those guns to choose from. Some of the advantages of carrying small guns in small holsters include:

- Concealing a small gun in your pocket is easy and convenient.
- You can have as many guns on you as you have pockets.
- You can have your hand on your gun at the ready, should you need to present your piece.
- You save valuable real estate on your waist and other areas of your body for things like cell phones and other devices.
- You can tuck your shirt in.
- You don't have to wear oversized or baggy clothes.
- You eliminate the need for cover garments.
- Pocket carry is more comfortable than hip carry for many folks who are very big around the hips and waist.

There are also a number of disadvantages to carrying a gun in your pocket, to wit:
- A gun in your pocket can be hard to access while seated.
- If you need to carry other things in your pockets such as keys and wallets, carrying a gun takes up valuable real estate.
- Unless you have a good pocket holster, the gun can end up upside down, with the muzzle pointing at your head!
- Unless you have the gun well secured in a good pocket holster, the trigger is dangerously exposed to foreign objects.

111

• Drawing a gun out of your pocket can be impeded if the gun is too big or if you are wearing other items on your waist.

• If the gun is too heavy, it can pull your pants down!

• If you choose the wrong pocket holster, that holster could come out of your pocket with the gun when you attempt to draw your gun.

Best of Breed .22 LR and .22 Magnum Pocket Guns

The .22 Long Rifle rimfire cartridge is inexpensive to shoot. That's a good thing, as the price of ammo has risen sharply in the past several years and it is important to practice with the guns you choose to rely on to defend your life. In my experience, there are several .22 LR and .22 Magnum handguns that are the best of the breed. One is the little .22-caliber Beretta Model 21A Bobcat semi-auto, with the its tip-up barrel feature for easy and safe loading and unloading. This cat will hiss with hot .22 LR loads, such as CCI's 40-grain Velocitor Gold Dot Hollow Points.

A second excellent choice is Smith & Wesson's eight-shot Chiefs Special Model 317 AirLite snub-nose revolver chambered for .22 LR. This is the lightest eight-shot revolver I've ever handled. It weighs in at 12 ounces with a 2-inch barrel and is made of high-quality aluminum alloy with a steel liner in the barrel.

A third top choice is the North American Arms line of single action .22 LR mini-revolvers. I also like the mean punch of this company's mini-revolvers chambered for the .22 Magnum. My favorite is the NAA Pug. NAA also has a new top-break version of the Pug called the Ranger. It allows for speed reloading of five .22 Magnums on the fly. Smith & Wesson's Model 351PD seven-shot .22 Magnum Airlite snubby revolver is another winner.

> Mouse guns aren't just the foundation for small calibers like the .22 Magnum and .380 ACP. Manufacturers are responding to a demand for larger calibers in small packages, with diminutive handguns chambered in 9mm and .40 S&W.

Best of Breed .32 ACP Pocket Pistols

The venerable .32 ACP cartridge was *made* for pocket pistols. Larry Seecamp's LWS .32 double-action-only mini-semi-automatic ushered in a new era of micro pocket pistols in the 1980s. His jewel of a gun functions as flawlessly as a Swiss watch, and I'm glad it's still viable and available new and used today. I must admit I am smitten by this gun, and I'm not alone. A host of manufacturers followed with their own versions. NAA produced their .32 ACP Guardian, a solid and reliable stainless steel truck of a pistol. Both the NAA Guardian and the Seecamp .32 pistols are of a quality suitable to be family heirlooms.

Like it's .22-caliber counterpart, Beretta's .32-caliber Beretta Tomcat semi-auto also features a tip-up barrel for easy and safe loading and unloading. Also like its smaller sibling, the Tomcat will really hiss with quality .32 ACP hollowpoints such as Speer Gold Dots, Federal Hydra-Shoks, CorBons, and Winchester Silvertips.

George Kellgren, the founder of Kel-tec firearms, contributed to the trend for high-quality small-caliber pistols by miniaturizing the .32 ACP pistol into a 6.6-ounce polymer wonder. My Kel-tec .32 pistols are my gym guns, as well as back pocket back-up guns. They never ever fail to go bang when I press the trigger, have surprisingly light recoil for such an ultra-light, ultra-thin pistol, and are so light weight that I have to add an extra magazine to my gun pocket just so I know I have a gun there!

The New Breed of Small 9mm Pocket Pistols

In a defensive semi-automatic pistol, 9mm is considered to be the minimum serious caliber for self-protection. Given the rise in popularity of the many mouse guns we just talked about in smaller calibers, there has been a growing demand by the gun-buying public for an ultra-compact 9mm pistol. With the success of its initial 9mm offering of the compact K9 in the 1990s, Kahr Arms responded to the market's desire for an even smaller version of this pistol by introducing its all steel MK9. This was followed by a .40-caliber version, the MK40.

These Kahr pistols are reliable, ultra-compact, and good shooters. They have excellent triggers—very smooth and consistent. These guns can work as pocket pistols, but buyers should consider that steel is heavy, and a heavy pocket pistol can pull your pants down. Justin Moon, the innovative President and founder of Kahr Arms, considered just that and went back to the drawing boards to introduce the P9 and PM9 line of 9mm pistols.

Kahr Arms' P and PM series of pistols are essentially the same size as its K and MK series, but they are significantly lighter, as they have polymer frames. Thus, they have become immensely popular given that they were made specifically for concealed carry. They, too, have been proven to be reliable guns and good shooters.

Kahr isn't the only manufacturer responding 9mm mouse-gun demand. Around 1995, George Kellgren, the founder and President of Kel-Tec, introduced the P-11 9mm sub-compact pistol. This 10+1 or 12+1 capacity polymer-framed pistol, at 14 ounces unloaded, rapidly attracted an avid and loyal following. Many P-11 owners adopted this handgun for pocket carry, although it is a little bulky in the pocket, but not as much as the heavier baby Glocks 26 (9mm) and 27 (.40 S&W) that many folks, including yours truly, already employ for pocket carry.

Following the success of the P-11 series, around 2006, Kel-Tec introduced an innovative single-stack 9mm pistol named the PF-9. Based on the P-11, this 7+1 capacity PF-9 weighs about as much loaded as does an empty P-11. It was advertised as the slimmest 9mm pistol on the market, and it is indeed very svelte. It feels more comfortable in the pocket than does the P-11, making it a very viable pocket carry pistol. As a result, the Kel-Tec PF-9 revitalized the trend in ultra-compact 9mm pocket pistols started by Kahr Arms.

However, even the slim PF-9 takes up almost too much pocket real estate unless you have pretty large pockets. As a result, many Kel-Tec fans and pocket pistol aficionados, such as yours truly, stuck with Kel-Tec's tiny, super-slim P-3AT and P-32 pistols as their primary pocket carry.

Still, the PF-9 is a good shooter, and mine have been reliable. It is a really comfortable IWB carry and has ridden a lot in my Don Hume H715 WC clip-on IWB holster.

As a side note, Colt had introduced its excellent Pocket Nine in the 1990s. I have several copies of this sweet little pistol. Unfortunately, production of this reliable little 6+1 capacity shooter was abruptly discontinued in the late 1990s, so buyers interested in this gun will have to source one on the used market.

In 2004, Karl Rohrbaugh, the founder and President of Rohrbaugh Firearms was on a mission to produce the "Seecamp" of pocket nines and introduced the ultra-compact R9. As it says on its website, www.rohrbaughfirearms.com, "Rohrbaugh Firearms was formed to fulfill the dream of its founder to create an ultimate-quality 9mm automatic pistol that is easy to carry and to conceal. After six years of painstaking development, this dream is now a reality." The 9mm R9 (without sights) and R9S (with sights) aluminum frame/stainless steel slide models are 5.2 inches long and 3.7 inches in height. Either weighs just 13.5 ounces unloaded. Based on my experience with my copy of this pistol, an R9S, I believe that the Rohrbaugh reality is a great one. The gun fits in my pocket like a glove, and it is extremely well made and aesthetically beautiful. It exudes quality, but this is not a gun you want to shoot hundreds of rounds through, due to its substantial felt recoil. As Karl Rohrbaugh has communicated to me personally and to many others, you need to shoot this gun as if your life depends on it.

Basically, that sentiment is true with most mouse guns. They are *not* target guns. They are last-ditch, in-your-face, bad-breath-distance, save-your-bacon, guns. But consider this. While practice may not be tremendous fun, if you needed to shoot the gun like your life depended on it, you would actually shoot it better than when you would taking your time on paper targets. This is because you are not thinking about recoil. You are just thinking about neutralizing your attacker.

To that end, the double-action-only R9 pistol is inherently accurate, shooting to point of aim. However, the long, but smooth, trigger pull and trigger reset in this DAO pistol and its stout felt recoil make it difficult not to flinch when you are shooting it, and this, combined with poor follow-through, can cause your group size to be large. There is a lot to be said for shooting this gun frequently enough to desensitize yourself to the felt recoil. You have to hold this puppy tight when you shoot it, though there's not a lot of gun to hold onto.

Given the above, Rohrbaugh felt the need to produce essentially the same gun in .380 ACP. I was sent an R380 for test and evaluation. Of all the mouse guns and .380- and .32-caliber pistols I have shot, this R380 has the least recoil, in fact, about as much recoil as I feel running light 9mm ball loads through a Glock 17! Shooting the R380 is a pleasure.

The last couple years have brought us to the introduction of several new 9mm pocket pistols, including the Ruger LC9 and SIG Sauer P290 in 2010, and the Diamondback DB9 in 2011.

Ruger (www.Ruger.com) introduced its 9mm LC9 as a follow-up to their .380 LCP it introduced in 2008. Both of these pistols are ergonomic, rugged, and reliable ultra-compact pistols, and both pocket pistols have "melted edges" for snag-free carry and use. The fit and finish on these polymer frame pistols are excellent.

The LC9 has a nifty and functional frame-mounted manual thumb safety, and it holds 7 + 1 rounds of 9mm. It is also a pistol that can tolerate +P ammo, if shot through it sparingly. (For the record, Rohrbaugh specifically states *not* to shoot any +P through its pistols. For me, this is a non-issue. I feel well defended with standard pressure jacketed hollowpoint 9mm. Nine millimeter +P ammunition really smacks you around in a small pistol, and getting accurate hits is more important to me than a more powerful bang that misses.)

As an eagerly awaited follow-up to its .380 DB380, in 2011, Diamondback Firearms of Cocoa, Florida, introduced its DAO 9mm DB9. Ever since I received this pistol, I have been in love with it. After breaking it in, this little ultra-thin 9mm pistol has earned a regular place in my pocket as an everyday carry in my RKBA leather pocket holster. It also carries nicely inside the waist band in an RKBA clip-on IWB holster. I have not been as much in love with a pocket gun since I discovered Larry Seecamp's .32-caliber jewel years ago.

The Diamondback DB9 shoots well, is solid, and the slide-to-frame fit is tight, but not so tight as to impede reliability. The recoil spring tension is taut. Operating the slide is not for the weak handed, but this quality promises exemplary function. And, when you shoot it, this gun delivers on what it promises: it is accurate. It is, in fact, the most accurate micro pistol I have ever shot, and that's saying something. The DAO trigger on this micro 9mm is excellent—crisp, smooth, and consistent, breaking around five pounds. And the sights are truly usable! Recoil is noticeable, but eminently manageable. In fact, it is remarkable how manageable the felt recoil is for this little gun with the high-pressure 9mm round.

Like its older but smaller .380 sibling, the DB9 looks like a micro-baby Glock, albeit a slightly bigger version. The DB9 is ergonomic and, like a Glock, is easy to field strip for cleaning and maintenance. The slide, barrel, and internal parts are also coated to resist corrosion, making this affordable, high-quality pistol a lifetime investment.

Last but not least is the SIG Sauer P290, a 6+1 capacity micro DAO 9mm pistol that was introduced in 2010. It weighs in around 20 ounces unloaded, and has a nine-pound trigger pull. Even though it's a DAO, this pistol has an external hammer that rests in a SIG-like half-cock position. Naturally, there is no decocker.

The factory three-dot night sights on this pistol are excellent. The trigger is long, but smooth and not too heavy. The size of the grip allows a surprisingly good hold on the pistol with my mitts. This pistol is accurate and relatively pleasant to shoot. You feel the recoil, but it is manageable. In my testing, it proved to be a reliable little shooter right out of the box, digesting every jacketed hollowpoint I fed it. While a bit heavy in the pocket, it is no heavier than my North American Arms Guardian .380, which I love. This SIG carries well in an ambidextrous Alessi leather pocket holster.

CHAPTER 20

Concealment Holster Primer

Holsters are basic equipment. You cannot safely carry a loaded handgun without an intelligently designed, comfortable, and functional holster that precisely fits your gun. Most importantly, the holster must cover and protect the trigger guard.

Holsters are exciting. Once you get "holster fever"—and you will—you want to own every fine piece of leather or Kydex made for your handguns. Then you end up with drawers full of holsters because you can only wear one at a time, and, truth be told, you really do want to wear one holster and one gun as your daily carry and train with that equipment. However, looking at and acquiring beautiful holsters for a gun lover is like a trip to Tiffany's for a diamond lover, and in defense of owning multiple holsters for the same gun, different modes of attire in differing circumstances will call for different holsters and carry options.

So, what is the secret to choosing the right holster? The answer is "intelligent design."

Essential Considerations in Choosing a Concealment Holster

Your concealed carry holster is your handgun's "safe home" on your body. As such, it's a very personal piece of equipment. If you carry concealed most of the time, you will grow attached to both gun and holster, and they will become a part of you. So, you must choose a concealment holster for your carry gun that fits your lifestyle, environment, modes of dress, daily habits, body shape, size, and fitness level. The choices in holster wear are finite.

In choosing the right concealment holster for you, some essential considerations are:
1. Wearer comfort
2. Excellent concealment given your wardrobe
3. The smoothness and speed of the draw that the holster facilitates
4. Fitting the size of the holster's belt clip or loop to the width of your belt
5. And, for other than pocket holsters, the ease of one-handed re-holstering.

Price is also a consideration. It is foolhardy to spend $500 to $900 on a handgun and then skimp on a cheap, floppy holster. Both the handgun and holster are an investment in your safety and survival. So, you should be willing to spend anywhere from $75 to $150 on a quality holster that will last many years. Additionally, you will probably want several types of holsters for different modes of dress and situations.

Cant

Strong-side holsters are made to ride or "drop" vertically, or to ride at some degree of forward angle or cant. The cant typically varies between eight and 20 degrees. The butt of the gun is raked forward and upward, and the muzzle is raked to the rear. Twenty degrees is considered an extreme, or radical, forward cant. The more extreme the cant, the better the concealment, as it is the handgun's butt that typically prints the most through clothing. I prefer a 15- to 20-degree cant with the strong side holster worn at the midline of my strong side. This facilitates quick acquisition of a good grip on the handgun in the first stage of the draw from the holster, as my hand is naturally pushed up high on the backstrap.

Holster Materials

Should you go with a holster made of leather or synthetic Kydex? Excellent holsters these days are made of both materials. In fact, some manufacturers have come up with holster solutions that are hybrids of the two materials. In making a choice, several considerations are pertinent.

An intelligently designed leather concealment holster is built of quality leather and other materials, is comfortable to wear, easy to conceal, easy to put on and take off, and provides a good fit for your carry gun. Leather rigs come in cowhide or horsehide. Cowhide is generally more supple and has more give than horsehide. Thus, a cowhide holster is easier to break in and usually more comfortable, at least initially, than the same rig made of horsehide. However, a horsehide rig does offer better protection against moisture, which is an important consideration if you live in a hot and humid climate. (If you are going to choose a horsehide holster, you should purchase one from a holster manufacturer that specializes in horsehide rigs, such as Kramer Handgun Leather and Milt Sparks,. Horsehide is typically stiffer but more durable than cowhide, though a good-quality cowhide holster will still last for years. Cowhide is typically prettier, too, because it is easier to dye and absorbs dye better than does horsehide. So, if looks and cosmetics are your main consideration, cowhide is the answer. But, we are talking about concealment holsters. This means they should never see the light of day, or something is wrong!

Often, a new leather holster is stiff and tight. This means it will be hard to draw your handgun from the rig, and it also may be hard to fully seat your weapon in the rig initially. Many leather rigs have adjustment screws, useful for adjusting to

An example of a "mouse gun" and a very discreet, inside-the-waistband, open-topped holster of comfortable, soft nylon construction. This holster is from Remora.

your gun both initially and when leather shrinks from heat, moisture, sweat, and humidity. Getting your gun stuck in your holster can be embarrassing to say the least, and fatal at worst.

If your leather holster does not have adjustment screws and is too tight to draw from effectively, the solution is to break in the holster with your unloaded handgun.

Also known as "working" the holster, this means pushing your unloaded handgun all the way into the holster, moving it around, and then drawing it out. This should be done 10 to 15 times. If the holster is really tight, then you need to carry out a simple break-in procedure called "blocking." This involves putting your unloaded handgun inside a plastic bag, such as the bag the holster came in, and then pushing the bagged, unloaded handgun all the way into the holster. You move it around as much as you can and then draw it and reinsert it 10 to 12 times. You then leave the bagged, unloaded gun in the holster for a couple hours. When you withdraw the unloaded gun from the holster and the bag, re-insert it and withdraw it again, you should find that the gun moves more easily into and out of the holster.

One of the author's favorite pocket guns, a Diamond Back 9mm, shown in and out of a leather pocket rig from RKBA Holsters, which neatly breaks up the outline of this square little pistol in the pocket and keeps it from printing.

Kydex is another holster material. It is a hard synthetic polymer that offers several advantages in a holster. First, it is very durable. It retains its shape and can be banged around without damaging the holster. Because it retains its shape, it doesn't have to be broken in, as does leather—Kydex does not stretch. What this means is that a Kydex holster typically needs to have a tension adjustment screw to enable you to adjust the fit of the holster by either loosening or tightening it. Most do have these screws, usually located behind or below the trigger guard.

Kydex rigs are typically more popular for competition and range training, because they offer a faster draw. But most Kydex rigs don't conceal as well as leather rigs, and they are typically not as comfortable as leather. Holster companies specializing in Kydex and thermoplastic holsters include Blade-Tech, Fobus, and Comp-Tac.

Beyond the material composition, there are four main categories of concealment holsters.

119

Concealed carry of a full-size pistol is entirely possible. The cant-forward ride of the outside-the-waistband holster rides tightly against the body and allows a natural and high grip on the gun as you lift it out of the holster. A thumb-break helps prevent a gun grab, and the snap-loop attachments make putting on and taking off the holster easy. These same loops also allow for a variety of positioning around your waist and hip. This holster is an Alessi CQC-S.

They are the paddle, inside-the-waistband (IWB) holsters, outside-the-waistband (OWB) belt, and pocket. Let's take a look at each one.

Paddle Holsters

As the name implies, these holsters have a paddle attached to the inside or body side of the holster. This paddle slides between the inside of the pants and the wearer's hip. Some paddles have a hook on the bottom of the paddle to keep the paddle and holster from coming up and off your trousers when the gun is drawn. The main advantage of a paddle holster is that it's easy to put on and take off. The trade-off is that most paddle holsters, especially with a heavy gun, tend to tip outward from the body, causing the gun to print through a concealment garment.

DeSantis makes paddle holsters with and without thumb-break retention straps. Gould and Goodrich only makes them with thumb breaks. Kramer makes a horsehide paddle holster that has an open top (no thumb break), but that offers excellent retention due to its precise molding to the gun.

Inside-the-Waistband (IWB)

These holsters are the easiest and most effective way to conceal a compact to full-size handgun. The body of the holster rides on your strong side between your body and your trouser's waistband—thus, you have to have enough room inside your waistband! When wearing an IWB, it is often necessary to wear slacks and a belt that are one size larger than what you normally wear.

An IWB is secured in place by either a single or pair of tunnel belt loops, snapping belt loops, or clips. The advantage of snap and clip attachments is that they make the holster easier to put on and take off. Excellent clip-on IWBs are made by Don Hume (the H715-WC), Alessi (the Talon, Talon Plus, and Deep Cover), Gould and Goodrich (the 890 Inside Trouser Holster), RKBA Holsters, Ted Blocker, Mitch Rosen (the Clipper), DeSantis (the Insider and Pro Stealth), and

High Noon Holsters. When it comes to loop designs, I find that those with snap-on belt loops are much easier to put on and take off than are those with tunnel belt loops that must be threaded through your belt. Look at the Milt Sparks Summer Special and Summer Special 2, Mitch Rosen's USD, Alessi's PCH and Hideout, DeSantis' Cozy Partner and Inner Piece, High Noon's Tailgunner and Down Under with Straps, and Galco's Royal Guard.

Within the class of IWBs, an ingenious adaptation for maximum concealment is the tuckable belt loop extension. The tuckable feature allows the wearer to tuck his shirt completely over the holstered handgun between the body of the holster and the extension strut, such that the only visible part of the rig is the belt clip, tunnel belt loop, or snap strap on the belt.

This smooth leather, inside-the-waistband clip-on holster by Alessi features a top-side flap of leather that helps protect the gun's sights from getting banged around and snagged on your shirt.

Like I said, this holster offers maximum concealment, but there are some serious limitations to the design. For one, getting to your gun when it is tucked under your tucked-in shirt can be difficult, especially for those with a bulging middle. Second, it makes for a much slower and cumbersome presentation of the gun, and this is a problem if you need your gun fast. Third, it can be uncomfortable to go through your day sitting, standing, and bending with the tucked-in gun in holster. Too, if you have a bulging middle, you are apt to experience your shirt coming untucked by itself frequently, and with it the fear of your gun showing.

It is important to recognize that, if you are going to carry in a tuckable IWB as it is intended, you probably have a definite need to carry in this manner. That is, you probably cannot rely on a smaller pocket pistol, and you probably have to take off your cover garment (e.g., your jacket or sweater) in order to blend in or to be comfortable. If that's the case, choose the thinnest gun you can rely on. With that in mind, here is my professional opinion on what makes a functional tuckable IWB.

A well-designed tuckable does not need a thumb break, as it is barely accessible to the wearer. To draw your handgun from a tucked-in tuckable, you need to pull your shirttail up out of your waistband, grip your handgun high on the backstrap as you would in the first stage of any draw, and then complete the draw. Such a holster should ride with enough stability to be worn as a traditional IWB, as well.

A tuckable IWB holster should be soft. Hard holsters of this design have a nasty habit of uncomfortably gnawing a hole into your side. With that same comfort in mind, the extending strut or band that holds the holster's belt clip or snap strap is best located in the middle of the

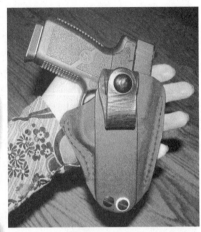

One of the most radical holster designs for concealed carry is the tuckable IWB. With this holster, the user will tuck his or her shirt over the gun. The design offers superior concealability, but does have its drawbacks, such as slowed ease of gun access and lack of comfort. They are best used with the smallest, slimmest guns, but, if your situation dictates it, bigger guns like the Glock can be accommodated. From left clockwise, Don Hume leather, a Kydex model by FIST, Inc., and an open-top leather rig by The Holster Store.

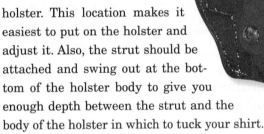

holster. This location makes it easiest to put on the holster and adjust it. Also, the strut should be attached and swing out at the bottom of the holster body to give you enough depth between the strut and the body of the holster in which to tuck your shirt.

It will be more comfortable if your tuckable IWB does not have a hard, reinforced mouth, and if it has a slight slide guard to prevent the rear of the slide, and all of the little levers on it, from biting into your side. If you must have a reinforced open top, which is desirable to facilitate one-handed re-holstering, that's okay, but it will compromise your tucking comfort.

A tuckable IWB holster that rides deep in your pants will also be most comfortable and functional. After all, when you wear a tuckable, the goal is excellent concealment. You don't want the butt or slide of your pistol flopping around. When you wear a tuckable tucked in, you are compromising speed of gun presentation for deep cover. Note, also, that a vertical drop with no cant on the holster usually works best, but a slight cant with the muzzle rake to the rear is okay and can improve concealment of your pistil's butt.

Given all of the above, in my professional opinion, there are very few holster manufacturers that have perfected the art of making a really functional tuckable IWB holster. The manufacturers that I recommend are High Noon Holsters, Elmer McEvoy's Leather Arsenal, RKBA Holsters, The Holster Store, Crossbreed Holsters, N82 Tactical, and FIST holsters. The tuckable IWBs manufactured by these companies fulfill all of my criteria for a comfortable and functional tuckable IWB.

Outside-the-Waistband (OWB) Belt Holsters

Within the class of OWB belt holsters, the pancake style, which has belt slots both fore and aft of the holster body, typically rides closest to the body and conceals best. Such a rig can be had with either an open top or with a thumb-break retention strap. Either way, the top can be reinforced to help it stay open for ease of draw and one-handed re-holstering. The downside to a reinforced top is that it can reduce concealability by giving the rig a wider profile.

A well-made concealment pancake holster is form molded and retains its shape. Recommended products include those made by DeSantis, Don Hume, Gould and Goodrich, Kramer, Ted Blocker, Alessi, Mitch Rosen, FIST, Inc., and High Noon Holsters.

This style comes both with and without a thumb break (without one is also known as an "open-top" design). A thumb-break retention strap provides secure retention of your handgun. This is a good thing, if you are going into a crowd. It retains the gun in the holster by preventing the gun from being drawn unless the retention strap is released first. This does, of course, add an extra step to the draw, so it requires practice. In one continuous smooth motion, your strong-hand thumb must come down and push through the snap-fastened thumb break to release the lock on the gun and permit you to grab it and draw it up and out of the holster. Note that, with some pancake holsters, a thumb-break tends to cause the rig to hug closer to your body, improving concealment—definitely a good thing! Excellent pancake belt holsters with thumb-break snap retention straps are made by Alessi, DeSantis, Don Hume, Gould and Goodrich, Ted Blocker, and Mitch Rosen. Their thumb-break scabbards ride high, close, and tight to the body for good concealment.

Pancake, or "belt-slide" holsters, as they're also known, are sometimes made with open muzzle ends, so they can holster the same pistol in different barrel lengths (e.g., all of the Glocks or various Colt 1911 styles). The advantage is that you save money being able to use one holster for multiple guns. The downside is that your muzzle and front sight are unprotected. Also, keep in mind that, if you carry in an open-muzzle belt or IWB holster any other gun than the gun the holster was molded for, you may compromise your gun retention. This is because if the gun fit is on the loose side, the handgun could be inadvertently pushed up and out of the holster from the muzzle end, either by a hand or if the muzzle happens to push up against something, like a counter edge. For these reasons, I prefer a closed-end molded muzzle.

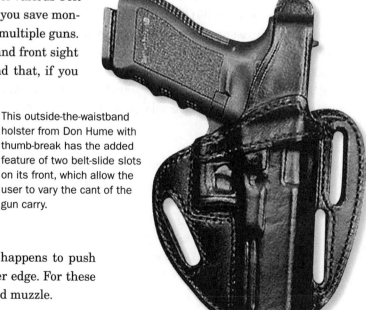

This outside-the-waistband holster from Don Hume with thumb-break has the added feature of two belt-slide slots on its front, which allow the user to vary the cant of the gun carry.

A beautiful leather, outside-the-waistband, open-top paddle holster from Kramer Gun Leather. Meant to be worn at the hip (the paddle will curve around your hips's curve to stay stable and comfortable) the paddle sits in between your trousers' waistband and your body. The snap-loop adds an extra measure of stability. This holster features a closed bottom, something the author prefers, as this design protects the muzzle and keep the gun from accidentally being pushed up and out, either by the muzzle's encounter with a hard surface or an intended gun grab.

A vertical drop (straight up and down carry) is desirable, if you tend to wear the rig on your strong side forward of your hip, at the strong-side appendix position, or in the cross-draw (non-dominant side) appendix position. If you wear your holster on your strong side at your hip, at your strong side midline, or slightly behind your hip, a slightly to moderately forward-angled cant or rake may be a better choice. In this angle of carry, your handgun's muzzle is raked to your rear and its butt is canted upward and forward. The strong-side forward rake typically enhances concealability.

One remarkable OWB concealment belt holster is Alessi's CQC/S. The CQC/S is a forward canted, reinforced open top, high riding leather pancake belt slide, with snap belt loops fore and aft. Its unique construction keeps the rig stable and close to the body. The snap belt loops make it easy to put the holster on and take it off, because you don't have to re-thread your belt! Many have copied Alessi's design, but no one has matched it in quality or functionality. It's a comfortable rig to wear all day, under a shirt, sweater, sweatshirt, or jacket.

Pocket Holsters

Pocket holsters are designed to carry small-caliber pistols or small-frame revolvers in a front or rear pants pocket or jacket pocket. In my experience, the most functional pocket holsters:

1. Are made for the front pocket.

2. Do not create a tell-tale bulge that prints through your clothing.

3. Keep the gun positioned upright and in a singular position in your pocket.

4. Are comfortable all day long in your pocket, to the degree that you can forget the rig is there unless you need it.

124

5. Stay in your pocket when you draw your gun. It is more than embarrassing in an unfriendly social situation to draw your pocket gun still sandwiched in its leather rig!

Here is a list of several manufacturers of very functional pocket holsters that fulfill all of my criteria. The first several are custom manufacturers, which make their holster to order one at a time, by hand.

Andrews Custom Leather manufactures some of the most intelligently designed leather pocket holsters on the planet. I use them to comfortably carry my Kahr PM9, Kel-Tec P-11, or Glock 26/27 in my strong-side pocket. Carrying a 9mm or .40-caliber pocket rocket in your pocket is easy and safe if it rides in a form-molded pocket holster made by master holster craftsman Sam Andrews. These cowhide leather gun sleeves fill your pocket and keep your weapon upright for a smooth draw. Their shape and rough-out finish keep the rig in your pocket when you draw your gun, and the fitted sleeve breaks up the outline of the gun to prevent printing.

Stephen McElroy, of RKBA holsters, manufactures some of the best, most attractive and functional leather pocket holsters I have ever used. The company offer a number of different models that include flat and curved bottom designs, wallet styles, and ambidextrous pocket holsters. The leather and stitching are high quality.

Randy Cooley, of Bulldog Custom Gun Leather, is a one-man custom shop and makes an excellent, ambidextrous leather pocket holster. Mine works extremely well with my Glock 26.

Robert Locke, of Meco Pocket Holsters, runs another fine pocket holster custom shop. He studied under one of the masters in the industry, the late R.J. Hedley, of Hedley Holsters. He has created a number of unique and very functional designs and will make his holsters to order out of high-quality cowhide or exotic leathers.

Kramer Leather makes a unique horsehide pocket holster that nicely disguises the shape of the gun as seen through the pocket. The outside of the holster is covered with a piece of plastic laminate that breaks up the outline of the gun, so the tell-tale bulge inside your pocket looks like a wallet. The side of the holster pressing against your body is smooth, comfortable, precisely molded horsehide. Also, Hidden Holsters makes fine, custom-crafted, front, rear, and wallet-style pocket holsters that hide extremely well in the chosen pocket.

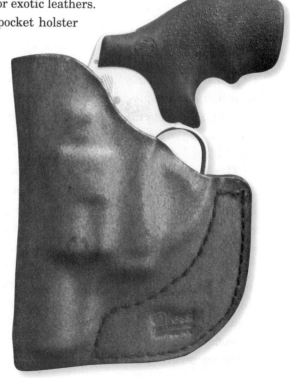

Remember, clothing choices go hand-in-hand with how and where you go about carrying concealed. So long as you're not wearing skin-tight designer jeans, the round cylinder of a snubby revolver will never show through your clothing in a well-made pocket holster, such as this one from Alessi Gun Holsters.

Alessi Holsters makes an excellent pocket holster that has the smooth side of the leather on the inside and the rough side on the outside. The holster is ambidextrous and has an edge on the rear that acts as a hook so that, when the gun is drawn, that edge catches on the pocket. This keeps the holster upright and in the pocket. The holster also allows for a full grip on gun while in the pocket. Alessi molds each pocket holster to a specific gun, provided those guns are in the small to medium range.

Larger production companies that produce very functional and affordable pocket holsters that are stocked include DeSantis, Uncle Mikes, Blackhawk, Don Hume, and Gould and Goodrich. The DeSantis Nemesis is made of a synthetic material that keeps the holster in your pocket and allows a seamless draw. This pocket holster is also very lightweight and affordable. The Uncle Mikes Inside the Pocket holsters come in four sizes to accommodate most small to medium size pocket-able pistols and revolvers. They are also very affordable, lightweight and functional.

> There is no such thing as a perfect gun and holster combination. Everything is a trade-off—weather, clothing, mode of travel, etc.—and a combination that works for one set of circumstances won't necessarily work for another.

Arm Both Pockets and Practice With Both Hands

It's best to have right- and left-handed versions of the same pocket holster for each pocket gun. Thus, when you're carrying a handgun of a more substantial caliber on your strong side in an IWB or OWB holster, you can carry your pocket gun in your support side pocket. Just make sure that you practice drawing from your support-side pocket! Become used to carrying a pocket sized handgun in your pocket. It's the best way to assure you'll be armed most of the time, and when you need to be.

The Perfect Gun and Holster Combination

Can't be found. There is no perfect concealed carry gun or holster. Everything is a trade-off, and what works well for one person may not work well for another. In choosing the right concealed carry gun and holster combination for your specific circumstances, you need to consider your mission, your capabilities, and your limitations.

Your mission is your purpose for carrying a concealed handgun. If you are not carrying on duty as a law enforcement officer or military operator, your mission is personal defense. With that established, consider your risk profile. Do you live in or do you travel through a high crime area? Are you someone violent criminal predators might view as easy prey? What kinds of predators are you likely to encounter? Recognize that, whatever your risk profile, violent crime can occur anywhere, and anyone can be targeted for victimization—so be prepared.

Your capabilities include your particular skill sets, as well as your legal rights and privileges. So, how well trained are you and what is your level of physical fitness? As I've discussed before, you should be thoroughly familiar with whichever gun you choose to carry and comfortable handling and shooting that gun under stress. Also, recognize that, as a civilian, you have the right to employ deadly force as a last resort against an assailant if you truly believe that the assailant is putting you or someone else under the mantle of your protection under an imminent and unavoidable threat of death or grave bodily harm. Self-defense is a right.

Your limitations include what you cannot do, as well as what you should not. Your concealed carry permit rights and privileges do not include police powers. You should focus on staying safe and keeping those under the mantle of your protection safe. This reasonable and legal mission is best served if you keep a low profile, and this is best accomplished by bearing yourself in a confident and unassuming manner while concealing your personal-defense weapons well. This demands you choose the right equipment and clothing for you.

Do Your Homework!

After studying this chapter, you need to do some research. Start by checking out manufacturers' websites. Call manufacturers, make sure you get a knowledgeable person on the phone, and don't be afraid to ask questions about how their products are made and how they should be used. A good manufacturer will gladly answer your questions. As an added bonus, if you can try before you buy, this is a good thing. However, this might only be possible at a defensive handgun training course, at a gun show, or in a reputable gun shop. All the more reason to take training, to go to gun shows, and to visit your friendly neighborhood gun shop!

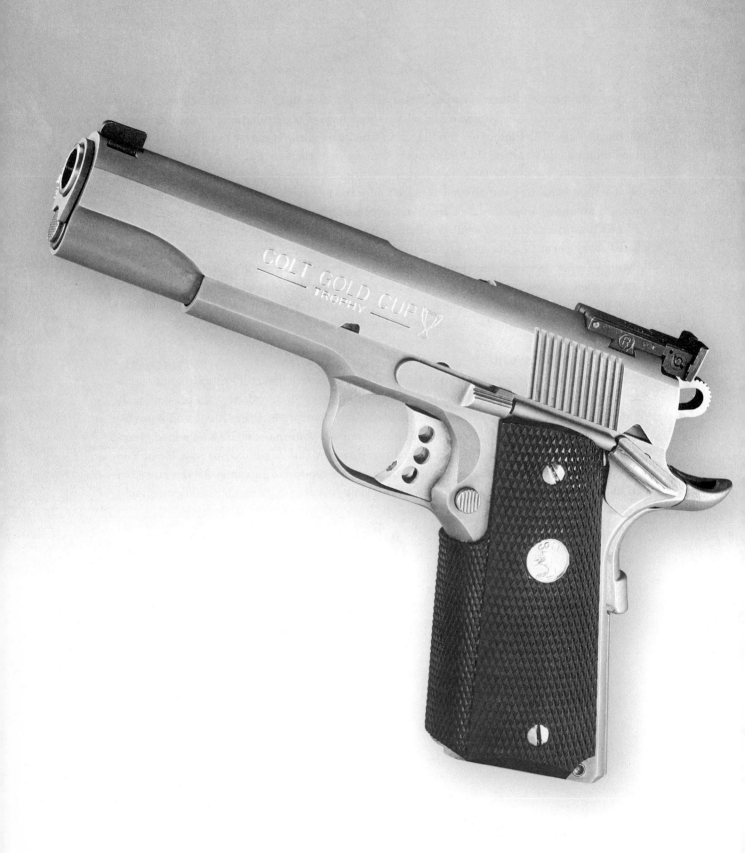

CHAPTER 21

Choosing A Comfortable Concealment Holster

One thing is for sure. Carrying a handgun without a holster, either loose inside your waistband or pocket, is a bad idea. For one, the trigger is unprotected, and, in that condition, it can get caught on clothing or other things. This could be a recipe for an accidental discharge. Also, with the gun in your waistband, it could get dislodged and end up in your socks or on the floor, certainly not something you would want to happen on the street, at work, or at a party. A loose handgun in your pocket could get turned around so that it's upside down, with the muzzle pointing up at your head, and then, when you reach inside your pocket to grip your pocket blaster, you'll end up grabbing the wrong end of the gun.

If you carry a concealed handgun for self-protection, you need a secure, stable, and safe way to carry it. That is the purpose of a holster. I am a holster enthusiast. I have tried a lot of holsters, and I own a lot of holsters that I don't use. For years, I searched for the "perfect" holster—I have still not found it. I don't think it exists. But don't give up on them! Holsters, just like firearms, are personal items. When you choose a carry gun and a holster for it, you have to make compromises.

You want to choose a quality holster that meets your individual needs. There are an abundance of excellent holster manufacturers nowadays that cater to different budgets and user needs. In fact, there are so many manufacturers who make quality products, and therefore, so many choices, that choosing a holster can be difficult.

As I've previously discussed, carrying a concealed handgun on a regular basis requires commitment and discipline. Training issues aside, this is because concealed carry is not at all convenient. To make it less so, and thereby encourage the commitment to carry, we each need a concealed carry system that is well suited to us each individually, one that will offset and alleviate the physical pain and strain of carrying a concealed handgun. My goal here is to help you design such a system so that you don't end up accumulating a box or chest of drawers full of unused holsters like I have. So, let's talk about how to choose a concealment holster that works with your body rather than against it.

Basic Functionality

What do we need to consider when looking for a functional concealed carry holster? The answer depends upon our physical issues, but all concealment holsters should be designed to perform certain basic functions:

1. **Fit**—Your holster should fit your particular handgun just right, not too tight and not too loose. Holsters should be molded to a specific handgun.

2. **Retention**—Your holster should retain your handgun securely until you decide to present it. If you are running or moving around a lot, you should not have to worry about losing your gun, therefore your holsters should be molded to each fit a specific handgun.

3. **Access**—When you need to present your handgun, your holster should permit you to access it rapidly. If your gun gets stuck in your holster when you need it, you might end up dead.

4. **Stability**—Your holster should ride securely in place wherever it is designed to stay, with no movement of the holster. It should be stable and not shift around, because, if it does, when you need to present your gun, it may not be there.

5. **Low profile**—Concealed means out of sight. If your holster is too bulky, if it pulls your pants down. If it leans too far away from your body, or if it flaps around, someone will be screaming, "He's got a gun!"

6. **Comfort**—Your holster should be comfortable to wear, otherwise you probably won't carry. I know some handgun gurus have said that carrying a gun should be comforting and not necessarily comfortable, but let's be real.

As we age, the cumulative wear and tear on our bodies takes its toll. The end result may include physical issues such as fatigue, stiffness, diminished range of motion, decreased hand strength and manual dexterity, overall weight gain or loss, weight gain in specific body parts such as the belly or waist, postural imbalances, muscle weakness, and chronic pain such as chronic neck, shoulder, arm, hand, and back pain, as well as arthritis. These physical issues can make carrying a concealed handgun even more of a chore. Even the process of simply putting on and taking off a holster can become difficult for someone with arthritis.

The bottom line is that if it hurts to carry, most people won't do it. The old adage that a .22 in your pocket is better than a .45 in the drawer at home is true. Wouldn't it be nice to be able to painlessly carry a .45 or whatever caliber you are comfortable handling? Of course it would.

If you carry your concealed handgun with a holster that helps you compensate for your physical problems, you will have less discomfort, strain, and fatigue. As a result, you will enjoy carrying more regularly. So, let's examine the types of holster designs that might allow you to accomplish this.

Compensating for Diminished Range of Motion

When you are stiff, your range of motion is limited and it is difficult to twist your torso. This can make it hard to put on and take off an outside-the-waistband slotted belt-slide or scabbard holster, or a snap-on inside-the-waistband holster, because you have to twist your body and maneuver your belt to do so. Typically, the belt fits tightly through the slots on the belt-slide or scabbard, making it tough to position the holster in just the right spot on your belt. (And, if there isn't a tight fit, the holster will flop around on your belt.) On IWB holsters, the snap-on belt loops on many are difficult to snap shut. By the time you snap them shut, if you can, and position the rig where you want it, you are all tuckered out! There are two solutions to this problem.

One solution is an OWB snap-on holster that is easy to snap on and snap off your belt with one hand so that you do not have to twist much. The CQC-S made by Alessi Holsters is one such holster. A second solution is an IWB clip-on holster that is easy to clip onto your belt or pants when you position the holster inside your pants. Excellent models include the Alessi Talon and Talon Plus with reinforced open top, Mitch Rosen's Clipper, Don Hume's H715-WC, Gould and Goodrich's Inside Trouser Holster, and Ted Blocker's ST17, which can be had with or without a thumb-break retention strap.

The bottom line is that, if it hurts to carry, you probably won't. You're better off with a small, .22-caliber pistol you'll carry in your pocket every day than you are a full-size .45 ACP strapped in a waistband holster that makes your back ache.

How would you wear either of these holster rigs? Imagine that you are standing in the very center of a clock face, with your belly button facing 12 o'clock. Either of these holster types may be comfortably worn on your dominant side at anywhere between the three o'clock and four o'clock position if you are right-handed, or anywhere between the eight o'clock and nine o'clock position if you are left-handed. Additionally, either type of holster can be comfortably worn in the appendix position at somewhere around one o'clock if you are right-handed, or around 11 o'clock if you are a lefty. However, appendix-carried holsters, and those intended to be worn between two and three o'clock by right-handed people, or between nine and 10 o'clock by left-handed people, should be cut so they ride straight up and down vertically. If they are designed with a butt-forward cant (with the muzzle raked to the rear), this can make it uncomfortable and difficult to execute a smooth draw. Butt-forward canted holsters work better worn past 3:30 for right-handed folks and earlier than 8:30 for left-handed folks.

Compensating for Diminished Hand Dexterity

If you have diminished hand strength and manual dexterity, you may not be able to operate the slide on a semi-automatic pistol. You might think about purchasing a pistol with a tip-up barrel, such as the Beretta Tomcat .32. Such a pistol allows you to chamber a round without manually racking the slide. Alternately, you should consider the pros and cons of carrying a snubby revolver. Either of these handgun choices can be carried comfortably in a good pocket holster that stays inside your pocket when you draw your gun. You might also do well carrying a revolver or semiautomatic pistol in a snap-on-the-belt holster similar to the Alessi CQC-S, in a vertical ride IWB clip-on holster such as Alessi's Deep Cover IWB, or in similar rigs made by other holster manufacturers such as Don Hume, DeSantis, Gould and Goodrich, Kramer Handgun Leather, High Noon Holsters, Mitch Rosen, Ted Blocker, and The Holster Store.

Compensating for Weight Gain at the Waist

Many of us with a bit of a stomach paunch have difficulty carrying in certain positions. A potbelly can make appendix or cross-draw carry uncomfortable. On the other hand, if you are built like an apple, holsters that do not snug close up into your side are likely to sag and print. To avoid this problem, you might try pocket carry. If you want to carry on your waist, you must search out a belt holster that rides tight and close to your body. If you want to carry inside your waistband, you may have the best experience carrying between three and four o'clock on your strong side. However, if you list to one side and are ambidextrous, you can figure out which side you need to carry on to keep your holstered gun closest to your body. Another option is carrying in a shoulder rig.

Two other considerations regarding waist-area comfort. The first is that the inner surface of an IWB, OWB, or paddle holster should ride flush against your body and be relatively smooth and free of uncomfortable ridges or seams. The second consideration is in regards to the flap of leather that rides up the inner surface and above the top of the holster to serve as a slide guard on some holsters. This slide guard is designed to protect your body's side from uncomfortable levers on the gun, such as thumb safeties, decockers, and slide locks. But if the slide guard is too high or floppy, this extension can actually get caught on the surface of your gun and interfere with drawing and re-holstering.

Compensating for Postural Imbalances

If you have back problems and are hunched over, or you have other postural imbalances such as a list to one side that places strain on your neck, shoulders, back, hips, and legs, a heavy gun worn on your side may create even more strain on your body. Consider carrying a relatively lightweight handgun in a snap-on belt slide or IWB clip-on holster. Or try carrying a lightweight pocket handgun that does not drag down your pants. Another option is to try wearing a well-balanced shoulder holster with the handgun on your non-dominant side and spare ammunition on your dominant side. Production manufacturers of excellent quality shoulder rigs include DeSantis, Don Hume Leathergoods, Gould and Goodrich, and Galco. Custom shops that produce superb shoulder rigs include Ted Blocker Holsters, Mitch Rosen, Alessi Holsters, Kramer Leather, and Andrews Custom Leather.

> A slide guard is a piece of leather that rides up the holster's inner surface and above its top. It helps to keep a gun's thumb safety, decocker, slide lock, and other sharp features from digging into your side when the holster is riding properly flush against you.

Sam Andrews of Andrews Custom Leather makes my favorite shoulder-holster system bar none. It is called the Monarch Shoulder Rig. It is modular and offers multiple carry options.

It is also very comfortable given the unique construction of the shoulder harness. Sam makes modules for the rig, such that you can carry two spare magazines, an additional gun of your preference on the side opposite your primary weapon, or an additional gun of your preference and two spare magazines for your primary gun.

Compensating for Chronic Upper Body Pain

If you experience frequent neck pain or shoulder pain on your strong side, you may have difficulty drawing your handgun. Consider carrying a relatively light handgun on your dominant side in a holster that rides lower on your hip, so that you need not raise your arm and shoulder too much on the draw. As a second alternative, you may choose to carry a light handgun in your pocket in a good pocket holster. A third option would be to carry in the appendix position, a fix that often eases shoulder strain during the draw stroke.

If you have back or hip pain and you want to carry in a traditional, strong-side OWB holster, such as a belt scabbard, you will want a holster that snugs up close into your body like the Alessi CQC-S. This puts less strain on your back and hips, and the CQC-S is easier to snap on and snap off than a belt scabbard or pancake holster with belt slots that you must thread through your belt.

Another viable alternative for some people might be a belly-band holster, such as the excellent one made by Gould and Goodrich. A quality belly-band holster keeps your handgun very close to your body and well concealed. In addition, on some level, it can function like a back brace. It also generates heat, which can be a good thing for sore backs.

The solutions I've just offered here are meant to serve as a guide to choosing the right holster or holsters for you from the plethora of choices out there. Ideally, it would be best if you could try before you buy. If that's not possible for you and you must buy off the Internet or otherwise sight unseen and untried, use this chapter as guidance and then make sure that the company you choose to purchase from is reliable and has a reasonable return policy. Some companies have well-educated, helpful phone personnel to help you choose the best holster for your particular needs. Others do not. Finally, consider taking this book with you to refer to when you go to a gun shop that sells quality concealed carry holsters.

CHAPTER 22

Beyond Gun and Holster

A s law-abiding citizens, we need all the help we can get in the judicious use of emergency rescue equipment, such as the defensive handgun. In this chapter, I shall discuss several types of equipment that are prudent to employ with your handgun. Many of these tools help protect innocent bystanders by making defensive handguns safer, more efficient, and more precise, and some can serve as alternative and backup equipment to your guns. Using them is the responsible thing to do.

Crimson Trace Laser Grips

Crimson Trace Laser Grips replace the stock grips of many types of semi-auto pistols and revolvers. When you firmly and properly grip the handgun, an activation button in the grip is depressed. This causes the laser unit to project a beam from the laser aperture, which is aligned with the barrel. (Like most sighting devices, the laser unit must be sighted in before use.) The laser aperture projects a dot of light onto the target to the same point of aim as the pistol's iron sights. It's a very simple and reliable system.

Also known as laser sights, the use of a laser can replace regular iron sights when it is too dark to see them clearly. However, laser sights are an *aid* to shooting in less than perfect conditions, and are not a *substitute* for good training and correct mind-set. Any target must still be clearly identified before shooting.

In the case of revolvers, Crimson Trace Laser Grips bring the .38 into the 21st century. They make little .38 Special J-frame snubbies and any semi-auto more user friendly in the following ways:

1. J-frames typically have vestigial sights and a short sight radius. Laser sighting makes using these sights unnecessary. This saves time in an emergency, when you have to deploy your firearm quickly. For example, if you were being attacked, you could rapidly acquire a sight picture by projecting the laser dot onto your target. You just need to point and shoot if necessary to save your life or limb.

2. Using a laser can serve as a deterrent. Just like the universally recognized sound of chambering a shell in a pump shotgun, a laser dot on one's chest or face communicates, "Stop your aggression now or be stopped!"

3. Laser grips are great training tools! They teach muzzle discipline by helping you learn

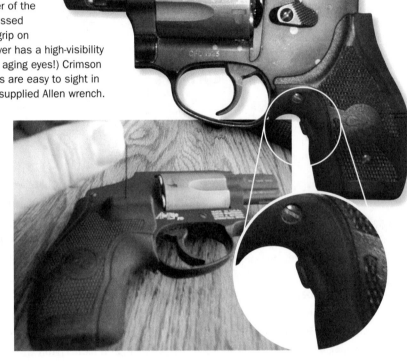

A S&W snubby revolver equipped with Crimson Trace laser grips. The activation grip (circled) in the front and center of the grip panels, is automatically depressed and activated with a proper hand grip on the gun. (Note also that this revolver has a high-visibility fiber-optic front sight, excellent for aging eyes!) Crimson Trace's grip-replacement laser grips are easy to sight in with a twist here and there of the supplied Allen wrench.

not to sweep things with your muzzle. They also teach trigger control, as the light will clearly display how big your "wobble zone" is when projected on a target. You can practice keeping your wobble zone small and the laser dot steady as you smoothly press the trigger. Finally, the laser teaches you how to acquire a good sight picture, especially for those of us with deteriorating eyesight. The unit's bright laser dot above the front sight serves as an aid to seeing our front sight and helps indicate where it's aimed.

4. Crimson Trace Laser Grips can help you learn point shooting. After sufficient practice with your laser sights turned on, you can switch them off and envision the laser dot as you point your handgun at the target. You will hit dead on, because you have developed a muscle memory of how your handgun points.

5. Laser grips help you train to firmly grip your handgun. A firm grip is necessary for many reasons: steady trigger press, recoil control, handgun retention, and adequate cycling of a semi-automatic pistol. With laser grips, unless you grip the handgun firmly, especially on the little J-frame snubbies, the laser will not be activated.

6. Having a set of Crimson Trace Laser Grips on your snubby will give you greater confidence in your ability to accurately and rapidly deploy your weapon, should the need arise. (Just remember that this confidence comes with smart practice.)

7. With your Laser Grips, you can rapidly and accurately deploy your handgun in an emergency from an unconventional or downed position. For example, a student of mine was knocked down by a vicious, attacking German shepherd. He was able to quickly project the laser dot of his Crimson Trace Laser Grip-equipped .38 onto the dog's snarling mouth and squeeze off a shot. This effectively terminated the dog's aggression and saved my student's life and limb.

8. Criminal justice statistics reveal that most criminal attacks and gun fights occur in the hours of darkness. Since one of the main tenants of firearms safety states you should be sure of your target and what is around and behind it, laser sights serve several purposes relative to this principle. First, understand that lasers are *not* the ultimate tool for helping you *identify* your target. (For that you'll need

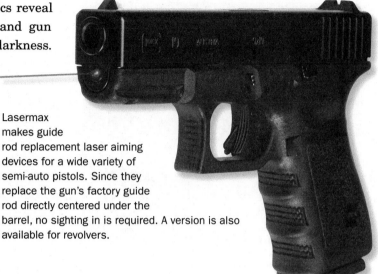

Lasermax makes guide rod replacement laser aiming devices for a wide variety of semi-auto pistols. Since they replace the gun's factory guide rod directly centered under the barrel, no sighting in is required. A version is also available for revolvers.

a good tactical flashlight and a good dose of common sense.) But, laser sights can help you to *locate* your target in the dark. Also, because the laser dot may serve as a deterrent, a laser dot on your target is likely to get a reaction such as, "Don't shoot, I'm in the wrong home."

Crimson Trace Laser Grips are made for a wide variety of semi-automatics and revolvers and are easy to install. You just replace your handgun's commercially supplied grips with the Laser grips (except for Glocks and Springfield XDs, where the Lasergrips are attached over the singular polymer grips). They are also simple, easy, and natural to deploy—all that's required is that you firmly grip your handgun. They come sighted in from the factory, but are also adjustable for elevation and windage fine-tuning. There are no switches to push or buttons to press that could slow you down. Now, with all that going for them, how could you not put Crimson Trace grips on every handgun you own?

Hollowpoint Bullets

We do not shoot to kill—we shoot to stop an attacker from trying to kill you or another innocent. The attacker may die as a result, since we are using deadly force, but that is not our intent. Our intent in using deadly force is to stop deadly force. For that purpose, we want to use the biggest caliber we can handle.

Now, there is no "magic bullet" with guaranteed instant stopping power. There is, in fact, no such thing as a "killer bullet" in a handgun caliber; handguns are inherently less powerful than long guns. However, handguns are what we are most likely to have on or around us when deadly force is necessary for defending against deadly force, and let's face it, bigger bullets make bigger holes and create larger temporary and permanent wound channels. *This translates into greater stopping power*, the only reason to use deadly force in a justifiable situation.

Now, if a larger-caliber bullet has greater stopping power than a smaller-caliber bullet, it makes sense that we just might need to shoot fewer bullets to accomplish our goal of stop-

Hollowpoint ammunition is a must for those carrying concealed. Such ammo makes bigger holes, which may mean you'll require fewer rounds to end an attack. They also have less pass-through penetration than full metal jacket ammo. These features together have the added benefit of reducing the risk of injury to innocent bystanders.

ping an attack. Although we should never count on a one-shot stop (and, truthfully, in most cases, more than one will be necessary to stop a determined bad guy), if we can do the job with fewer bullets, all the better. Fewer bullets fired reduce the chances of innocent bystanders being hurt. Also, fewer bullet channels in the aggressor means there is a lesser chance of killing the aggressor. So, let's now talk about hollowpoint bullets, and, lastly, wadcutters.

Hollowpoint bullets are designed to mushroom and expand as they penetrate flesh. As they expand, they will ideally create bigger holes and greater temporary and permanent wound channels. Also, when hollowpoints expand like a parachute, this action slows their penetration. Full-metal-jacket or hardball rounds tend to over-penetrate in calibers 9mm and greater, as they don't expand or deform to the degree hollowpoints do. Thus, there is always the possibility that hardball rounds can over penetrate, exit the target's body, and keep on traveling. This endangers innocent bystanders.

Of course, it makes sense that we must use whatever rounds we have on hand should we need to defend our lives. But, the advantage of hollowpoints is that they have all the above-described properties, plus they are more humane.

More humane? Indeed. As pointed out by Massad Ayoob, hollowpoints are more humane, because you are likely to need fewer rounds to stop the attacker.

If you are new to handgunning, you need to know that hollowpoints are not "cop-killer" bullets, nor are they "armor-piercing," as some misinformed (or intentionally misleading), zealous anti-gunners would have the others believe. What they are, instead, are modern bullets, manufactured to exacting standards and designed to stop an attacker with minimum collateral damage. Therefore, and unless ruled illegal in your jurisdiction, hollowpoints are your preferred bullet choice for self-defense.

One last point. Full metal jacket and hardball rounds are still likely to get the job done. Despite arguments to the contrary, they have had a history of doing so for many years. This is especially true in larger calibers such as .40 S&W and .45 ACP, as well as in smaller, less-powerful calibers such as .380 ACP, .32 ACP, and .25 ACP, where a hardball round's extra penetration may be just what is needed to compensate for what can be a lack of reliable expansion.

Wadcutters

Wadcutter, or flat-nosed, bullets have been used for years in revolvers for target shooting, because they make big, round, easy-to-see holes on paper targets. The bullet design is a lead cylinder that's seated internally to the cartridge case, so that the tip is flat and flush with the top of the case. They generally weigh in the intermediate range in grain weight, but they generally have a lower powder charge, thus, they are easier to shoot and promote better shot-to-shot recovery. They are a viable alternative for defensive carry, because you need not worry about bullet expansion and the bullet plugging up with debris.

Wadcutters make consistent round holes of the same diameter as their caliber—remember that bigger holes are better than smaller holes, when you are trying to stop someone from killing you. Bigger holes will cause more rapid blood loss and, hopefully, more quickly terminate an aggressor's aggression.

Six Rescue Tools that Could Save Your Live

Spare keys, smoke alarms, carbon monoxide detectors, fire extinguishers, electronic security systems, flood lights, cellular phones, first aid kits, flashlights, safety matches, butane lighters, candles, knives, hammers, and axes are emergency rescue equipment. All these tools go together as part of an emergency rescue system, and no well-equipped home should be without any of them. Defensive firearms are also emergency rescue equipment. However, many folks who choose to own a defensive firearm do not realize the necessity of coupling their guns with other essential defensive tools as part of their complete defensive emergency rescue system.

The problem is that a firearm is viewed, as it should be, as a tool of last resort, one to be used only in the gravest extreme. If you aim a gun at a person, you had better be certain that person possesses both the ability and the immediate opportunity to cause you death or grave bodily harm, and that he is acting in such a manner that a reasonable and prudent person would assume he was using those powers to place your innocent life in jeopardy.

It's been said that, if the only tool you have is a hammer, every problem may look like a nail! But, with gun ownership, this viewpoint isn't an option. In any situation where force is indicated, a sane person uses only the amount of force necessary to solve the problem at hand. If you locked yourself out of a room in your house, you wouldn't use an axe to break down the door if you had a spare key or a tool to jimmy the

> If you're new to hand-gunning, you need to know that hollowpoints are not "cop killers," as the anti-gunners would have you believe. Rather, they are modern bullets made to exacting standards and specificallt designed to stop an attacker with minimum collateral damage.

lock. Similarly, only a crazy person would use a firearm to repel a low-level threat, when less-than-lethal force—a verbal warning, pepper spray, a hand strike, a knee to the groin, etc.—is all that may be necessary to take care of it. So, then, the well-prepared person is equipped with a range of less-than-lethal force options to deal with social threats where ultimate force is uncalled for.

If you choose to own a handgun for home-defense, or if you carry a concealed handgun for self-defense, there are six essential, defensive, emergency rescue tools that you should always have at the ready and carry with your handgun as components of a total defensive, emergency rescue system. Let's take a look at each.

Tactical Flashlights

Criminals, like roaches, come out at night. That's why more violent criminal attacks and gunfights occur at night or in low light conditions. So, if you carry a gun, you should be prepared to light up the night. You must carry a reliable and powerful illumination tool. In my opinion, a personal, tactical flashlight is an essential companion to your carry and home-defense guns. The defensive flashlight partnered with the defensive handgun serves several purposes:

1. **Locates the Threat**—In order to deal with a threat, you have to first locate it. Ergo, the flashlight.

2. **Identifies the Threat**—We do not want to shoot at shadows, nor can we ever condone shooting at anything that we are not 100 percent sure is what we think it is. Recall the universal firearm safety rule, "Be sure of your target and what's around it."

> A personal tactical flashlight is a must. It can locate and clearly identify a threat, verify a safe direction to point your gun, and can be used at its own impact weapon or to blind and disorient an attacker.

3. **Verifies Safe Direction**—We must never point a gun at anything we are not willing to destroy. A hand-held flashlight permits you to identify a threat without pointing a gun at it until you confirm it's warranted to do so.

4. **Disorients the Threat**—A super-bright flashlight beam in an attacker's eyes is sure to temporarily blind and disorient him. This can buy you, the defender, valuable time to either escape or establish dominance in the confrontation.

5. **Serves as an Impact Tool**—If you are surprised by an attacker close in, a solid flashlight can serve as a less-than-lethal impact weapon. This could possibly make the use of deadly force unnecessary, if your response is delivered with enough impact and the attacker gets the message.

Surefire and Streamlight are two companies that pioneered tactical lights, and both continue to manufacture the best tactical illumination tools on the planet. With the most choices of any flashlight company, you are certain to find one among either's line-up to serve your needs and budget.

Reliable Spare Magazines

If you carry a semi-automatic pistol, you should consider carrying at least one tried and tested spare magazine. Two or three are even better, especially as many gun stoppages or malfunctions are attributable to faulty magazines.

In addition to reducing the chances of a malfunction, a spare magazine can, of course, get you out of a jam if you run out of ammo. More shots are generally better than fewer. This follows the theory of the gun itself, as stated by Ayoob, when he said, "It is better to have it and not need it than to need it and not have it."

Emergency rescue equipment is no place to compromise on quality, especially when you are talking about the heart of your pistol. There are numerous after-

You must have backup. Backup gun, backup knife, backup magazines, and backup ammo. This user has an off-side attachment on his Alessi shoulder holster rig, so that he can reload his revolver quickly if needed.

market bargain magazine manufacturers, but only one company stands out when it comes to quality and reliability, and its name is Mec-Gar. This Italian firm, with U.S. headquarters in Connecticut, once was, and still may be, the original magazine supplier for many of the world's leading firearms manufacturers, including Beretta, Browning, Kel-tec, Para Ordnance, SIGarms, Smith & Wesson, Taurus, and Walther.

Mec-Gars are the only after-market magazines I would bet my life on. In many cases, I have found them to function more reliably than the original factory magazines.

Pepper Spray

If you carry a gun, you should also carry pepper spray. Obviously, a gun is a deadly weapon, while pepper spray is not. A defensive firearm is a rescue tool of last resort, while pepper spray is a

tool of first resort to be used after a verbal warning is given and that warning does not deter a physical aggressor. Pepper spray is jerk repellent. A firearm is a killer.

Pepper spray should be a no-brainer for everyone wanting to protect themselves. The potent capsicum contents are a top less-than-lethal option for incapacitating an arm's-length attacker enough to let you escape and get help. Every cop in this country carries pepper spray, and isn't that enough reason you should, too?

141

Pepper spray should only be deployed in an up-close situation. To be effective, it must be sprayed at the face so that it will inflame and close up an attacker's mucous membranes (eyes, nose, and mouth). This and the burning will temporarily shut down your attacker's sensory capabilities and give him something else to think about, hopefully giving you a chance to escape. If it stops your attacker, great, you have just avoided employing deadly force. But if all it does is slow down your attacker, it will give you a tactical advantage, for now your attacker has to react to your actions, propelling you ahead on the reaction curve. Remember, action is faster than reaction! Finally, if pepper spray doesn't work, then you have a good reason to up your level of defensive force.

One handy pepper spray dispenser I like to use is the ASP OC Defender. This lightweight, high-strength, aluminum mini-baton is a pepper spray dispenser that attaches to your key chain with a quick-release option. It has a positive and secure safety to prevent an unintentional discharge. Intentional discharge of its contents requires two distinct movements. First, the user releases its positive safety ring. Second, the user presses the spring-loaded button attached to the key ring, releasing a cone-shaped spray of 2,000,000 Scoville heat units of oleoresin capsicum protection on target. The ASP Defender can also serve double duty as a defensive flail or thrasher, and as a contact-distance, impact and pain compliance tool, such as a Kubotan.

Tactical Folding Knives

The term "defensive tactics" refers to lines or strategies of counterattack. To counter a gun grab, it makes tactical sense to carry a defensive folding knife on the side of your body opposite the side where your gun rides. With appropriate training, knife carry can enable you to cut off an attacker who is attempting to disarm or otherwise harm you. Plus, shooting to wound makes no sense. Cutting to deter further aggressive action does.

A knife, whether folder or fixed blade, should be on your body every time you carry a firearm. It can be a less-than-lethal option before you go to the gun, and it can deter a gun grab in a close-quarter attack situation if you can easily unsheath and deploy it.

The key is a concealable folding knife that can be quickly deployed. Emerson Knives which is owned by noted author and edged weapon combatives trainer Ernest Emerson, makes a line of serious tactical folding knives with the company's patented Wave feature. With a bit of practice, this feature enables you to open the knife as you draw it from your pocket. These knives are faster to deploy than an automatic knife or switchblade, and they are legal in most jurisdictions, whereas automatic knives are not. The pocket clip on most of Emerson's tactical folders can be switched for right- or left-sided carry.

Cold Steel and Columbia River Knife Tool also manufacture a wide variety of quality, reliable, versatile, affordable and innovative, defensive folding knives, and these knives are razor sharp. TOPS knives is another company I'd recommend, one that makes a large line of innovative, functional, rugged use combat and tactical fixed blades.

Cell Phone

Nowadays, there's no good reason not to carry a cellular phone. In an emergency, you can dial 9-1-1 from wherever you are, as long as there is service. Were you aware that your old, deactivated cell phones will still dial 9-1-1 when charged?

The Ayoob D-Jammer

This handy device, designed by Massad Ayoob, conveniently attaches to your keys along with your pepper spray. It can serve a number of useful functions. It was primarily designed as an emergency tool for removing an obstruction from the barrel of your handgun, dislodging jammed bullets or cases in a revolver or autoloader, un-jamming stuck mechanical parts in a pistol or revolver, and it can also serve as an emergency cleaning rod in the field. Secondarily, it can enable you to use your keys as a defensive flail or thrasher, and it can also be used as a close-up impact and compliance tool, such as a Kubotan. The D-Jammer has been available from Armor of New Hampshire.

The long skinny baton attached to the author's key chain is an Ayoob D-Jammer tool. It is a great defense tool for gouging an attacker's throat or eyes, and can also be used as a handle for flailing the keys into some punk's face.

Does all of the above seem like too much to think about and carry? If it does, then ask yourself the question, "How much effort is your life worth?"

It is really just a matter of developing an at-the-ready, defensive emergency rescue system and integrating it into your lifestyle. This type of integration and habit formation comes naturally, for, in fact, we do it all the time in other areas of our lives. For example, those of us who are smart carry a spare tire in our vehicles, a spare gas can, spare cans of engine oil, jumper cables, a flashlight, and other such tools. If we are smart, we change the batteries in our home smoke alarms annually, we install anti-virus software on our computers, and we purchase life insurance, disability insurance, home owner's insurance, property insurance, car insurance, and so forth. Be smart with your personal-defense solutions, too, and survive.

CHAPTER 23

The Necessity of Knives

Concealed means out of sight and that only you should know you are armed. However, there are myriad ways in which you can inadvertently announce that you are carrying. For example, if your gun prints through your cover garment when you bend or reach for something. Another is if you are in a crowd and someone brushes up against you. If you are not the only one who knows you are carrying, you run the risk of someone attempting to relieve you of your firearm. It is imperative that you remain prepared and ready to defend against such threats.

The immediate goal when defending against a gun grab is to disable the offending hands and disrupt the attacker's plan. As discussed in the preceding chapter, the action of thwarting an attempt to disarm you (a whole book in itself) is referred to as "weapon retention." One of the simplest and most effective methods of maintaining handgun retention is to cut off the hand or arm that is trying to disarm you. There are various techniques for doing so, and the details are beyond the scope of this chapter, but the tool needed for the job is a sharp, reliable blade, a quality folding- or fixed-blade knife that can be carried on the side opposite your handgun. A rapid-deploy blade reserved solely for defensive purposes constitutes essential equipment for the legally armed citizen.

As stated above, the immediate goal when defending against a gun grab is to disable the offender's hands and disrupt his plan. A well-targeted and timely slash with a sharp blade that cuts the tendons that control movement of the attacker's hands and fingers will do the trick. You may also need to trap the offender's hands before, during, and after making your cuts. Recognize that a slap or a parry may not be the thing to do, if the attacker already has his hands on your handgun, as this could propel his inertia in getting your gun out of your holster.

Get Schooling

There are many simple martial blade techniques that are easy to learn and practice, and good training is available for citizens needing to learn these skills. The Sayoc International Group, under the leadership of Grand Tuhon Chris Sayoc and Master Trainer Tuhon Tom Kier, offers seminars and training DVDs on the Filipino-based Sayoc Kali martial arts system of blade, stick, and empty-hand fighting methods (www.Sayoc.com). Master edged weapons trainer and combat knife manufacturer Ernest Emerson, of Emerson Knives (www.EmersonKnives.com), offers edged weapon and defensive tactics seminars, as well as training videos, as does noted author and master edged weapons instructor Michael Janich, of Martial Blade Concepts (www.Martial-BladeConcepts.com).

Action is Faster

You cannot be fast enough to catch up if you have to react to a vicious attack. Therefore, you must not only be aware and anticipate when an attack is imminent, but you must also be the "feeder" and not the "receiver." The feeder, or actor, lives to see another day, and the receiver, or reactor, dies. You must disrupt an attacker's plan and reverse the tables on him by turning him into the receiver.

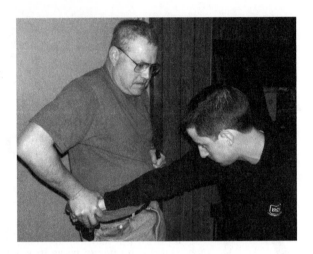

The author (left) in an edged weapons training class, demonstrating how to thwart a gun grab by an assailant. As with anything, and especially the tools you choose to carry, training such as this is paramount to effective deployment and use of your chosen defensive tools.

This is done by transforming instantly, explosively, and aggressively into the feeder and disabling the bad guy's body and mind in an aggressive, offensive counterattack.

You must never underestimate your attacker. This may sound silly, but you should assume your attacker has combatives training and truly knows how to disable, maim, and kill. To prevail if you are assaulted, your mind-set has to be that the best defense is a good offense. Be the feeder. You must act decisively and aggressively to end the fight *fast*. A physical attack on your person calls for an all-out, full-court press against your attacker that overwhelms them.

> In the event of an attempted gun grab, deploy your knife with an underhand grip and slash upward into your attacker's arm. Your primary goal here is to disable your opponent by cutting the tendons that control the movement of the hands.

When you are dually armed with a knife in addition to your gun, a simple underhand grip on your blade's handle and an upward slash into your attacker's arm, followed by a powerful stab to the assailant's neck will typically do the job. You can practice this drill with a training blade and dummy handgun at least 1,000, times so it is installed into your subconscious as a motor memory.

Blade Choice and Carry Considerations

I prefer plain-edged over serrated or partially serrated blades, as the former are easier to sharpen and maintain. For stabbing, spear-point and drop-point blades, such as the Crucible II folder and Crucible FX2 fixed blade by Blackhawk Products Group, are more efficient than are tanto style blades. I also prefer designs with convex, belly out edges for slashing, such as the Crucible II folder. However, straight-edge and concave-curved karambits and hawkbill-shaped blades, such as the Garra II folder, will also serve just fine.

This folding knife rides subtly on the author's blue jeans waistband and belt loop. It is easy to access with either the weak- or strong-side hand as needed.

If you choose to carry a blade or two for personal-defense, you need to think about how you are going to deploy it if you need it in a hurry—just as you think about how you'll deploy your gun. There are multiple options. Folders, for instance, are easy to stow, but they are not always easy to deploy in a hurry. Nor are they typically as sturdy as fixed blades. Fixed blades, while sturdy and fast, are less convenient and less comfortable to carry unless they come with a concealable sheathing system that offers adjustable or multiple carry positions.

When you choose a folder for defensive carry, you want to choose a sturdy one that opens smoothly and reliably, as well as one that is razor sharp and holds its edge. The knife should also permit multiple carry positions because how you carry it should be a function of what other weapons you are packing and your attire. Therefore, in a folder, it is desirable for the pocket carry clip to be movable so that you can carry the folder in your left or right pockets, and with the blade tip either up or down.

CHAPTER 24

The Importance of Follow-Through

Follow-through is important in every endeavor. It means simply completing what we aim to do effectively. It also means communicating clearly in words and making our actions match our words. In a stressful situation, such as in a fight, following through requires that we remain at the ready, that we don't let down our guard, and that we don't quit before the job is completed.

Follow-Through Language

In life, following through isn't always easy. It takes hard work and the wherewithal to think through problems. But, we live in a time when people often do not say what they mean—especially if speaking the truth requires verbalizing opinions, beliefs, attitudes, or facts that are considered to be "politically incorrect."

Tom Givens, master firearm instructor and author, and John Farnam, my good friend and sensei, summed up the language part of the issue well.

Givens: "When asked why you routinely bear arms, albeit concealed, what is your answer? Do you shrewdly couch your response in ostensibly inoffensive phrases like, 'personal-security,' 'self-protection,' or 'accessing the full spectrum of the force continuum?' … . When asked that same question, my unmistakable and unapologetic response is ever, 'I carry a gun so I can shoot people!'"

Farnam: "Under some circumstances, some people need to be shot dead, on the spot! Indeed, there are times when shooting people, while always regrettable, is still acutely necessary in order to prevent the innocent from being hurt. That's what guns are for, and we carry them constantly, because we cannot know when the pivotal moment will be upon us. I don't keep a fire extinguisher in my home because I harbor some secret, pestilent desire to put out fires! On the contrary, it is my sincerest wish that I never see a fire. Still, most regard keeping a fire extinguisher handy to be a reasonable precaution."

These two respected teachers are arguing that we stop worrying about being politically correct, because it leads us to use the same type of weasel words so many politicians do to rationalize or soften the impact of what they are saying so their real intentions are not apparent. When legally armed citizens use weasel words to explain or justify why we carry concealed, we are delivering points to the enemy, as Farnam points out, by "pseudo-apologizing for refusing to be the perpetual victims that politicians and the media, at every level, so desperately want us to be. We need to speak clearly, without apology."

Follow-Through Actions

The legally armed citizen must be prepared to follow-through with every action he takes. A predatory threat won't just go away if we do nothing—this is not the time to "give peace a chance."

Working up the force continuum is, on its own merits, follow-through. The law requires that we meet force with a little more than like-force. And, if an attacker escalates his level of force, we must be prepared to immediately escalate our level of force. The late Colonel Jeff Cooper pointed out in his classic book *Principles of Personal Defense* that the best defense against a vicious attack is a more vicious, explosive, and overwhelming, offensive counter-attack *followed through to the very end*, with the attacker being down, disabled, and out of the fight.

If we have to shoot, following through with the shot means that we must maintain our aim for a fraction of a second or more *after* the sear releases the hammer or striker, to allow time for the bullet to follow-through and exit the barrel.

The "surprise break" is a concept that is germane here. It is a concept frequently used with beginning shooters, yet one that is too often misunderstood. It does not simply mean being surprised by the shot. Rather, it means continuing to apply all the shooting fundamentals—power stance, hard combat grip, front sight focus, sight alignment, sight picture, trigger control—throughout the break of the shot. In order to place an accurate shot, you simply must continue to maintain your concentration on sight alignment right after the shot is fired. In addition to giving the bullet enough time to exit the barrel, this is the element that makes the breaking of the shot a surprise. This is so very important, because it prevents you from anticipating the shot and flinching or jerking the trigger.

Almost everyone suffers from a lack of follow-through in their shooting at one time or another. I first learned this from my friend and teacher, master firearm instructor and author Louis Awerbuck, who is the director of the Yavapai Firearms Academy (www.YFA-Inc.com), and a senior instructor at Gunsite, in Arizona. Awerbuck is an expert at diagnosing students' marksmanship problems. When I trained with Louis, he diagnosed the first of my shooting problems as a lack of thorough follow-through. I was dropping my shots, because I wasn't giving the bullet a chance to exit the barrel after the gun fired. It takes a little more than a fraction of a second for the bullet to exit the barrel after the round is detonated. If you fire at the target and don't hold the gun on target long enough after the gun fires, the bullet will be sent on awry.

Louis suggested the following remedy. After taking one shot, stay on target and prep the trigger as if you are going to take another shot. Thus, one shot means remaining ready to take a second, two shots means remaining ready to take a third, and so on. One shot means two sight pictures, the before and the after. Two shots mean three sight pictures, before the first shot, before the second shot, and after the second shot. And so on. What Louis explained is that you actually fool your brain (your subconscious shooter) into thinking that you are going to take another shot (one more than you actually take). Not only does this give the bullet the time it needs to exit the barrel, it also keeps you at the ready to take the next shot if necessary. After I started practicing this, I no longer found myself dropping my shots.

Following through after the shot is the act of *recovery*. It is the act of letting the pistol return in recoil to your original holding position from which you aimed your shot. Master firearms instructor and author Andy Stanford, formerly of Options for Personal Security (OPS), points out in his book *Surgical Speed Shooting* that, "To shoot accurately at the maximum rate of fire, you must be ready to apply the final pressure to the trigger at the instant the sights settle back on the target." To accomplish this, you must keep your finger on the trigger at all times while in the act of shooting. As the handgun is recoiling, you must ride the trigger forward to its reset point (i.e., the point at which you can pull the trigger again) by keeping your finger on the trigger, and then depress it again to let off another shot.

This constant readiness to follow through is a necessity for accurate marksmanship, irrespective of shooting speed. Stanford discusses in his book, "Whatever the action type of your gun, one key to accurate rapid fire is to keep the trigger busy. Instead of the traditional recipe of 'aim then fire'—which often results in the shooter jerking the trigger in an attempt to take a snapshot of a good sight picture—correct the alignment of weapon and target while you are pressing/stroking the trigger." In other words, the act of firing a shot isn't complete until the sights have come back on target after recoil and the shooter is prepping the trigger for the next shot. This reset-prep process each time you fire the gun needs to become as ingrained as a reflexive, subconscious habit, though the conscious part of the sequence is your brain commanding you to continue firing or cease firing. If the command is to continue firing, your finger must stay on the trigger. Only when it's time to cease fire does your finger need to come off the trigger.

Follow-Through on Your 360

Follow-through also means continually maintaining awareness of your 360-degree environment. Stanford explains in his *Surgical Speed Shooting* book that, after shooting a string and taking down your adversary (even if it's a square paper target), get into the habit (i.e., repetitive practice) of taking the following steps:

1. Stay on target with the trigger prepped for just a moment to keep yourself from dropping your guard too soon. If the threat is stopped …

2. Take your finger out of the trigger guard and lower your weapon to a combat-ready position.

3. Assess the situation to ensure your adversary is really out of the fight and then …

4. Scan a full 360 degrees for additional threats. Turn your head to the right and right rear, then the left and left rear. This also will break the tunnel vision you'll have on your adversary.

5. Reload your handgun during any lull in the action or while moving to or behind cover, so you are prepared to resume fighting if the need arises. As Clint Smith is fond of saying, "Reload when you want to, not when you have to."

6. Call for help.

CHAPTER 25

What's Your Stance?

T he goal of any combat shooting stance is to put your handgun into the position where you can make the most accurate hits in the shortest amount of time. Your stance functions to align your point of aim, the front sight, rear sight, and your dominant eye. It is your shooting platform for launching bullets and, as such, needs to be stable, balanced, and mobile. It needs to be a fighting stance, a *power* stance.

One component of this is to hold your handgun the same way every time. This grip needs to be firm and consistent, while allowing us to retain the gun and isolate the trigger finger. If you're all over the place with this, you're shifting the aiming burden to and overloading the dominant eye, when, if fact, it should be your whole body that's indexing and aiming the gun. Let's look at a couple proven platforms for accomplishing this.

The Isosceles Stance

This stance, or way to hold the gun out, is basically like a tripod, or isosceles triangle. It is a two-handed technique in which the dominant hand holds the handgun and the support hand wraps around the dominant hand. When seen from above, the shooter is pushing, or punching, the gun outward towards the target with his arms, and the handgun makes the apex of an isosceles triangle, the equilateral legs of the triangle being the shooter's arms, and the base being the shooter's body. Different shooters will have different degrees of bend in their elbows, and that's just fine.

A combat Isosceles is more aggressive. Viewed from a side profile, the shooter should be leaning forward aggressively in a vulture-like position—the shooter's nose in front of his shoulders, his shoulders in front of his hips, and his hips in front of his feet. The knees should be slightly bent.

The author target shooting in a classic Isosceles stance. Both legs are parallel and slightly apart for a solid base, the knees slightly bent for flexibility and reaction. He is leaning forward aggressively, but not so far that he will cause himself to be unbalanced.

153

The shooter's feet should be shoulder-width apart, and the leading foot should be the foot opposite the shooter's dominant hand. The shooter's dominant side foot should be to the rear, heel wedged into the ground, toes pointing outboard to about the one to three o'clock position for a right-handed shooter, and to about 11 to nine o'clock for a left-handed shooter.

The Weaver Stance

This shooting platform was developed by Los Angeles Counter Deputy Sheriff and IPSC pioneer Jack Weaver, and popularized by Col. Jeff Cooper. The Weaver stance is a two-handed technique in which the dominant hand holds the handgun and the support hand wraps around the dominant hand. Unlike the Isosceles stance, with the Weaver, the elbow of the dominant arm is bent

The classic Weaver stance, demonstrated by the author. His body is bladed away from an oncoming attack, and his strong-side arm is slightly bent. This particular stance offers a very solid shooting base, and one that handles recoil well.

slightly towards the ground, while the support arm elbow is pointed straight down towards the ground. The shooter pushes forward with his dominant hand, while the support hand exerts rearward pressure. The resulting isometric tension is intended to lessen and control muzzle flip when it is fired.

In the Weaver stance, the shooter is "bladed" toward the target. That is, the chest of the right-handed dominant shooter is facing forward canted to a roughly two o'clock position; the chest of the left-handed dominant shooter would be opposite, toward the 10 o'clock position.

A couple things to know about the Weaver stance. It is not a problem if your elbows are too far out. "Chicken winged" is okay. Also, if your gun rotates slightly counterclockwise (for right-handed shooters), or clockwise (for lefties) this is not a problem.

The Chapman Stance

This shooting platform was developed by the late Ray Chapman, a champion police combat pistol shooter, IPSC pioneer, and a range master at the Los Alamitos County California Police Department. The Chapman stance is a two-handed technique in which the dominant hand holds the handgun and the support hand wraps around the dominant hand. It is a variant of the push-pull bladed Weaver stance, but here the dominant arm is held rigidly, like a rifle stock, with the elbow locked and parallel to the ground. The non-dominant arm's elbow is pointed down towards the ground, as in the Weaver.

Don't Fight Recoil

You must accept the fact that the gun is going to jump—recoil—in your hand. It's not going

Defensive shooting is *not* target shooting. You must be able to address any and all possible attack situations you may find yourself in. That requires practice. Make sure you get off your two feet and a solid platform, practicing your aim and live-fire control from prone, one- and two-leg kneeling, crouching, and moving-as-you-shoot positions.

to hurt if you have the right gun for you. If a gun's recoil does hurt you, then you may have the wrong gun for you or you may be holding it improperly.

While you should not fight with recoil, you should not ride it either. Riding the recoil can serve to exaggerate it, and this brings the gun much further up than it needs to be before it settles down. You need to be in control of the gun as you shoot it, not vice versa. A wide and stable power stance in any of the above modes will help you control your gun's recoil.

You should also not anticipate recoil and shove or jerk the gun forward to fight it. Let the gun recoil naturally. You need a firm hard grip, but not a death grip. Shooting a gun is a process. The process will go off naturally if you don't try to over-control or over-think it.

Personalizing Your Stance

Every shooter must find or adopt a stance that is comfortable for him or her, based on their body type and physical condition. It is not necessary to perform a perfect Isosceles, Weaver, or Chapman. A less-than-perfect stance that is consistent can still function to reliably index the gun and deliver the front sight to the target.

It's okay to have an imperfect stance, but there are some things to keep in mind. Don't lean too far forward or backward, and keep both feet on the ground. Remember that, if you have to draw your gun on someone, you must be prepared to fight. Your stance should be a fighting stance that keeps you stable so that you cannot be knocked off balance by your opponent. You must also stay balanced to be mobile.

> The goal of any combat shooting stance is to put your handgun into the position where you can make the most accurate hits in the shortest amount of time. Your stance functions to align your point of aim, the front sight, rear sight, and your dominant eye.

Again, your fighting stance needs to be aggressive—your shoulders should be in front of your hips and your hips slightly in front of your feet. Knees should be slightly bent. The non-dominant foot should be forward, while the dominant foot is rearward and digging into the ground for stability. Keep in mind you may need to fight in any direction, so do not thrust yourself too far forward, for, if your opponent is smart, he will outflank you and take the upper hand.

A Solution for Inadequate Platforms

There are situations in which it may not be possible to get into a good shooting platform or stance, for example, when you are behind cover or concealment. Another situation would be if you are physically disabled to the point where you cannot adequately align your point of aim, front sight, rear sight, and dominant eye, so as to get all four points into a straight line. This could be due to diminished eyesight, range of motion limitations in the upper extremities, or being confined to a bed or wheelchair, among other factors. For these situations, good technology, along with training with the right equipment, may provide a viable solution. Here, I am talking about laser sights.

A laser sighting system can facilitate accurate shooting from behind cover and concealment and in low-light conditions. That is why S.W.A.T. teams using full-cover ballistic shields often employ laser sights. If you have to hide behind an automobile, bed, bookcase, or some other available barricade, or if you have to shoot from a prone position or with your weak hand, a reliable laser sighting device on your handgun may still afford accurate shot placement.

Earlier, I discussed the Crimson Trace laser grips. I also like the ones from LaserMax (www.LaserMax.com), a company that has been making reliable laser sighting devices for the major brands of handguns for years. These sighting devices are rugged, user-friendly, and easily installed by just about anyone. The lasers fit internally in your handgun, as close to the bore of the firearm as possible, thus allowing for the closest and most consistent relationship between your point of aim and point of impact. Because LaserMax sights feature a distinct on-off switch that can be easily activated by both right-handed and left-handed shooters, there's no need to alter your grip and potentially compromise your shooting accuracy to activate the laser beam, as can happen with the Crimson Trace grip lasers. Additionally, the laser need not inadvertently reveal your position while you're drawing from your holster, such as can happen with a tactical flashlight. Last but not least, an intuitive, easy-to-operate laser sighting system such as the LaserMax can help new shooters learn sight picture and trigger control more quickly.

CHAPTER 26

Skills Maintenance Drills

G iven the fact that yours truly is physically challenged with neck and back pain, fibromyalgia-related inflexibility, degenerative arthritis, and a bunch of other muscular-skeletal issues, I am often asked how I regularly train. In this chapter, I shall address this question, discussing several skills maintenance exercises that I have learned over the years for both live- and dry-fire practice.

Visual-Motor Coordination Exercises

I frequently practice two visual-motor coordination exercises without a gun. In the first, I pick a spot to aim at. Then, I visually focus on that spot and simply point my finger at that spot. That's the exercise. It's one smooth flow.

Exercise two builds on the first. I again pick a spot to aim at. Keeping my visual focus on that spot, I imagine drawing my handgun and acquiring a sight picture on that spot. Together, these exercises build muscle memory.

Dry-Practice Drills

The following exercises involve working at home with an unloaded handgun (emphasis on unloaded and verifying that condition of your gun). Make sure you have a safe backstop regardless how many times you have verified your gun is unloaded, and make sure there is no live ammunition in the room.

Dry-Practice Exercise One

Staying in sequence is the key to hitting what you are aiming at when you get to firing live.

1. Pick a target and a small aiming point (aim small, miss small). Focus on that point.

3. Bring your unloaded handgun up, with your finger off the trigger and alongside the gun's frame. When your gun intersects your line of sight, pick up the front sight.

4. Superimpose your front sight, as seen through your rear sight, on top of your aim point.

5. Establish that there is good sight alignment.

6. Focus on your front sight and establish a good sight picture (your front sight centered in the rear sight notch).

7. Repeat this drill 10 times.

Dry-Practice Exercise Two

This drill repeats all the steps of the first exercise, but now you'll bring your finger onto the trigger and slightly press the trigger rearward without taking the shot. Take up the trigger slack, but do not press the trigger all the way back to the point where the shot breaks. Repeat this drill 10 times.

Dry-Practice Exercise Three

Now, practice 10 repetitions of acquiring your sight picture and fully working the trigger.

Some things to consider when practicing Exercise Three. If your handgun is a double-action revolver or a double-action-only (DAO) trigger-cocking semi-automatic pistol with a hammer, you can simply and easily dry-practice double-taps. A double-tap refers to firing two shots in rapid succession. Of course, with most semi-automatic pistols, in this drill you'll have to manually cycle the slide to simulate the gun's action. This will be a slower drill than with a revolver, but still useful.

Safe Room Dry-Practice

Another exercise that you can do at home is to simulate working within your safe room, where you'll visualize home invaders breaking in. Make sure you're working with an unloaded gun and sequester all live ammunition.

The sequence entails verbalizing appropriate commands from behind cover: "Stop! Drop your weapon! I'm armed! Go away! Leave this house now!" Acquire a sight picture on your imaginary home invader and dry-fire if necessary. You should practice this drill with your trigger finger first in register, then taking up the trigger slack, and both with and without dry-firing. Remember, you hope that you do not have to fire, but you must be prepared to do so if the threat does not back down.

As part of this drill and the others like it, it is prudent that you learn to really notice and study multiple targets. This involves scanning and verifying each target in an array. As you verify each target, you establish an aim point and acquire your sight picture. This type of practice builds your perceptual and awareness skills. It also transfers to live-fire drills.

Live-Fire Drills

I try to get to the shooting range for skills maintenance practice at least twice a month. When I go, I try to make the most of my time and ammunition, and so I have found the following live-fire drill to be an excellent way to keep my skills intact. The drill incorporates multiple skills: stance, grip, draw from concealment, trigger control, sight alignment and sight picture, varying distances, follow-up shots, speed, and accuracy. It is not a beginner's drill, nor is it a skills *acquisition* exercise. It is a skills *maintenance* drill. It requires just 50 rounds—one box of ammunition. It does not require a shot timer.

The target used is a humanoid silhouette, either a Q, a B-27, or some other equivalent. I like to paste a five-inch orange circle at the high center of mass for focusing purposes.

With all shots taken from my concealment holster, 10 rounds are shot at each of the following distances: five, seven, 10, 15, and 20 yards. That makes for a total of 50 rounds. At each distance I clear my covering garment, then draw and fire a double-tap at the pasted-on orange circle. That's five draw-and-fire double-taps (10 rounds) at each distance. That's the drill. The greater the distance to the target, the more I rely on my sights and the more time I take for each shot.

Secondary Live-Fire Drills

Here's a drill I find useful, if you have the time and ammunition. It is a tracking drill that lets you practice visually scanning and shooting multiple targets. To practice this, set up and number four, five-inch orange circles in a square target backer. Acquire target No. 1 and fire. Then move your eyes to target No. 2. Your muzzle follows, you verify your target, acquire your sight picture, and fire. Repeat with target Nos. 3 and 4, then you track backwards counter-clockwise through the rotation you've just shot. That makes a total of seven rounds. Two complete cycles are shot at each distance of five, seven, 10, and 15 yards. That makes for a total of 56 rounds. If you started with three boxes of ammunition, you are now left with 44 rounds with which to practice the third drill, what I call the rhythm drill.

The rhythm drill entails loading your handgun to capacity and discharging your loaded gun as quickly as you can, maintaining a rhythm, and keeping all your shots in a respectable grouping on the target. I like to perform this drill at distances of three, five, and seven yards. Thus, with 44 rounds, I can shoot the rhythm drill nine times with my five-shot J-frame revolver, three times with my 13+1 capacity .40-caliber Glock 23, and three times with my 17+1 capacity 9mm Glock 17. You get the idea. This drill also entails doing emergency reloads—nine speed-loads with my J-frame revolver, using either a Bianchi Speed Strip or HKS Speed Loader, and three magazine changes with my Glocks.

Going through all the drills in this manner, you'll expend 150 rounds—three boxes of ammunition—and gotten a great shooting workout. That's doable for most people a couple times a month or more, but if your time and budget are more limited and you can only do one drill, do the first one with one 50-round box of ammunition. The other drills are very valuable, but optional if you have limited time, energy, or ammunition.

CHAPTER 27

Advanced Dry-Practice Drills

If you go to a shooting school or study with a qualified firearms instructor and learn a basic set of good marksmanship, gun handling, and tactical skills, you need to practice—a lot—to imprint those skills into your subconscious and into your muscle, or motor, memory. Then you have to keep on practicing regularly in order to maintain those skills and keep them sharp.

If we can get to the range once a week, that's great, but, for a lot of gun owners, that kind of dedicated practice never happens. Fortunately, there is a solution. It is called "dry practice."

Dry practice refers to working with a thoroughly verified unloaded gun in a designated safe area and practicing the gamut of gun handling and tactical skills. These include marksmanship, drawing the gun from concealment, performing reloads, strong-hand and weak-hand shooting, shooting and moving, moving to cover, using cover and concealment, barricade shooting, clearing malfunctions, and just about any other skill you need to know in order to survive in a fight for your life. In addition, dry practice has some great side benefits. In the safety of your home, it provides exercise, it costs little to nothing, and it keeps you sharp. Also, without the recoil of live fire, it's easier on the joints.

It is important to remember that it's not practice itself that makes perfect, but rather perfect practice that gets the job done. If you practice poor or sloppy technique, then it's poor or sloppy technique that will come out when you most need good technique to survive. Garbage in, garbage out. So, what makes for perfect practice, when it comes to gun handling, marksmanship, and tactics?

The simple answer is that you first need to learn viable skills and techniques, then practice, practice, practice. I have been a student at a number of shooting schools. All of them were excellent, the instructors first rate. But, each teaches differently, so it was my job to figure out which techniques and ways of doing things worked for me. I have been able to do this through dry practice, which I then validated through trips to the range. I have improved my endurance, my draw stroke from concealment, my quickness and precision in acquiring and maintaining good sight alignment and a good sight picture, and my trigger control and shot-to-shot follow-up. Such practice has also helped my strong- and weak-handed and one- and two-handed shooting dexterity, my malfunction clearing, reloads, the ability to shoot and move, and how I use cover and concealment. I do my dry practice with my various concealed carry guns belt holstered, inside-the-waistband holstered, and pocket holstered.

With dry-fire practice, first and foremost you must establish a designated safe area. You should be alone and undisturbed. There should be no live ammunition of any sort in the room. The direction in which you aim should be a safe backstop. That means that, if there ever were a negligent discharge, the wall should be able to absorb and stop the bullet. I use the stone foundation wall in my basement, in front of which I have filled bookcases. As an extra precaution, I've modified and marked as training magazines several old 10-round magazines for my Glocks. I've done this by removing the follower, spring, and magazine insert and replacing the floor plate. Thus, I know that these magazines cannot hold ammunition. This modification also allows me to keep a magazine in the gun and still be able to rack the slide and reengage the trigger bar and striker to reset the trigger without the slide locking back.

Before you begin your dry-practice session, you must have decided how long your session will last. I have found that 10- to 20-minute sessions avoid fatigue and the resulting sloppy practice. Once I've set the kitchen timer, I begin my dry practice by saying out loud, "I am now beginning my dry practice session. My gun is safe, and there is no live ammunition in this room." I then proceed through the following drills.

Drill No. 1: Sight Alignment, Trigger Press, and Trigger Reset Practice

1. Double-check to make sure your gun is unloaded.
2. Pick a spot on the wall on which to visually focus your aim point.
3. From a low ready position and with your firm two-handed grip, bring the pistol up on the target and acquire a sight picture.
4. Take up the slack in the trigger and continue to smoothly press the trigger rearward to break the dry shot, all the while concentrating on keeping your front sight steady on the target.
5. After the dry shot breaks, hold the trigger to the rear, keep the gun extended and pointing down range, and use your weak hand to rack the slide in order to get the trigger bar and striker to re-engage.
6. Reestablish your firm, two-handed grip and let the trigger go forward until you hear the reset click (and no further), as you re-establish your sight picture and press the trigger rearward from the reset point to break another dry shot.
7. Repeat these steps for about five minutes, click-bang, click-bang, click-bang, and so on.

Remember that when you do this drill with a Glock or any type of single-action pistol, you need to make sure that you don't put too much trigger finger on the trigger. It's best to touch the trigger with the mid-tip of the pad of your trigger finger tip, so that you can press the trigger straight back. For traditional double-action or double-action-only pistols or revolvers, you may want to use a little more trigger finger, up to the first crease of the finger.

Drill No. 2: Drawing the Empty Gun and Firing One Shot

This drill is for practicing the draw stroke out of the holster. Cock your empty pistol before holstering it. For every shot you fire, you should take two sight pictures. Your second sight picture is your follow-up to the shot. It counters jerking the gun in anticipation of recoil and keeps the barrel and muzzle on target, thus giving the bullet enough time to exit the muzzle in a live-fire situation. Repeat these steps 25 times, less if fatigue sets in.

1. Pick a small spot on the wall on which to visually focus your aim point.

2. Perform your draw stroke out of the holster, drive your empty gun to the target, and press the trigger. Make sure to hold the trigger rearward and maintain your sight picture as a follow-up to the shot. With live or dry fire, every shot should have two sight pictures, before and after.

3. With your finger off the trigger, rack the slide to cock your empty pistol.

Drill No. 3: Draw and Fire While Moving

This drill is for practicing drawing and firing at the target while moving laterally, alternately moving left and right. As above, verify your gun is unloaded, and cock your empty pistol before holstering it.

1. Pick a spot on the wall on which to visually focus as your aim point.

2. Perform your draw stroke, drive your empty gun to the target, and press the trigger, while you move laterally to the right and off the line of attack. Make sure to keep your front sight on your aiming point as you move and press the trigger! Also, make sure to hold the trigger rearward and maintain your sight picture as a follow-up to the shot. Again, moving or stationary, with live or dry fire, every shot should have two sight pictures, before and after.

3. Finger off the trigger and rack the slide to cock your empty pistol before re-holstering.

4. Repeat these steps, only this time moving laterally to the left.

5. Continue the drill one to four times each side, again being aware of fatigue setting in and causing your skills to become sloppy.

Drill No. 4: Emergency Reloads

When you begin this drill, verify that your gun is unloaded. Make sure that you have two empty spare training magazines on you such as you would carry on the street.

1. Insert an empty magazine into your unloaded gun and lock your slide back.

2. Keep your out-of-battery/locked-back pistol in your line of sight so that you can reload your weapon while keeping an eye on the imaginary battle in front of you. Press the magazine release button and drop the empty magazine, letting it fall without catching it. Simultaneously grab your spare training magazine tap it into the empty magazine well.

4. Rack the slide into battery (as if you are chambering a round), using your support hand.

5. Drive your pistol back on target, assess, and scan.

Repeat this exercise 10 to 15 times, as your session practice clock allows. Remember, the goal of an emergency reload is to do so when you *have* to, so it must be done smoothly and rapidly.

CHAPTER 28

Weapon Retention and the Draw Stroke

As a responsible gun owner and concealed carry permit holder, the last thing you ever want is for someone else to use your own gun on you or on anyone else. This can be prevented through proper equipment selection, the judicious and tactical use of well-rehearsed avoidance and disengagement strategies, and learning some basic weapon retention skills.

Scope of the Problem

A responsible gun owner would never leave a firearm lying around unsecured in their home or in anyone else's. When your defensive firearm isn't on your person, you must lock it up in a safe or a lock-box, so it is secure and inaccessible to unauthorized persons.

That same mentality and commitment should also apply to how you carry concealed, and this is one of the reasons that, unless you are a uniformed patrol officer, open carry is a bad idea. A recent, tragic case illustrates this point.

An off-duty officer was responding to an on-duty officer's call for backup help with an arrest. He arrived on the scene in plain clothes, with a .38 Special revolver openly carried in an open-top belt holster. During a struggle, the off-duty officer was disarmed by the suspect, who shot both officers, murdering one in cold blood.

This is why uniformed patrol officers carry their duty sidearms in what are known as Level Two- and Level Three-retention holsters that are reinforced with additional mechanisms that make gun grabs by an opponent difficult to nearly impossible. Indeed, open carry of a handgun in anything with lesser retention is irresponsible. On the other hand, when you carry concealed, your firearm is (or should be) out of sight and protected by one or more layers of covering garments. This gives you the element of surprise, should you ever have to draw your weapon, and, more importantly, if you get into a close-quarters tussle or are in a crowded place where you're in bodily contact with a lot of people, your concealed weapon is less compromised.

For concealed carry, a quality, Level One-retention holster with a thumb-break retention snap strap makes a lot of sense. At the very least, if you have to run or find yourself in any position other than straight up and down, this will give you a comfortable extra edge of security.

The solutions to the problem of firearm retention cut across four categories: attitude and mental preparedness, physical preparedness, good equipment, and well-rehearsed psychomotor skills

Concealed carry practitioners think of gun security as preventing a gun grab. That is part of the definition, but not all of it. You cannot leave your guns lying around—ever. Keep your home guns that aren't in your immediate presence in an easy-access mechanical or cipher lock safe.

for protecting your weapon against a gun grab, both when your gun is in the holster, as well as during and after your draw stroke. As we've covered attitude, physical preparedness, and equipment at length elsewhere, let's focus on the skills that can prevent or rescue you from a gun grab.

Certain criteria must be met for retention to be effective:

1. The psychomotor skills have to be simple to learn and retain.

2. The techniques have to work against a larger, stronger assailant. This is known as the "Bambi vs. Godzilla" criterion.

3. They must work with any duty or concealment holster.

In the past, retaining or regaining control of your weapon was simply thought of as a matter of brute strength—the strongest person won. All that changed after the 1970s and '80s, when Jim Lindell, Chief of Unarmed Tactics with the Kansas City PD, was tasked with the goal of coming up with teachable techniques for preventing officers from being disarmed and shot with their own guns. He came up with a system of structured weapon retention and disarming techniques. These proprietary techniques are now taught in police academies throughout the country.

Lindell's methods focus on the use of leverage versus brute strength. This is obviously important for female officers and older officers, as well as for civilians and old geezers like me. Without giving away any of Lindell's proprietary secrets, the basic weapon-retention formula for preventing a gun grab attempt by a bad guy is to keep your weapon secure and grab-resistant by holding it in a "crush grip" close in to your body (where you have the most strength and leverage), while you keep moving to a position of advantage over your attacker:

1. Always be aware that you are carrying a gun. Watch how you sit, stand, bend, reach, and move so as to not flash or lose your gun.

2. When you are standing and talking with someone, get into the habit of assuming a

bladed interview stance, with your body angled so that your gun side (usually your strong side) is the portion of your body furthest away from the person opposite you.

3. When you sit in a restaurant, it is better if your gun side is facing away from the aisle where people walk.

4. If you must draw down on someone and present your gun, keep your firearm close in. The biggest mistake you can make is to extend fully—that's like asking for your gun to be taken away.

5. You should develop a habit of moving your head 360 degrees to scan your environment before and after you draw so that you are not flanked by an opponent or his accomplice.

When you hold your gun with both hands close into your body, you have more strength, leverage, and control over your gun, making it harder for someone to take your gun away. You should also be in a power stance, as we've previously discussed. In this position, you are facing a stranger in a bladed and well-balanced position, keeping your distance. Your strong/gun-side is canted away from the person opposite you, and you are leading with your support-side foot. Your gun is protected and you are ready to move if you have to. (See the earlier chapter, "What's Your Stance?") This hold on the gun is variously called, "compressed ready," "close ready," or "combat ready."

You must always protect and secure your carry gun from unauthorized hands. When you go armed, keep the awareness of that first in your mind. You must never get too close to the wrong people. Maintain healthy physical boundaries and protect your personal space. Do not let anyone violate it. Know where your gun is at all times. This is a good argument for carrying the same gun in the same holster all the time, so as to develop a subconscious muscle memory of where your gun is. Too, it is also an argument against carrying too many guns or a different gun each day. In an emergency, when you are on autopilot, you could subconsciously reach for a gun that is not where you remember it to be.

Presenting the Gun

The standard draw sequence is to index your non-dominant hand out of the way. The non-dominant hand may be placed on your abdomen or chest, or may be occupied striking or parrying to fend off an attacker. If your left hand continues to be busy, you must draw one-handed.

In a one-handed draw, you must use your dominant or strong hand to clear your cover garment, so that you can acquire a good grip on your holstered gun. Once you have a good grip, you lift your piece up out of the holster, your strong-side elbow rising up as you do so. As soon as the gun's muzzle has cleared the top of your holster, you rock your elbow down, pushing the gun out and parallel to the ground so that the muzzle points at the target. In close quarters, the hand holding the gun should be pressed against your third rib or there about.

This is a *retention* position. From this position, close in, if your body is indexed facing the target, you can point-shoot at the opponent's center of mass. Keep in mind that this type of one-handed retention shooting should be practiced at a distance of six feet and closer at the range, so that you develop a feel for it. You may find that it is best to cant the slide of the pistol slightly outwards so that the slide doesn't rub against or strike your body as it cycles. If you can back up or move laterally to gain distance from your attacker, keeping the gun aimed at him, you can keep shooting as necessary as you go into one-quarter, one-half, three-quarters, and full extension, depending on the distance from your opponent that you can gain.

There is also a two-handed retention draw. If your non-dominant hand is not occupied as you bring the gun up vertically out of the holster (elbow moving up), you can prepare your non-dominant hand to meet your dominant hand in order to acquire a two-handed grip on the gun. If you are close to your opponent, you must remember to draw into a close-in retention position to avoid a gun grab, backing up to gain some distance if you can. Distance, in most cases, is your friend.

In the two-handed draw, with your non-dominant hand at midline and palm facing against your chest or abdomen, you lift your gun up vertically with your dominant hand to clear the holster. You'll then rock your gun arm elbow down and push the gun up into a position horizontal to the ground and pointing at the target. At this point, for retention, keep your gun pressed against your third rib or there about.

Keeping contact with the front surface of your body, your non-dominant or weak hand next begins to slide over your body towards your dominant gun hand. Move your gun slightly forward so that your weak hand can meet your gun hand and merge with it, behind the gun, into a full two-handed grip. (Caution! You must always be sure to avoid covering, or "lasering" your weak hand with your gun as your gun hand and non-gun hand come together). Now

you can push out as much as is tactically judicious, given the distance from your opponent. You will try to move as you get off necessary shots, scanning and moving when you are not shooting. You want to gain as much distance as quickly as possible from your opponent and his partners.

Though some speak of it, there is really no such thing as a non-retention draw. You should always be mindful of gun grab attempts and be focused on gun and weapon retention. However, if you have distance, or you can gain more

The author demonstrating a close-in two-handed retention draw. His elbows are in, the gun aimed at an assailant. He can shoot from this position in a close-quarters combat situation if need be, keeping his gun potentially safer from a gun grab and his body more stable and ready to respond, should his attacker move to knock him off balance.

Another close-in retention draw, this time one-handed. This leaves the non-gun hand ready to push an attacker away or pull a knife or even a weak-side concealed gun, if need be.

distance by moving backwards, laterally, or diagonally away from your opponent, you may be able to push or punch your gun in a two-handed presentation out into a full Isosceles or Weaver platform.

The draw stroke has to flow in one continuous motion, and it should be practiced that way, not as a sequence of separate steps. Drawing your handgun should be as natural as reaching for something and pointing at it.

Worst-Case Scenarios

What do you do if your opponent gets his hand on your gun while you have it presented? A simple technique that works most of the time is to push the gun's muzzle into your opponent and then abruptly pull back, keeping the gun close in to your body and using your full body weight. What this will accomplish is to throw your attacker off balance so that you can get him off your gun. For this reason and others, it is essential to maintain a crush grip on the gun. If you are responding to an attempted grab for your gun, your full awareness must remain on what you are doing, and you must keep your wrists locked, because locked wrists give you added strength.

What do you do if someone attempts to grab your gun out of your holster? In such a case, you must immediately trap your attacker's hand or hands. Recognize that this is your first goal. If you begin to pivot away from your attacker *before* you trap his hands under yours, and you have on an open-top holster, you will simply be assisting your attacker in lifting your gun out of the holster. Once you trap his hands by clamping down on them with yours, then you can turn in towards your attacker to throw him off balance and possibly throw an elbow strike or make some other defensive move before you abruptly and violently change direction and pivot the other way. You can also strike down on his elbow as you move, which should loosen his grip on your gun and peel him off of it.

Disarming skills require as much practice as retention skills. I'd strongly encourage everyone who carries a gun to seek out professional training from schools that offer classes on this specific subject.

The Need for Speed

Whether you carry a pocket gun or a larger handgun in a belt holster, you must be prepared

171

to get your gun into action as soon as you realize that your life is in imminent danger of great bodily harm or death from the attacker's actions. If you cannot bring your gun into action fast enough, it does not matter how good a shot you are.

It is important to realize that combat shooting is not bull's-eye shooting. You don't even want two-inch groups. In fact, if, when you practice, you are shooting two-inch groups, then you should speed up. Conversely, if you are shooting 13-inch groups, then you should slow down a bit.

Surviving a violent attack requires ingrained, subconsciously imprinted, automatically deployable fighting skills. If you have to think about it, you will die thinking. You must build into your training regimen drills for practicing your ability to draw from the type of holster you carry every day and shoot, putting multiple rounds with speed into the center of mass of your target.

> **You must be prepared to get your gun into action, as soon as you realize your life is in imminent danger. If you cannot bring your gun into action fast enough, it won't matter at all how good a shot you are.**

Eyes in the Back of Your Head

All is for naught if you are asleep at the wheel. You need to remain in Condition Yellow until something comes into your radar screen that moves you into Condition Orange. When you are in Condition Yellow, you need to maintain a continual state of free-floating attention to everything within your 360-degree world. This means exercising your peripheral vision and your incidental hearing. It means having eyes in the back of your head.

Surprisingly, this state of being and awareness is not psychologically taxing. Quite to the contrary, it is invigorating! It wakes you up to the world around you. It enables you to see everything with fresh vision and greater depth. You take nothing for granted. You are at the ready so that no one can sneak up on you.

Gun Presentation

The draw of the handgun from the holster is really easy, so why make it complicated? It's really as simple as "Hi. How are you?" Surprise!!! With the proper grip, trigger control, and visual and kinesthetic reference points using your natural pointing and visual abilities, you can be rewarded with combat-accurate hits on your target.

Hits without speed are like driving without a functioning transmission. You have to get the gun out fast and pointed on the threat, then start getting bullets on the person who is trying to kill you before you take damage yourself. It is all about getting right into the bad guy's reactionary curve and beating him to the punch.

The trick is to *not* stop and think about it you fire. The fundamentals are a power stance, a crush grip on your handgun, focus on the front sight, good trigger control (smooth roll of the trigger), and good follow-through. With perfect practice, you can build your natural ability to:

1. See your target.

2. Focus on a small aim point on your target (aim small, miss small).

3. Draw your handgun. Get a good grip on it in the holster, then lift it out of the holster and clear leather, rock the gun forward towards the target, punch it out into your line of sight, bring your front sight into visual focus, and achieve as much sight alignment as necessary given target size and distance.

4. Make combat-accurate hits on your target.

When you practice the above, the idea is to let your mind and muscle memories do their thing.

CHAPTER 29

Reality-Based Skills

Sometimes, new shooters find themselves training with instructors who are dogmatic, egotistical, and too heavily invested in their own training methods (i.e., they are not open to expanding their own base of knowledge or refusing to acknowledge other methods as valid). According to such dogmatic instructors, there is only one right way to shoot. Their students learn that particular instructor's "right way," but that often leaves them unexposed to other methods that are also effective.

Recently, this problem was driven home over the course of a day of private shooting instruction with a student who had served as an American reserve soldier with the Israeli military. He had been trained in Israeli combat point shooting. As I routinely do, at the day's outset, I had this student shoot from a ready position at a target set at seven yards, in order to obtain a baseline assessment. His stance was an exaggerated telegraphing crouch, both arms locked straight out in an Isosceles position, as he looked at the target and not at his sights. He was shooting a 9mm Glock 26, which was too small for his hands, and his shots were all over the B-27 target. This gentleman had also taken several NRA pistol courses, but he thought his Israeli method was specifically designed for close-quarter combat, that it did not involve any aiming (rather, he believed it required he only focus on the target), and that it had to be superior since it was supposedly created by special Israeli military units.

On another occasion, a private student had taken several advanced and specialized combative pistol classes. He was trained to shoot in an extremely compressed Weaver-type stance. He was also trained to shoot while moving. Here again, this student's combat accuracy was awful. In both cases, we needed to go back to basics.

In the last several years, several combat shooting terms have gained popularity. Among others, these include "threat-focused shooting" and "reality-based shooting." It is my opinion that these terms have no specific, independent meaning, because all combative or defensive shooting is threat focused and needs to be reality based. Additionally, there are schools that only teach point shooting or one particular stance or shooting platform, such as the Weaver or the Isosceles stance. It is my opinion that this type of rigidity does the student of defensive handgunning a disservice.

What good would a boxer be if he was limited to only one type of punch? Similarly, how versatile is a combat shooter who only can shoot from one stance? Fighters need to be flexible and need to be able to apply the right technique for the job at hand. They need to be able to flow from one technique to another as a dynamic fight unfolds, and fighters need to maintain a stable, balanced, and mobile stance that can be adjusted to the changing demands of the fight.

The study of defensive handgunning is the study of fighting with the handgun. There is no one way that is better than all other ways. Different stances (Weaver, Chapman, Isosceles), different grips (one-handed, two-handed, thumbs forward, flying thumbs, thumb print over thumb nail), and different trigger finger positions are required for people of different sizes with different hands to effectively run a variety of guns in a variety of circumstances.

> As a fighter, you need to be flexible and able to apply the right technique for the job at hand. You also need to be able to flow seamlessly from one technique to another, as a dynamic fight unfolds.

Learning "reality-based" defensive handgun skills must begin with the fundamentals and then progress into specialized applications. Every student with whom I work privately first gets a solid presentation about firearms safety—I never take safety for granted. One misstep, one bit of stupid or negligent behavior, and a firearm will bite you just like a poisonous snake.

Once safe gun handling has been gone over emphatically, I typically assess the student's baseline shooting skills. From there, we proceed to going over the fundamentals of marksmanship. Following the "Stressfire System" developed by Massad Ayoob, I teach the student how to adopt a stable and mobile base, the "power stance," how to acquire a high hand grip on the pistol, how to employ a crush grip on the gun, how to use a classic sight picture after aligning the gun's sights on the target, how to focus on the front sight, and how to smoothly press the trigger at the same time. These items comprise what Ayoob calls his "five-point pre-flight checklist".

I then take into account the student's body type, flexibility, and strength and assist the student in fine-tuning his or her stance, grip on the gun, and finger position on the trigger. We begin with single shots from a low ready position and eventually progress to multiple shots so that the student can learn the best way to ride and reset their gun's particular trigger. We cover the concept of follow-through, so that the student learns the importance of holding the gun on target to give the bullet enough time to exit the barrel, and so the student learns how to prep the gun for a next shot. Since trigger control is a central feature of good marksmanship, we spend adequate time on fine-tuning the student's command and control of the trigger through a variety of drills.

The student is reminded to not worry about the last shot as it is gone, nor the next shot that is going to come. The Zen-like concept of focusing on the present task in the moment—the process of making the shot—is emphasized. If appropriate, the student might be encouraged to think of the shot he is taking as if it's a rescue shot to save a child's life. The student's focus is directed to where it should be, on the task (taking the shot) and not on the goal (hitting the mark). If the student follows good mechanics, all other things being equal, it will be a good shot.

Given the importance of mastering different shooting stances and different handgun grips, we go over the Isosceles, Weaver, and Chapman shooting stances. There is a need for *all* of these in the combat shooter's toolbox. The student is helped to adapt the ideal stances to his or her body mechanics, and they are also taught to shoot one-handed with both the strong and weak hands.

Depending on the student's baseline level of shooting and their progress, we might then address the presentation of the handgun from the holster. We always start with the draw from an unconcealed holster, and then progress to drawing from concealment.

Holster work is conducted from an open-top reinforced holster that allows one-handed re-holstering. Proper form is emphasized at first, not speed. Eventually, smooth turns into fast. It is important to make sure that, when the student draws from the holster, as well as when the they re-holster, they do not cover, or laser, their support hand or other parts of the body. The student is taught to re-holster slowly, or reluctantly—seldom is there a rush to re-holster in a real-life situation. Proper technique demands that the student's trigger finger stay out of the trigger guard to avoid an unintentional discharge. Eventually, typically on the second day of training, we move to having the student work from a retention holster.

In terms of stances, we also address shooting from the cover crouch, high kneeling, and low kneeling positions. This then progresses to shooting from behind barricades, and shooting over cover using the cover crouch stance is also addressed.

Finally, we address sighted, semi-sighted, and unsighted point shooting. Point shooting is just one method in a bag of tools intended for close-quarter situations, especially because using sights, even peripherally, is superior to unsighted fire.

Is the thought process becoming part of you? Shooting schools claiming there is only one right way to shoot ignore the complexity of reality, and reality is indeed complex. You cannot afford to be limited in your defensive arms skills set. It is essential to learn a variety of techniques that can be drawn upon if and when the need arises.

CHAPTER 30

Defensive Shooting Fundamentals

As a defensive firearms instructor, I work with many students of all ages on a private basis. Over the years, numerous students have come to work with me to learn advanced defensive shooting techniques. In many cases, initial evaluation of their shooting skills revealed that they were terribly incompetent with a handgun, and often unsafe, as well. In almost every case, these people had never gotten the basics down, and that phenomenon left me wondering how they had missed the boat. (I was also left wondering how it was that some big-name firearms instructors with whom they said they'd trained, in some cases privately, never straightened them out!)

A shooter must understand and be able to perform the basics before he or she can expect to move on to develop competence in advanced shooting skills and tactics. That's what we'll cover in this chapter, a blueprint for learning the basics well, so that you can then move on to develop advanced competence with the defensive handgun. Take this blueprint, work with a qualified shooting instructor, and practice.

Massad Ayoob has been a pioneer in teaching people the fundamentals of defensive shooting in ways consistent with what happens physically and psychologically when you are fighting for your life. In the 1970s, he developed the Stressfire System, and it has evolved and been refined over the years. Ayoob studied what happens to the human mind and body in the "stress flood" of a fight-or-flight scenario. Based on what he learned, he created techniques that not only wouldn't fall apart under stress, but would, in fact, feed off the effects of the body's alarm reaction and become more effective under stress.

The Stressfire shooting program emphasizes techniques that depend on simple gross motor skills, since fine motor skills deteriorate under life-and-death stress. Also, gross motor techniques can withstand the tremors and increased physical strength attendant to the body's alarm-triggered adrenaline dump into the bloodstream.

Stressfire emphasizes a five-point checklist that comprises the fundamentals for accomplishing the above, and also serves as a blueprint for practicing the fundamentals of marksmanship. Let's look at each.

The Power Stance

More times than not, when I work with shooting students, I have to correct their stance.

Many initially stand with a backwards lean, and either too rigidly or too floppily. Some stand like a pole, while others square to their target with both feet parallel. None of these stances are aggressive fighting stances. Sure, you may have to shoot in a rapidly unfolding dynamic gunfight from an unorthodox and non-choreographed position. However, you must start from an aggressive and powerful stance that gives you a solid foundation.

> A slightly forward-leaning power stance gives you a wide base that provides stability and balance. It keeps you from being pushed backwards by the recoil of your gun—or by an opponent.

A power stance gives you a wide base for stability and balance. It keeps you from being pushed backwards by the firearm's recoil or by your opponent. It entails leaning aggressively forward from the hips—head in front of shoulders and shoulders in front of hips. Knees should be slightly bent to absorb shock and facilitate mobility. The non-dominant foot, the one opposite your strong shooting hand, should be forward, and your dominant foot should be rearward and digging into the ground. This power stance can be applied while static or moving (this will be familiar to anyone with experience in wrestling, boxing, or the martial arts).

The High Hand

The lower a handgun bore's axis, the easier it is to control the gun during recoil and deliver accurate follow-up shots. One can make the bore's axis sit lower in the hands by gripping the handgun with their master hand as high up on the back strap as possible. This increases your control over the gun, whether you are shooting with one hand or two.

The Crush Grip

You cannot grip a handgun too hard or too strongly. In real combat, defensive shooting means you are fighting for your life. Are you going to be relaxed at such as time? Of course not. You are going to be holding onto your life-support system—your weapon—as if your life depends on it. Get used to it now. A crush grip, or convulsive grip, will make your handgun more difficult for your opponent to take away from you. It will also help you control recoil. Additionally, a crush grip will help you better isolate the movement of your trigger finger so that you have more trigger control.

Ayoob points out that the crush grip, or hard grasp, may be applied with the thumbs in virtually any position, but it will benefit most when the thumbs are curled tightly down. The crush grip is one of the elements of Massad Ayoob's five-point "pre-flight checklist," comprising the fundamentals of solid combat handgun marksmanship. When a shooter uses a crush grip or hard grasp on the handgun with the thumbs curled down, the curled thumbs promote a stronger and tighter grasp. Yet the thumbs curled down do not shift the windage on the muzzle direction. My experience, and the results with my students, validates that one can absolutely shoot with combat accuracy using such as grip. Furthermore, as demonstrated in Massad Ayoob's *Stressfire* combat handgun training program, when a shooter intentionally "gorilla grips" the handgun to the point of tremor, the resulting "wobble zone" results in shot groupings on target at combat distances that are still within a combat accuracy-acceptable three to four inches.

There is one other essential point that makes the crush grip beneficial. The harder you grasp the handgun, the better you will control the gun. Too, the harder you grip, the easier it is to isolate your trigger finger. Just perform this little experiment:

Make a fist with your dominant hand and keep your thumb pointed forward. Now, extend your trigger finger and press it to the rear just as if you were working a trigger. If you watch your hand as you do this, you may notice that your other fingers are also moving. If that's the case, you haven't completely isolated the movement of your trigger finger from the rest of your hand. This is called "milking," and, if you do this while you are shooting, it typically results in shots that are low and to the left.

Now make a much tighter fist and curl your thumb down. Now when you extend your trigger finger and press it to the rear, again mimicking the working of the trigger, you will notice that your other tightly clasped fingers do not move in unison. You have isolated your trigger finger.

The Front Sight

The bullet will go where the muzzle is pointed. To ensure the muzzle is pointed where you want the bullet to hit, you must have a reliable way of indexing the muzzle on target. That is the purpose of the front sight. Verifying that the front sight is centered in the rear sight notch is called "sight alignment," and superimposing your aligned front and rear sights onto your point of aim on the target is called getting a "sight picture." The smaller your target is, the greater the distance you are from your target, or the more accurate your shots need to be, the more precise your sight alignment and sight picture need to be and the more time you will need to take those shots. The closer the distance, the faster the shooter can afford to shoot and the more margin of error you have for a slightly off sight picture. At close, bad-breath distances, point shooting is the way to go. So, to learn to shoot for combat accuracy, the shooter must learn to shoot both with and without their sights.

> The harder you grasp your handgun, the better you will control your gun. Too, the harder you grip, the easier it is to isolate your trigger finger and smoothly draw back the trigger.

The Smooth Roll

Good trigger control is the most important aspect of getting good hits. It becomes even more important under stress. It is logical that, to keep the muzzle on target, the shooter needs to smoothly operate the trigger. Erratic trigger control will drive the muzzle away from the point of aim.

The goal is to smoothly press the trigger all the way rearward, without hesitation, until the shot breaks, and then ride the trigger forward as the trigger resets for the next shot. Ayoob notes that, "Each activation of the trigger is done with a single-stage movement. We use the term 'roll the trigger' to convey the smooth, uninterrupted, straight back pressure on the trigger."

If the handgun fits the shooter's hands, poor trigger control is typically caused by a combination of factors. These can include poor isolation of the trigger finger (also known as "milking" the gun), inadequate placement of the trigger finger on the face of the trigger, an inadequate or unstable grip on the handgun, flinching, anticipating the shot, jerking the trigger, trying to stage the trigger, and not keeping the finger on the trigger throughout a string of shots (also known as "trigger weld").

Trigger control can be practiced through dry-fire and live-fire. So can the other fundamentals of marksmanship. An excellent dry-fire drill for practicing all of the fundamentals is the "wall drill." This drill requires sustained focus and concentration, and it builds a muscle memory of the key marksmanship fundamentals. Here's how it goes.

1. Make sure that the handgun is unloaded, that there is no ammunition in the room, and that the backstop wall is safe.

> # The closer the distance to your target, the faster you can afford to shoot and the more margin of error you have for a slightly off sight picture. At close-in distances, no-sight point-shooting is the way to go.

2. Pick an aim point on the wall or surface in front of you, and point your unloaded handgun about an inch away from the aim point such that your front sight is right over the aim point.

3. Go through your pre-flight checklist of marksmanship fundamentals: power stance, high hand, crush grip, front sight, sight alignment, sight picture, and smooth roll of the trigger.

4. Think or say to yourself *Front sight*, keep your sight alignment and sight picture steady, and then say to yourself *Smooth roll*, as you retain your visual focus on the front sight while smoothly pressing the trigger all the way rearward.

5. Ride the trigger forward until the trigger resets for the next shot; you'll hear and feel a click as the sear mechanism is re-engaged. (Note: you will have to rack the slide on guns such as Glocks that do not have an auto-resetting trigger).

The One-Hole Drill

This is an excellent live-fire exercise for when you've mastered the dry-fire drill above. It makes use of the principle that, if you aim small, you will miss small.

1. Start out at a reasonable distance from your target. Don't be ashamed for this to be three yards—that's nine feet! Pick a small spot on your paper target as your point of aim. You can draw a one-inch circle in black magic marker to mark the spot.

2. Go through your checklist of marksmanship fundamentals as you focus on your aim point. Punch your handgun out towards your aim point, focus intently on your front sight, and acquire a sight picture. Your front sight should be in sharp focus, in contrast with a slightly blurred target and rear sight (you can only focus sharply with your eyes on one object at a time).

3. Keeping your gun steady (you should be in a power stance, with a high, two-handed hard grasp on your handgun), smoothly roll your trigger rearward while staying focused on your front sight. Watch your front sight as the shot breaks and through the gun's arc of recoil. Don't peak over your gun to see the shot!

4. Hold your trigger to the rear as the gun recoils, and then ride your trigger forward until it resets as the gun settles back on target. Prepare for your next shot by taking up any slack in the trigger, your follow-through.

You can run this drill one of two ways. One is to take a string of shots without checking where those shots went until after shooting the string. The other way is to drop the gun to the ready position after each single shot or pair of shots. Your goal is a perfect one-inch group. You want to exercise your fundamentals at the target distance at which you are working until you attain this group, then move backward to repeat the drill at a greater distance. For example, if you started at three yards, move to five, then seven, 10, 12, and so on out to 25 yards and beyond, if you wish. Keep moving backwards until you can no longer shoot a perfect group at a given distance, and then you stay and work at that distance.

Individualized Handgun Training

Most people who are new to the world of firearms quickly realize that they are going to need more intensive instruction than what is offered in a beginning handgun safety class. Even many students who have some experience with firearms also conclude that they could benefit from more intensive instruction on the defensive use of the handgun.

Going to gun school can be very expensive, both in terms of time and money, especially if you have to travel out of town to take a three- to five-day course. So, many people choose to find a local, certified firearms instructor who can provide them with competent, individualized, private instruction on the defensive use of the handgun. With such instruction, students can begin or continue their handgun training at a point that takes into account their background, personal-defense needs and goals, and unique life situation.

Assess the Student

I typically begin an individualized, private-instruction session by assessing the student's level of experience, goals, and needs. Why is the student seeking firearms instruction at this time? What types of firearms has the student shot before and how much experience have they had with them? What makes and models of firearms does the student own, if any? What does the student want and need to learn at this time? How does the student live with or intend to live with their firearms?

Legal Issues

Once I have these and other basic questions answered, we review the current legal standards that define lawful self-defense and the use of force by private citizens, including the lawful use of deadly force for self-defense. I then cover the prevailing legal standards relating to the transportation and concealment of firearms.

Handgun Safety

I typically review the safe handling, checking, loading, unloading, storage, and carrying of both revolvers and semi-automatic pistols, something I think should always be part of the curriculum. I also review proper range etiquette.

Mechanical Operations

With safety covered, I next go over the mechanical operation of both revolvers and semi-automatic pistols. This involves a review of handgun nomenclature, identification of the basic parts of a handgun, how they function. I then talk about different types of mechanical safeties and their functions, emphasizing that no mechanical safety is a substitute for safe handling of a firearm. The student is shown how to check both a revolver and a semi-automatic to ensure proper function of both the firing and safety mechanisms.

Ammunition Basics

I always cover various types of ammunition and discuss the differences between centerfire and rimfire. The student also learns the components of a round of ammunition: case, primer, propellant, and bullet. We discuss the physics of handgun fire and the types of ammunition most commonly used for personal protection, in particular, how to choose the appropriate ammunition for the student's firearm given the considerations of caliber, bullet type, and what the ammunition will be used to accomplish. We also discuss how to inspect ammunition for imperfections and the potential problems that can occur with the use of light loads, heavy loads, and reloads.

Marksmanship Fundamentals

I can't count all of the experienced people I have trained who demonstrate faulty habits and poor technique, when shooting a qualification course on the range. Therefore, I make sure to cover the fundamentals of shooting a handgun and the basics of marksmanship. First, we identify the student's dominant eye, and then I teach the student how to grip the handgun properly with both one and two hands. I help the student find the best two-handed shooting stance for that individual, be it Isosceles, Weaver, or a hybrid of the two. I cover the fundamentals of sight alignment and sight picture, then how to smoothly press the trigger so the student learns good trigger control. Finally, we work on integrating all these components into one smooth flow, with proper follow-through after each shot.

Appropriate Distances

We begin with the student shooting at close-in targets, to develop and imprint basic marksmanship skill and to build the student's confidence. Distance is gradually increased. We perform drills that involve shooting from the on-target position and from the ready position. With more advanced students, we work on drawing and shooting from the holster. The students also practice retrieving their handguns from a shelf I've placed at the head of the shooting lane and firing at the target.

Dry-Fire Drills

Dry-fire drills are also built into the training, in order to diagnose faulty techniques and to reinforce good habits. We typically provide the student with a safety-conscious dry-fire routine for practicing marksmanship fundamentals that integrate grip, stance, sight alignment, sight picture, and trigger control.

Shot Strings

We begin with one-shot strings of fire, then gradually progress to multiple-shot strings. We teach students how to double-tap two rapid shots at close range, both one-handed and two-handed.

Sighting Techniques

I teach the student how to shoot using the handgun's sights and also how to point shoot without using the sights at close-range targets. We work on these skills using both two-handed and one-handed shooting grips. With targets at close range, I teach point shoulder shooting, as well as retention shooting techniques with the handgun held close in to the body to prevent a gun grab, reviewing when each type of defensive shooting is appropriate.

Malfunction Clearances

I teach the basic "tap, rack, re-assess" (or "tap, rack, bang") and other routines to follow if the student has a malfunction on the range, such as a stove-pipe feed, a failure to eject, a magazine not fully seated, a hang fire, a squib round, and so forth. I also instruct how to reload the handgun in an emergency and as a tactical reload.

Maintenance and Cleaning

I always discuss the importance of regular cleaning and maintenance of firearms, safety considerations when cleaning a firearm, and specifically how to clean each student's pistol.

Mind-set

Before and after shooting, I discuss situational awareness, mental preparedness, confronting a threat, management of fear, and the fight-or-flight body alarm reaction. I also go over a mental rehearsal technique for developing and fine-tuning mental preparedness for self-defense.

This is the mode of training I follow with my students. I encourage interested readers to shop around and converse with prospective trainers (and their students, if at all possible.) It is important to note the general atmosphere in each training environment in order to determine the best instructor to meet one's individual training needs. You have to feel comfortable in order to absorb information.

CHAPTER 32

Training for a Gunfight

Most gunfights occur at close distances of nine feet or less. At such range, the gun will have to be presented and kept close to your body in some type of retention position to avoid a disarm, and, if you need to shoot, you will need to do so without using your sights—that is, you will need to point and shoot. Having point-shooting skills allows you to be 100-percent threat focused and focused on where you are aiming on the threat or target.

Point shooting is often misunderstood. Many people erroneously believe that no aiming is involved, because point-shooting techniques do not involve using your gun's sights. The fact is that, when you are point shooting and threat focused, you are still aiming the firearm. You're just not focused on the gun or your sights. You are focused on the threat. We all have a natural ability to point at objects. When we engage in point shooting, we are simply pointing with a handgun.

Awareness is and always will be a key ingredient of survival—that is, your ability to be aware of who and what is in your immediate vicinity and their actions or apparent intent. With that said, to be competent in the defensive use of the handgun, you must continually work on developing and practicing skills that allow you, to access your handgun immediately and deploy it with as much speed as possible, to produce combat-accurate hits at normal self-defense distances. Let's look at several useful techniques that enable such hits.

Elbow Up/Elbow Down

I learned this term from master combat firearms and defensive tactics instructor, Robin "Brownie" Brown. I believe it was coined to describe the physical action that occurs at, or just above, hip level, to effect instant hits on threats at close distances—nine feet and closer. You grip the gun in the holster. *Elbow up* lifts the gun out of the holster such that your muzzle clears the leather. *Elbow down* rocks the handler's forearm and gun into a horizontal position, parallel to the ground, so that the gun is pointing at the target.

The Zipper

Flowing from that first skill is the technique known as the "zipper." After the gun is horizontally pointed at the threat and the elbow is indexed at the hip, you extend your arm out towards the threat and run bullets up the center of the threat's body, stitching him up the middle.

Quick-Kill Hip Shooting

Robin Brown also taught me what he terms, "quick-kill hip shooting" for use when you are confronted by multiple assailants. In this technique, upon drawing the firearm, your elbow gets tucked into the body's pocket that exists in front of your hip bone, and the handgun is held about 45 degrees outboard to keep your wrist straight. This technique is more effective for battling with more than one assailant, as it allows you to turret your upper body while having your shooting arm remain locked into the position.

Live-Fire Practice

Relative to the distance one should train at, most people would be well served to spend some of their training time at distances of no more than 12 feet, with some of that training under eight feet. Practice drawing the gun and firing as soon as the handgun clears the holster and the muzzle is horizontal to the ground at distances of 10 feet or closer from the target. (Remember to keep your finger off the trigger until your handgun is pointed at the target.) Learning to draw and fire your weapon immediately from below your line of sight has many advantages not the least of which is a faster first shot on the threat before that threat might be able to get a round on you.

Relative to the point-shooting skills themselves, an indoor range is typically not the most conducive place to practice effective techniques that reduce the time it takes to put shots on the threat, and many indoor ranges do not allow such practices. However, with that said, when I am under these typical indoor range constraints (often), I practice my eye/hand coordination skills with the firearm so that I can maintain my ability to point the muzzle as naturally as I can point my index finger at an object, without waiting to find my sights or front sight. The goal here is to not directly look at the firearm before getting rounds down range and into your target's high center of mass. It is imperative you are be able to just instinctively put rounds on the threat without hesitation and as soon as the muzzle is aligned properly.

Finally, you need to practice one-handed shooting skills up close. If you have to use your gun at 10 feet or less, there will probably be no time to get into a two-handed stance, let alone verify a sight picture. This should constitute the substantial portion of your realistic training.

Gunfights

The title of this chapter is intentionally misleading. That is because you cannot realistically train for a gunfight. But you should practice being able to make combat accurate hits as fast as possible and with unconscious thought while still focusing on the threat itself. For this type of shooting, it is counter-productive to worry about shooting small groups. You want to get upper center-of-mass torso hits as fast as you can. These skills give you options based on variables that may present themselves on the street or in our homes.

Heated arguments have occurred between point-shooting and sight-shooting advocates. It is important to recognize that threat-focused point-shooting skills are not meant to replace sighted fire, but, rather, as a compliment to the skills people already have using their sights. It's not an either or situation, but both, and people who carry a handgun with self-defense in mind should get as much practice time in with close-in point shooting as they do with front sight work.

Small Guns

People typically choose lightweight, small-frame, snub-nosed revolvers for concealed pocket carry. They're cool to look at, simplistic in operation, and offer good concealability and ease of carry. Snubbies also lend themselves to close-in point shooting. A colloquial term for a snubby is "belly gun."

Trigger control is paramount to handling double-action revolvers. Recoil management is also extremely important. People who carry a five-shot usually carry one that is light weight, as a matter of convenience. Five rounds are a limited number, so gun owners need to make sure they practice enough to be able to make every round count under pressure. You just cannot afford to waste shots when you only have five or six on hand before you reload, especially as there is usually no time to perform a reload in a self-defense situation.

This is shooting from the hip, or quick-kill hip shooting, practiced at the appropriate range—very close up.

Snubbies are some of the hardest handguns to shoot well. They require dedicated practice in recoil management and trigger control. So, your best ammunition load option in an Air Lite or Airweight snubby is an intermediate-weight cartridge that reduces recoil impulse and, thus, allows faster follow-up shots. The less the recoil, the faster you can shoot the gun and stay on the threat.

If you carry a small-caliber, or even a 9mm, pocket pistol, you should practice shooting one handed, and you would be well-served to learn to use your gun instinctively. That means practicing with the gun you'll likely have on you when something happens that necessitates your needing it. Practice employing your peripheral vision skills, while shooting your gun one-handed and below your line of sight. Learn to use your gun without having to look at it. When you practice in this way, you will develop the confidence to shoot as fast as possible so you can get shots on the vital areas of the threat/ target as quickly as possible. Also, by not having to visually verify where the gun's sights are at the time you fire, you save valuable time. Visually verifying that the front sight of your handgun is on a threat takes 30 to 50 percent more time for the average concealed-carry practitioner—and time is one of the key factors you must have on your side of the reactionary curve in order to survive a gunfight.

CHAPTER 33

Training as We Age

This chapter addresses the range of problems we face from a personal-defense standpoint as we get older, past middle age, and the accompanying waning abilities. With our decline in physicality, we must adjust our shooting and training techniques, our choice of carry and home-defense guns, and our gear. Let's look at a wide range of problems affecting the aging body and what you can do to adjust your emergency rescue equipment and skill set.

Loss of Visual Acuity

Wear your prescription glasses when you shoot, because, if you can't see your target, how are you going to hit it? In addition, wear safety glasses over your prescription lenses to protect your eyes from ejected shells and other flying particles. If you are nearsighted, your shooting will benefit from wearing progressive bifocals. They will enable you to adjust your visual focus and head position to accommodate for the distance of the sights from your eyes.

Consider adding high-visibility night sights to your defensive handguns, because most lethal force incidents occur in dim light or at night. XS Sight Systems manufactures Big Dot 24/7 Express tritium sights that facilitate fast sight acquisition in all light conditions. The full circle of the Big Dot front sight is easily acquired and superimposed on your point of aim.

I'd strongly advise learning a viable system of point shooting, as discussed earlier. Most defensive encounters occur at close range. At the shooting range, practice the following drill: focus on your target, choose a small point of aim, bring your gun up to the target, and fire. Keep your visual focus on your point of aim—aim small, miss small. This can work well if you're near-sighted and your distance eyewear gives you a clear picture of the target.

When you do use your sights, get used to shooting with a less than crystal-clear front sight picture—you don't have to see the serrations! As long as your front sight is on your point of aim, you can still get good fast hits out to about seven yards by using the alignment of the front post in the rear sight notch, even with the front sight sticking up out of the rear sight notch. This has been termed "getting a flash sight picture." The key to success is lots of repetitive practice on the range. You should also dry-practice train with an unloaded gun at home.

Finally, don't forget to always have on hand a powerful, portable flashlight as an essential handgun accessory. A firm knock on the noggin of an attacker may work better than a firm, verbal command, and, as I've discussed previously, it can help you locate and identify threats and possibly temporarily blind your attacker to provide you with a chance to get to safety or take some other appropriate course of action.

Hearing Loss

Purchase a good pair of passive or electronic hearing protectors. They will dampen the decibels on gunshots at the range and save your remaining hearing. Electronic muffs will also *amplify* other essential sounds, such as the sounds of footsteps on the stairs, a doorknob turning, the sound of breathing, and so forth. I keep my electronic ears by my bed. It just makes good sense.

Loss of Fine Motor Skills and Dexterity

Keep your training techniques simple. Learn and practice handgun manipulation techniques that rely less on fine motor dexterity and more on gross motor dexterity.

From the standpoint of handgun choices, carry a gun that you can handle and shoot. A revolver really is the easiest to manipulate, as you don't have to pull back a heavy and tight slide. Too, the trigger is the safety, because it requires a long and deliberate pull to fire the gun.

If a semi-auto is just more your thing, make sure you can operate the controls. Make sure you can firmly grasp the slide. Make sure you can operate the magazine release button, the slide stop and any manual safeties. Make sure you can charge and unload the magazines, and make sure you can manage the trigger pull. Make sure the pistol fits your hands. Some semi-autos require more dexterity and strength to grip and retract the slide back than you may have. Also, some semi-autos have magazines that are very uncomfortable and difficult to charge and unload. You may want to stay away from semi-autos that have slides with very little surface area to grip on their sides, as well as those that have slide-mounted levers that will bite you.

Fine motor tremor can be its own problem. However, you would be surprised at how possible it is to keep your shots within the torso area of a man-size target at seven yards, even while you are shaking considerably, as long as your front sight or the end of your barrel is superimposed on your aim point. Of course, as discussed earlier, adding a laser sighting system to your handgun can be a great help, and they have the added plus of greatly assisting aiming in low light and stress-fire conditions, vastly improving shooting accuracy and speed. An additional benefit is their possible deterrent effect on an attacker once he sees a red dot aimed on his chest.

Just because your hand strength isn't what it used to be doesn't mean it can't be improved. A great way to improve your fine motor strength and dexterity is through the use of a "Gripmaster" hand exerciser, which strengthens and conditions each finger individually, and also increases endurance, dexterity, and control in the hand, wrist, and forearm.

Loss of Flexibility

If you have difficulty with flexibility and range of motion, a small-of-the-back holster is probably not a good idea. You may want to experiment with appendix or hip-bone carry (inside-the-waistband or outside-the-belt), so you can easily access your holstered gun. Pocket holster carry for a pocket gun is also an excellent way to go armed.

Flashlights have dozens of useful purposes, but none more than that when paired with a handgun. Used aside from the gun or paired with the gun as part of the overall grip, they help identify a target and what's around it.

Loss of Endurance and Reaction Time

Build your endurance through supervised weight training and cardiovascular exercise (brisk walking, bike riding, and swimming). Work out with a personal trainer at a gym, if you can. For your shooting, purchase a shot timer, such as a Pocket Pro made by Competition Electronics (www.CompetitionElectronics.com). Use it at the range to speed up your gun presentation from concealment and your shot-to-shot transitions, while, at the same time, improving your shot placement accuracy.

Take some one-on-one instruction with an experienced shooting instructor to improve your shooting skills. Also, take a defensive handgun class. Practice with your carry gun at the range at least twice a month. Aim for quality, not quantity, of rounds fired.

Increased Feelings of Vulnerability

This can be a natural occurrence as we age. To keep it under control, build your network of personal safety and defense resources. Keep a cell phone with you at all times, and keep it with its charger by your bed when you sleep.

Be cautious as you go about your day, but not timid. Don't walk where angels fear to tread. A gun does not make you invincible. Basically, don't go anywhere with a gun that you would not go without a gun, and carry pepper spray.

Lock the door to your house, apartment, or condo as soon as you enter. Watch that you are not being followed. Practice awareness drills. Look all around you. Watch your 360. Every time someone comes up on you and surprises you, shame on you! Give yourself an "F." Practice noticing others before they notice you. For this, give yourself an "A."

Get to know your neighbors. Be friendly, but not overly so—let people earn your trust. Don't volunteer unnecessary, personal information about yourself. However, be a good, helpful neighbor. Make friends. Help each other. Keep an extra key with a trusted neighbor or two, but don't lend out your key to handymen, etc.

In your home, have some sort of quick-access lock box or gun safe near your bed. If you live alone, you might want to consider keeping your home-defense gun directly by your bed, but, remember, make it a caliber and size that you can handle. Do not keep it on the night table or in the nightstand dresser, because this is the first place an intruder will look. By the side of the bed on the floor or in a holster mounted to the side of the bed or floor would be much better. Frontier Leather Works makes a nice leather holster for multiple guns that can be strapped on your bedpost for bedside protection. Make sure to lock up your bedside gun whenever you leave your home.

You can downplay feelings of vulnerability by practicing issuing commands with authority in front of a mirror. Use a tape recorder to record your voice and play the tape back. You'll learn to be convincing fast! Also, practice your moves and draw with an unloaded gun in front of a mirror regularly. Eventually, you'll be convincing to yourself, and, if you can convince yourself with your demeanor, you'll surely sound and look convincing to others.

Staying Armed and Safe in a Wheelchair

Having to use a wheelchair to get around is no reason to be without personal protection. You may look like a target of opportunity to Mr. Bad Guy, but your physically challenged setup can actually serve as your cover, as, in some cases, it also appears to widen the disparity of the strength and force gap between you and an attacker.

There are two ways to carry a concealed weapon when you're in a wheelchair. The first is *around* your person. When you're sitting in your wheelchair, you can carry your firearm in an appropriate type of bag or pouch secured to the chair. For example, most of the fanny packs or gunny sacks for on-your-person carry can be strapped to the arms or back of your wheelchair. One fellow I know keeps a revolver in a small knapsack tied to the side of his wheelchair.

There is nothing wrong with this mode of carry, but you should make sure you have quick, unimpeded access to your weapon. In my opinion, it makes the most sense to fasten the gun pack to the inside arm of your wheelchair (preferably the strong side) for security reasons. If you leave the wheelchair, the gun should leave with you.

The second way to carry in a wheelchair is *on* your person. The concealed carry fanny packs are probably the most efficient and unobtrusive way to carry a concealed handgun, if you use a wheelchair. The pouch, which will contain a compartment for your firearm, is best worn in the cross-draw or strong-side appendix position. For folks who spend a lot of time sitting, the high ride cross-draw position keeps the gun comfortably out of the way, but easily accessible with the strong hand.

There are many excellent products of this type on the market. DeSantis and Uncle Mike's make excellent and affordable concealment fanny packs. In fact, many enable you to pack a large-bore pistol with no one to know but you, and most also have multiple compartments

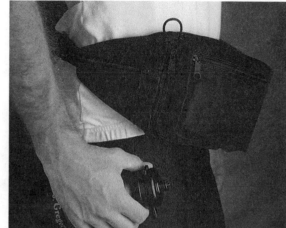

Using a wheelchair to get around doesn't mean you have to go unarmed. A fanny pack holster (right) or a super-comfortable belly-band holster (below) are terrific options for those lacking physical mobility. Shoulder holster rigs are also a great option.

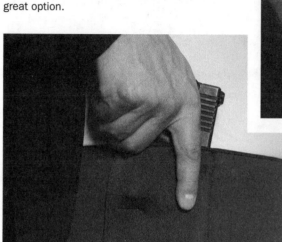

in which to carry your wallet, keys, change, a flashlight, a folding knife, OC pepper spray, and so on. This fact also can normalize the perceived purpose of the pouch and enhance concealment. Purchase one with a rip-open gun compartment. These may come either with Velcro and snaps or zippers with loops to grab onto and pull open (you don't want to have to fiddle with finding the zipper when you need fast access to your handgun).

A cross-draw outside-the-waistband belt holster (CD-OWB) is probably the next best mode of concealment carry for those who are seated in a chair. It allows comfortable, unimpeded access to the handgun in the sitting position. There's also nothing wrong with a cross-draw inside-the-waistband holster (CD-IWB), if you can carry your handgun this way comfortably and access it easily. However, many folks who have a big waist find that an IWB rig pinches them in the cross-draw position when they are seated. They also may have a more difficult time accessing the gun.

Also worthy of consideration is the shoulder holster and harness, with one recommendation. If you get a shoulder rig, get one that holds the handgun in a horizontal position with the butt vertical and the muzzle facing the rear. Products that hold the muzzle up into your armpit laser you, and I don't like that concept. Also, products that hold the gun muzzle down make it harder to acquire your grip and draw the gun. With any and all these holster choices, you should try before you buy, especially if you're in a wheelchair. One size rarely fits all.

Epilogue

The basic right to carry a concealed deadly weapon for personal-defense comes with a moral imperative and legal obligation to walk the moral high ground. Unfortunately, the road is not always well paved, and there are stretches where there is no road. So, how do we who go armed stay on the right path? I have thought about this question ever since I began carrying concealed firearms, right after September 11, 2001.

As a child, I was an avid fan of TV westerns (and I still am!). The most popular of this genre included such programs as *Gunsmoke, Bonanza*, and *The Rifleman*. These shows were dramas and not mindlessly violent shoot-'em-up action shows. Typically, they depicted human tales with moral lessons. For example, *Gunsmoke's* Marshal Dillon character, played by James Arness, was typically reluctant to go to the guns and shoot people, even bad guys. Similarly, the Ponderosa's Cartwrights of *Bonanza*, who weren't lawmen, were reluctant to shoot people. They only went to the guns when they had no other choice and when it was in defense of innocent life.

The TV westerns of the 1960s depicted a simpler time, one that is long gone. Today, the world is far more complicated, yet the dialectic of good versus evil continues to play out. This, among other reasons, is why keeping and bearing firearms remains an absolute necessity, and why those of us who lived, the armed lifestyle must walk the moral high ground.

So, what is the moral high ground? It all boils down to good intentions and appropriate restraint. Have you ever watched a movie in which the protagonist finally overpowers and captures the bad guy alive, then wants to play out his longed-for vengeance? In most scenarios, unless the bad guy continues to be an immediate threat, the hero lets him live to face justice. In every fiber of his being, the hero might want to deliver a *coup de grace*, but he does not. What makes him the "good guy" is that he exercises appropriate restraint. Having good intentions means you avoid doing unnecessary harm. Now, let's apply this concept to one aspect of every-day reality.

In an extended thread on the online forum www.DefensiveHandguns.com, members examined the following scenario. A middle-aged man is leaving a restaurant some time after 1:00 a.m. and walking to his parked vehicle among several female friends with whom he has shared a pleasant evening. Suddenly, three 20-something gang-bangers walk up to them and verbalize inappropriate and invasive sexual comments to the women. Two of the punks slap one woman's rear end—and she flips out. The man confronts the three gang-bangers, telling them that they have committed an assault and that they need to go away and leave him and his friends alone. The gang-bangers then physically assault the man. Two of the women call 9-1-1, but, at the same time, the man is being beaten—three young men against one middle-aged man. The women do not jump in. They continue to witness the thrashing, becoming hysterical as the drama plays out.

This event actually happened in downtown Philadelphia, earlier this year. The man was not armed. The three gang-bangers brutally beat this man, causing him to sustain a severe concussion and other serious injuries, though he survived. The gang-bangers fled into the night, as the police sirens approached.

Now, let's slightly modify the story, as was done for purposes of discussion on www.DefensiveHandguns.com. In this version, the man is armed, and the question is whether this man would have been in the right to present his firearm, when the three attackers made it clear that they were about to assault him.

Some forum discussants opined that, in this case, he would not have been in the right to present his firearm because, by verbally confronting the attackers, he had instigated the fight and escalated the altercation. They also argued it would be a different story if he was unarmed and had the skill set of a Chuck Norris, saying that then he might have been in the right to confront them. Since, in reality, the man was in fact unarmed and did not have advanced martial arts or hand-to-hand combative skills, these discussants reasoned he should have avoided altogether verbally engaging the offenders and he should have tried to move away with his friends. Their argument was that the man was beat down because it was just him against three younger and stronger men (disparity of strength and numbers) and that he foolishly erred in brazenly confronting greater power and strength. He was lucky he hadn't been killed.

On the other side of the debate were those who argued that whether or not the man was armed, he had the right to verbally confront the offenders and take defensive actions when they attacked him. Some of these discussants argued that if he had been armed, he would have been in the right to present his firearm given the immediate threat of grave bodily harm and death with which he was confronted due to the marked disparity of force.

Which side of the debate do you fall on? If you carry a firearm for self-defense, does appropriate restraint mean you must avoid *all* confrontations? Does being discreetly armed mean you must abdicate your right to confront bad or inappropriate and aggressive behavior? If you have no intention of employing deadly force or using your gun to intimidate, is the wisest course of action to keep your mouth shut when you witness an assault?

Every situation is different, given the totality of the circumstances. But, the common thread that runs through every social problem is the importance of exercising appropriate restraint. It cannot be reduced to a formula, because the dictum is that *you must employ good judgment* in order to exercise *appropriate restraint*. Your mind must be in control of your emotions.

Common sense and survival dictate that you calculate the odds before you commit yourself to a course of action that is likely to lead to a fight. In the case above, given a clear disparity of force against him, would it have been cowardly if the older man had chosen to strategically appear without reaction to the insult, for the sake of the greater good of keeping everyone safe?

Now, think about this. If the older man had been armed, and if he'd had to shoot the attackers afterwards in self-defense, a grand jury would ask whether he responded to his attackers as he did because he knew he had the power of deadly force with him. You see, the common sense dictum and legal standard is that one should walk away from a fight if one safely can.

So, this goes forth to the question of intent, and it is an important question. If the man was armed and he chose to confront, the question would be, what was he thinking? Was he thinking that he could and should confront because he was armed, and, therefore, he could handle the situation if the attackers escalated? In fact, another question would be, was he thinking, or was he just reacting? And, if he was just reacting, was he exercising appropriate restraint?

Let's be clear. I am 100 percent for immediately countering violence with greater violence to neutralize the attackers. But here's the problem. When we are carrying, we are held by the law to a higher standard than when we are unarmed. If you are attacked and your life and limb are in immediate danger, you must do whatever you must do to survive without grave bodily injury. But, do we sacrifice the right to respond with righteous anger to clear wrongs, when we are armed and such response could result in our having to use the deadly power at our disposal? I do not have a clear-cut answer to that, but what I want to leave you with is this. You must think before you act and stay in control of your emotions, for your own and everyone's good. So, be smart, use your head, and stay safe. Our mind is our greatest weapon.

—*Bruce N. Eimer, Ph.D.*

COMBAT
SHOOTING
with Massad Ayoob

Competition As Training

" *very bit of information that may be picked up on the range will prove useful in war. True, it will not always – nor often – be possible to assume the exact, orthodox positions used in competitions and there is the matter of adjusting oneself – mentally and physically – to the stress and strain of battle but, just the same, all those fundamental principles will have an important, even if sub-conscious influence, tending to increase the rifleman's effectiveness."*

--From Herbert W. McBride's introduction to his classic book, A Rifleman Went to War

Earlier in this book, we saw that one thing Wyatt Earp, Charlie Askins, and Jim Cirillo had in common was that they competed in the pistol matches of their time. All seemed to feel that this experience stood them well when they had to "compete" against men who were pointing their guns at them instead of at the same bank of targets as they were.

Early in my career I had the good fortune to know and be mentored by Lt. Frank McGee, the legendary NYPD firearms trainer. Frank was the one who turned the department's firearms training unit into the Firearms and Tactics Unit (FTU). He incorporated practical shooting stances instead of target shooting into the marksmanship side of it. He was the first on NYPD to use role-play training. He emphasized such tactical elements as the use of cover, arraying automobiles, mailboxes, and telephone poles on the ranges of the training facility at Rodman's Neck in the Bronx to get the cops accustomed to putting something between them and the incoming fire that at least some of them would inevitably face.

Frank's unit was responsible for gathering the information for SOP-9. Inaugurated circa 1970, Standard Operating Procedure Number Nine was an in-depth debriefing of every MOS (Member Of the Service) involved in any sort of discharge of a weapon outside the training ranges. The debriefing included such questions as, "Did you use your sights? Did you fire double action or single if you used a revolver? What was your shooting position at each point in the fight? Did you hold the gun with one hand or two?" The responses would be correlated with facts learned from the investigation, such as how many shots were fired vis-à-vis how many hits, at what distance, and similar things.

It occurred to members of the Firearms and Tactics Unit that it would be useful to cross-reference the hit percentage in actual gunfights of each member of the department, with what that member's score was in regular qualification at the main NYPD range at Rodman's Neck and the satellite indoor ranges around the city. Quite apart from the obvious benevolent interest in officer safety – if the more highly skilled shooters were more likely to survive, the city might budget more money to train more officers to that skill level – the FTU also stood to benefit from a positive correlation. If their training in marksmanship skill was saving more lives, they would get much positive reinforcement.

Alas, Lt. McGee told me, there was no correlation to be found. Not the expected positive correlation of high scores equaling high field performance, but no negative correlation either that might have indicated good shooting skills were somehow deleterious to survival-oriented performance. With this in mind, the FTU simply redoubled its emphasis on tactics and mind-set, which unquestionably did improve gunfight outcomes and save officers' lives.

In the years since, other instructors around the country came to the same conclusion. However, while never officially studied by a police department to my knowledge, there is another comparison that results in a different conclusion. Those who shoot in competition seem to have a remarkably high hit potential and survival ratio in actual gunfights.

Historical Precedent

This seems to have been pointed out by soldiers before it was pointed out by cops. In his book *A Rifleman Went to War*, H. W. McBride wrote extensively of his experiences in the trenches and on the battlefields of WWI. He had been a competitive rifle shooter before signing up so he could fight in The Great War. Once on the battlefield he killed soldier after enemy soldier, one bullet at a time, with the unerring marksmanship he had learned on competitive rifle ranges in North America.

After WWII, Lt. Col. John George wrote *Shots Fired In Anger*, subtitled *A Rifleman's View of the War in the Pacific, 1942-1945*. He had begun his adulthood as a skilled competitive rifle shooter. He felt that skill would serve him well in the jungles of the Pacific Theater. It did. His outstanding book shows multiple cases where he used essentially the same techniques, and the same coolness under stress, in combat that he used on shooting ranges. The result was a very significant number of enemy dead, and an American fighting man who'd returned home both victorious and unscathed after extensive mortal combat.

Fast forward to the Vietnam conflict. The most famous rifleman to emerge from it was Carlos Hathcock, memorialized in the biography *Marine Sniper* by Charles Henderson. Hathcock was credited with 93 confirmed kills of enemy personnel, some at extraordinary distances and under extraordinary circumstances. Perhaps the most storied was the incident in which he faced another master sniper. The man was aiming at him as Hathcock put a bullet through the enemy's telescopic sight from front to back, into his eye, and thence into his brain, killing him barely in time to save his own life.

Hathcock had been a member of the U.S. Marine Corps rifle team, the crème de la crème of American military marksmanship, and had won the Wimbledon Cup, which is essentially the United States Championship of long range shooting with high powered rifles, before ever seeing an enemy combatant in his gun sights. It is apparent that the 93 confirmed kills were merely the tip of the iceberg, due to the strict reporting requirements of the USMC Scout Snipers, and that his actual body count was well into three digits. It is clear that the coolness, the focus, and the mastery of his weapon under pressure that he learned on the rifle ranges of Quantico and Camp Perry translated extremely well to the jungles and rice paddies of Southeast Asia.

Over the years, police learned the same lesson when they bothered to look for it. One of the most legendary police gunfighters was Delf "Jelly" Bryce, who first earned his reputation as a street cop in Oklahoma and was subsequently recruited – purely for his gunfighting prowess, it is said – by J. Edgar Hoover in the formative years of the FBI. A master gunfighter, Bryce earned his first badge by winning a pistol match in front of a very impressed chief of police.

In another section of this book, we note that Wyatt Earp, Charles Askins, and Jim Cirillo all shot competition and did very well at it prior to the gunfights that made them famous. Earp did not discuss it much with his biographer, Stuart Lake. However, it's abundantly clear in Askins' writing that he was as proud of his match shooting awards as he was of his victories in gun battles, and the correlation between the two was just as abundantly clear without saying. In his book *Guns, Bullets, and Gunfights*, Cirillo came out of the match-shooting closet and flatly stated that the competitive shooters had the highest hit ratios – and the most dramatic win records – of all the thirty-plus members of the NYPD Stakeout Squad.

Competence develops confidence; confidence, in turn, leaves one cool enough under pressure to exercise competence. Decades of studying and teaching this full time have convinced me that the two are inextricably intertwined. There is no centrifuge into which we can throw those two elements, spin them, and determine that the formula is X% competence and Y% confidence. It suffices to know that they feed off each other and become more than the sum of their parts. If one had to make a diagram of the two factors interrelating, it would probably look like a circle, or perhaps a yin/yang symbol.

Cirillo and Askins were not by any means the only police champions who became gunfight survivors after honing their skill and confidence. Ohio police officer Kerry Hile had won multiple consecutive national championships in PPC, or "police combat shooting," before he was invited to join the SWAT team. He accepted the invitation. He had never been in a shooting before. The night came when the SWAT team was arrayed in plainclothes on stakeout for a particularly dangerous suspect. When cops moved in, the man came up with a gun and opened fire. Multiple other officers shot at the gunman without effect. Hile, some 35 yards away, coolly raised his service handgun and rolled off four fast, smooth shots. The gunman collapsed, killed by four center hits from Hile's gun. The superb marksmanship and coolness under life-threatening stress that Kerry Hile had learned on the ranges in the pressure of top-level championship matches had saved his life and the lives of his brother officers.

It takes a bit of digging beneath the surface to see the difference between a soldier or peace officer who passes a qualification test, and one who shoots in competition, as it relates to preparing either gun-wielder for maximum performance under life-threatening stress. The soldier or Marine would certainly like to win an expert medal to pin on his chest after qualification, but knows that if he doesn't earn the higher honor, merely passing the test at minimum qualification level will suffice to keep his job and career. There is motivation, but not huge motivation.

That military man or policeman also knows that even if he fails to qualify, he'll get another chance. In between the last failure and the next try, there will also be remedial training, perhaps one-on-one coaching, and perhaps even another attempt in the future if the next one fails, too.

The competitive shooter is different. He is acutely aware that he will get no do-over. He knows, in the immortal words of the great International Practical Shooting Confederation champion Tom Campbell, "practice ain't race day." The match is a do-or-die performance on demand experience. He's not there to finish in the middle of the pack, he's there to win, and that raises both the stakes and the blood pressure.

The competitive shooter puts his or her ego and reputation on the line. It becomes intensely personal. Being a denizen of the "middle of the pack" is not going to be good enough. Often, that intense "this is it!" element tricks the lizard that lives in the base of our brain into thinking it's a real fight or flight situation, and the body actually goes into body alarm reaction. Any of us who have shot a lot of matches can tell you we've both seen those manifestations in others and felt them in ourselves.

The heart pounds. The proverbial butterflies in the stomach flutter. We look down and see that our hands, and perhaps even our knees, are trembling. We suddenly experience "dyspnea," or air hunger, as if we're beginning to suffocate. We experience dry mouth. The fingers and lips may tingle. The shooter's face may be seen to go suddenly very pallid.

All of these things are manifestations of body alarm reaction, the highest form of which is the true fight or flight response. The tremors are a direct side effect of epinephrine dump, as the body's endocrine system goes into action to strengthen us for the great effort it instinctively senses may be about to come. Vasoconstriction occurs; blood flow is redirected into the major muscle groups and the internal viscera, again to "fuel the furnace." This means that blood flow is taken away from the extremities. That's why fingers and lips go numb, and why Caucasians under either match pressure or genuine danger are so frequently observed to go deathly pale. Blood flow away from the fingers seems to be the real reason we become clumsy under stress, not the epinephrine-generated tremors. It is what makes crime victims and gunfighters alike feel so terribly clumsy, and why a person in this condition feels as if "they're all thumbs" as they handle what used to be a gun so familiar to them that it felt like a natural extension of their hand.

The air hunger comes from another element of body alarm reaction. Anticipating a need for explosive, sustained physical exertion, the human body begins to pump blood and suck in oxygen at an accelerated rate. However, no muscular exertion is yet "burning off" that surplus of oxygen racing through the bloodstream, and hyperventilation takes place. One of its side effects is tricking us into thinking we need more oxygen, not less, so we start breathing more desperately, compounding the problem. If it goes unchecked, it will cause us to pass out.

We are used to framing these experiences within the context of the circumstances that trigger them. If it happens in ordinary life without a particular "trigger moment," it is generally diagnosed as an anxiety attack. The soldier or cop experiencing it in the course of human conflict comes to call it "pucker factor." The hunter calls it "buck fever," experienced when a trophy male deer is spotted within shooting range. And the competitor calls it "match nerves."

It's all different terminology for the same effect.

There is a definite element of "stress inoculation" in match shooting. It gets you accustomed to trembling hands, shaky knees, and all the rest, with a gun in your hand.

And ... *it makes shooting under pressure the norm, instead of a terrifying "this is it" experience.*

No one is ever going to say that shooting a match is scarier than shooting for your life, least of all this writer. The fact remains that some who have survived gunfights have found it so.

One was Dave Wheeler, who retired from a distinguished career with LAPD that encompassed multiple shootings in the line of duty. Dave was a competitive shooter for most of that same period in his life, and a damn good one. I would always pick his brain when we shot together at a major IPSC match or at the Second Chance shoot "back in the day." Dave told me that, every time he had to shoot a man, he felt a sense of palpable calmness that allowed him to stay steady and get the hit in time to win, and that he often felt more stress in a match than he felt any of the times he was aiming at an armed antagonist and pulling the trigger, with his own survival or that of a citizen on the line. Dave is one of the few men I know who ever actually shot a hostage taker out from behind a hostage. He did it with a single shot from his service revolver, and the shot was so perfect that the gunman and his weapon hand were both limp and dead before his corpse began to fall. The hostage survived unscathed.

Jim Cirillo figures prominently in this book. Jim and I shot on the same squad at the first Bianchi Cup event in 1979 at the Chapman Academy in Columbia, Missouri. Of all the matches I ever shot, Bianchi Cup was unquestionably the most intense pressure cooker. The first one was intended to be "the Wimbledon of handgun shooting," a championship of champions. That first year, you needed to have won at least one state championship or equivalent to even get an invitation. There was a bunch of money on the line – something like $30,000 for first place if I recall correctly, unprecedented at that time – and you knew that one bad shot could theoretically cost you every penny of that if you were hoping to win it. (Startling revelation: every one of us there hoped to win it.)

Cirillo and I had just completed the Barricade Event up on the hill, and were walking down the trail together and over the little bridge on the Chapman Academy range to shoot the Moving Target event. Jim told me, "Jesus Christ, I never felt pressure like this in any of my (expletive deleted) gunfights!"

A bit surprised, I asked him why he thought that was.

"Because there wasn't all this (expletive deleted) time to build up to it! And there weren't all these (expletive deleted) people watching," he replied.

After I left the pro shooting tour I thought I had retired. It turned out to be semi-retirement. During the time I was away from it, I realized competitive shooting had become my personal "pressure laboratory" to gauge and maintain not only my ability to draw, fire, and hit, but my ability to do so under stress.

The beauty of competitive shooting, and the real reason it did far more to prepare soldiers like McBride and Marines like Hathcock and cops like Cirillo to win gunfights, was that in this seemingly sporting environment, handling their guns swiftly and surely under significant pressure had caused that expert handling to become a reflexive norm.

Cops who are known by their opponents to be skilled with guns have found that their repu-

Armed The Essential Guide to Concealed Carry

tation alone can prevent bloodshed. If you study the history of the aforementioned Jelly Bryce, you'll find that his reputation was so imposing that armed, barricaded felons surrounded by police and ready to shoot it out, were known to surrender when they realized that Bryce had arrived on the scene.

My time as a police officer has been entirely in the state of New Hampshire. I was proud to be a friend of Andy Cannon, one of the finest police marksman (and police instructors) the Granite State ever produced. New Hampshire's only statewide newspaper was and is the *Manchester Union Leader*, which continues its policy created by its famed publisher William Loeb, a member of the National Rifle Association's board of directors when he lived, that shooting was a legitimate sport and was therefore to be covered just like baseball or football in sports pages of his statewide newspaper. Therefore, whenever Andy Cannon won the state championship, or a lesser match of note, the story and his picture got in the newspaper.

Andy worked for the NH Department of Fish & Game. The night came when he was staking out a field where he had a tip that jack-lighting poachers were going to show up. They did, and soon Andy was on them, in his patrol vehicle with lights and siren. The poachers jumped in their vehicle, and the chase was on. Andy radioed that he was in a high speed pursuit.

There were four suspects in the vehicle, two in front and two in the back seat. In his headlights, Andy could see that one of the two men in the rear compartment was raising what appeared to be an M1 carbine and trying to bring it to bear on him from the left rear window. Ducking down behind the dashboard for cover until he could barely see the road and the car in front of him, Andy broadcast on the radio that an M1 was in play and he was about to come under fire.

Suddenly, he saw a violent flurry of movement in the back seat of the fugitive vehicle. The carbine went sailing out the window, and seconds later, the car pulled over and parked, and three of the men inside raised their hands and sat meekly still. Cannon couldn't see the fourth. Opening his door and angling his engine block for cover, Andy parked behind them with his roof lights still flashing, covered them with the same Smith & Wesson .357 Magnum Model 19 he used in competition, and ordered them over the cruiser's loudspeaker to remain still and not move. Soon, assisting units arrived, and the felony stop was completed without further incident.

The resultant tally was three meekly-surrendering game law violators, and one groggy and bloody suspect dragged semi-conscious from the left rear seat. He was the erstwhile gun-wielder, and turned out to be the brother of the man sitting to his right. The weapon that was thrown from the vehicle turned out to be not an M1 carbine, but a .30-caliber selective fire M2, fully loaded with a 30-round "banana clip" and its selector switch set on full automatic. The gun had been illegally brought back to the U.S. from the Korean War by the father of the two outlaw brothers.

Police soon learned what had happened. The violators were well aware that there was one particular conservation officer who patrolled that part of Moultonboro, New Hampshire…and they read the newspapers like everyone else. When the one brother raised the machine gun to fire at the pursuing officer, the other brother ripped it away from him and beat him unconscious, screaming at him at the top of his lungs as he did so. What the desperate brother was yelling was, "You God-damned fool, that's *Andy Cannon* in that police car! You shoot at him, he'll kill us all!"

Getting the Most "Training" From Matches

Shooting bulls-eye pistol – standing in a rigid duelist's position, carefully thumb-cocking his revolver in the centerfire event, and firing no faster than five shots in ten seconds – Col. Charles Askins, Jr. developed skills and confidence that saved his life and the lives of many other good people he was responsible for protecting. That tells us that any trigger time under pressure can be valuable in the training context.

Obviously, Askins didn't shoot that way when the chips were down. We recall that he was smart enough to move behind cover, firing as he went, in the incident where he was alone against three gunmen – one a proven cop-killer – and shot them all, decisively winning the battle.

That said, though, the more the match experience replicates good tactics – use of cover, tactical movement, etc. – the more valuable and "job-related" it's obviously going to be. With that in mind, it makes sense, if you only have limited time to devote to competition shooting as part of your training regimen, to give priority to the matches that will inculcate the most relevant possible skill sets.

For that, it's hard to beat IDPA, the International Defensive Pistol Association. Let me tell you about the most recent IDPA National Championship in which I competed before writing this book.

Lessons From An IDPA National Championship1

We would probably all agree that a shooting match is not a gunfight.

However, *a gunfight is a shooting match!*

In either case, two people are testing their skill at hitting man-size targets that might be running, bobbing or weaving, or partially obscured behind hard cover. Each of those two people might themselves be moving, ducking, pushing someone out of the way, or attempting to keep awkwardly-positioned cover between themselves and incoming fire.

Does it not stand to reason that the person most experienced in doing those things, and in combining those skills while under some degree of pressure, might have some advantage over the other when the stakes on the table are their own lives instead of trophies and plaques?

An Example in Point

In late September of 2010, a few hundred of us convened at the fabulous U.S. Shooting Academy range complex in Tulsa, Oklahoma, to compete in the fourteenth annual National Championships of the International Defensive Pistol Association (IDPA). Founded by IPSC (International Practical Shooting Confederation)/USPSA (United States Practical Shooting Association) veteran competitors at a time when those other games seemed to be more run and gun athletic marksmanship than anything else, IDPA's purpose was to return to the simulated gunfighting envisioned by IPSC founder Jeff Cooper.

Most stages, or shooting scenarios, require the gun to be drawn from concealment. All require the gun to be carried in a concealable, practical holster. All demand a "street-type gun" with no recoil compensator, and no optical sights. Ammunition must meet a power level of roughly 158 grain .38 Special +P revolver ammo for Stock Service Revolver, Enhanced Service Pistol, and

Stock Service Pistol divisions, and approximately that of a 185 grain jacketed hollow point .45 ACP round out of a short barrel pistol in the Enhanced Service Revolver or Custom Defense Pistol divisions. The complete rule book can be downloaded at no charge from the organization's website, www.idpa.com. *(Author's note: in early 2011, power floor in Stock Service Revolver was lowered to equal standard velocity 158 grain .38 Special ammunition.)*

The 2010 Nationals consisted of seventeen challenging stages. A few were pure tests of shooting skill. Some happened indoors in "shoot-house" format: moving in dim light, you had to grab a gun from a table and engage multiple targets at close range, or negotiate through a "building search" and shoot the bad guys without shooting the good guys.

Any match, any contest, is a skill test. The question is, are the skills being tested relevant to real-world needs? Take a look at some of the challenges created by the team led by Match Director Curt Nichols, himself a four-time National Champion IDPA shooter and an experienced street cop, and see for yourself.

"Standards" That Go Beyond Standard

Stage 3, called "National Standards," was the longest course of the event. It encompassed 42 shots at distances from six to twenty-nine yards. There was a lot of potential for missed shots, so it was a real "deal-breaker" for those more into speed than accuracy. Scoring was "Limited Vickers." In most IDPA stages, "Vickers Count" is your elapsed time, with half a second added for each point down from a perfect possible score, but you can fire extra shots to make up for bad ones. In Limited Vickers, you can fire only a specified number of shots, no make-up allowed.

This stage included "weak hand only" and "strong hand only" firing. It included speed reloads and tactical reloads, head shots, and firing from either side of a vertical barricade at the longest distance.

Lessons: Because we all like to look good and perform well, we generally shoot two-handed when we're practicing. Trouble is, real-world problems often require one-hand-only manipulation of the defensive sidearm. At longer ranges, supporting the firing grasp against the solid barricade gives you better hits. Many have confused "search techniques," where you stay well back away from the wall because someone might be hiding in that undiscovered territory to grab your gun, with pure cover techniques that maximize the protection of the barrier you're hiding behind, while simultaneously letting you deliver more accurate fire to extinguish the threat. It was my experience and observation that bracing on the barricade at long range was the most successful strategy.

The Standards weren't the only place where one-handed shooting proved effective, either, which leads us to...

"Weak Hand" Only

The Nationals put significant emphasis on firing with the non-dominant hand only in 2010. In Stage 16, titled "Wrong Number," course designer Nichols at one point put you into a situation where you had to dial the phone for 9-1-1 with your dominant hand, holding your gun in your non-dominant hand. At that point, a target sprang up that you had to shoot multiple times.

Those who regularly practiced with their "weak hand" were grateful for that experience in this dimly-lit scenario.

(Another lesson emerged from this stage: one was required to speak into the phone at the moment the target was attacking. Many who hadn't planned for this real-world need did not have time to transition from talking to shooting and still get all their hits.)

In Stage 1, "A Day At the Range," designed by former national champ Jerry Biggs, the shooter faces a scenario that in 2010 took the life of a gun club member in Pennsylvania: the bad guys attack a lone shooter on the range to steal his gun. At one point in the scenario, the shooter's gun arm is presumed to be wounded, and he or she has to "finish the fight" weak hand only.

Relevant? Oh, yes. Tactical instructors call it "target focus" and expert on eyewitnesses Dr. Elizabeth Loftus calls it "weapon focus," but whatever you call it the fact is when someone is up against an armed person, they tend to focus on the weapon the other person is holding. "Where the head goes, the body follows" is a truth of physiology and armed combat alike, and since where the head is looking is where the shots go, people on either side of the fight tend to shoot one another in the gun hand or gun arm with a disproportionately high frequency. I recall a New York City officer who dropped his gun after being hit in the upper arm/shoulder area by his antagonist. He picked up the dropped gun and, using his weak hand only, shot and killed his assailant.

Lesson: In a gunfight, the gunfire goes in both directions. We all have to be prepared to take a hit and keep fighting. The single most likely place we're going to be hit may well be somewhere in the gun arm. It is imperative to a "full survival skill set" to be able to shoot fast and effectively "weak hand only." Kudos to IDPA for making that "part of the program."

Shooting From Vehicles

In recent decades, "carjacking" became an American crime phenomenon. More recently, so did "road rage." Each has resulted in a significant number of situations where good people who could shoot back saved their lives from modern "rustlers" who were prepared to murder them to steal their "ride."

This reality was well reflected in the 2010 IDPA Nationals. There were stages where we had to shoot from the driver's seat out the driver's window. There were stages where we had to shoot from the driver's seat to our right, out through the passenger's window. There were stages where we had to get out of the car to not only take maximum cover, but to get an angle of fire where we could aim and shoot the opposing "target" at all.

In 2010, there was a gunfight in middle America where a bunch of punks who had already become cop-killers were cornered in a parking lot. They were taken down by a courageous conservation officer who had responded to this high-priority scene and rammed the suspects' vehicle from behind with his own heavy-duty vehicle. Taking fire from the suspects' van, he unlimbered his own patrol rifle and simply fired through (his own) windshield, neutralizing the threat. This hero cop used successful out-of-the-box thinking that all of us can emulate if we're ever fighting car-to-car with multiple, heavily armed, homicidal criminals, as he was.

In one scenario at the Nationals, Stage 15 (another one designed by the redoubtable Curt Nichols), each of us was put in a situation where we were sitting center in the back seat of a full-size sedan and suddenly had to draw our guns and engage threats to the outside. This was a meaningful experience to me, since I had researched and written about the situation that occurred at the Little Bohemia shootout in the 1930s with the Dillinger gang. A coupe with three lawmen all jammed together in the front seat pulled up to question a suspicious person. Seated in the middle was a local constable who had a Smith & Wesson .38 Special in a shoulder holster, and should have been the one person in the car most capable of drawing from a seated position and neutralizing an attacker outside the vehicle.

The man they had stopped to talk with turned out to be perhaps the most psychopathic killer of the whole Dillinger Gang, known as Baby Face Nelson. When Nelson came up with a machine pistol and opened fire, the man in the middle seat was too cramped by the lawmen on either side of him to get to his gun. Everyone in the car got shot up, and the agent sitting to one side of the constable was killed. We can learn from this.

Lessons: If you're shooting out the left side driver's window and the deadly threat moves in front of the car, you'll have to lean out the window to keep line of sight and get a stopping hit. Put the car in Park, brace your right foot on the floorboard, and you'll be able to lean your head, shoulders, and upper body far enough out the open window to keep the threat in line of sight and put some fight-stopping bullets in it. Bracing the inside of your left arm on the outside of the door can help you pull your upper body outward, to give you a good, continuing track of fire on such a target.

The vehicle might be one-passenger style, and that changes the dynamics. In Stage 13, "Motorcycle Mania," former National Champ Jerry Biggs' course design put us astride a recreational vehicle with a heavy pack on our back. Feet had to stay on the pedals as we shot an array of targets nearly 180 degrees apart.

Lesson: The ability to flow between a bent-arms Weaver and a straight arms Isosceles position from the waist up when pivoting from weak side to strong side was advantageous here. A one-punch fighter won't last long in the ring, and a one-stance shooter is handicapped when he can't step to face his target.

You might even be under the vehicle when trouble starts. Nichols' Stage 11 had you begin supine on a rolling mechanic's creeper under a jacked-up Jeep. (It was titled "Jeepers Creepers" – cute!) Remember that a man on his back under an obstacle is vulnerable to attack by standing men he'll have trouble seeing coming.

Lesson: Sometimes you have to get up before you can fight. Grabbing the undercarriage of the Jeep, lifting your feet, and pulling the whole rig with you on it quickly out from under the vehicle turned out to be the smart plan here. Whenever we're in a disadvantaged position, we need to have a plan for getting out of there quickly.

If you need to get to one side or the other of the car when you're on the wrong side or in the middle, *lean forward and then pivot your upper body "gun turret" toward the threat!* This can give you more range of movement and allow you to safely extend your handgun past a passenger on either side of you.

Use your feet, extending them sideways. This will allow you to push much more toward the window on either side, and give you far more range of movement with which to engage the threat. If the constable at Little Bohemia had been taught to lean forward and do this, he might have been able to shoot Baby Face Nelson before Nelson could shoot him and his brother officers. The foot pushed against the floorboard of the car extends both your body and your weight forward, toward the threat to give you more range of movement and toward the recoil of your own gun, to give you faster recovery time between shots.

We Ain't Just Woofin' Here

Cops and armed citizens alike are often required to shoot vicious dogs to keep themselves or other good people from being horribly bitten and mauled. There may also be times when the shooter is trying to keep his own dog under control with one hand, and having to deliver rescuing gunfire with the other hand.

Both of these scenarios were played out for the hundreds of contestants at the 2010 IDPA Nationals.

In Stage 14, "Who Let the Dogs Out," the shooter begins standing in the bed of a pickup truck , both feet on the lowered tailgate, and faces a dozen "dog targets," representing a whole pack of feral canines. The shooter is required to get one shot into each without hitting the innocent human targets mixed in, one of which is moving.

Lesson: Even a parked pickup is not the most stable firing platform. The vehicle's suspension means springs, and springs mean bounce. The winning strategy was to take a deep backstep to place your standing body over the rear axle, where bounce was least. In a real-life attack of this kind, it would also put the body far enough back to be better placed against a mad dog or wolf that was fast and strong enough to jump up onto a truck bed.

The flip side of this situation was perhaps the most ingenious of the match. In Stage 5, "Can I Bite Em? Can I Bite Em Now?" the shooter began holding the leash of his own agitated dog, represented by a cantilevered weight on the other end of the leash. The mission was to maintain control of the "dog" while shooting the bad guy targets. That shooting is not easy when something is pulling on your support hand!

As I fired it, I was reminded of a friend of mine who worked K9 for a southern Sheriff's Department, who had to kill an armed fugitive one-handed with his SIG .45 while holding his lunging dog's lead in his other hand. Yes, this sort of situation does happen.

Lesson: The winning strategy proved to be simply holding the leash in one dedicated hand, and firing the pistol with a dedicated strong-hand only grasp. I discovered that too late, midway through the stage. Learn from those of us who did it poorly, and have a plan for this situation beforehand. That's one of the things IDPA competition is all about.

Bottom Line

A gunfight simulation match that's based on things that have been known to actually happen gives the participant authentically replicated experience. Those lessons stick. A friend of mine in the Carolinas is a street cop and an avid IDPA competitor. He feels that the competition did more

213

than his training to make use of cover second nature to him. Some months ago on a routine call he was confronted by a man who raised a Mossberg 12-gauge at him. He reflexively dove to the side, evading a shotgun blast that otherwise would have killed him, and firing from cover with his Glock 21, he shot and killed his attacker. This lawman credits IDPA in part with saving his life.

Like I said … the shooting match isn't a gunfight, but the gunfight is a shooting match. The more experience you've deposited in your "long term muscle memory bank," the better your chances of successful outcome in either scenario.

IPSC/USPSA

In the 1950s, Col. Jeff Cooper created a sport of simulated gunfighting that drew in some of the defining champions and great teachers of the era that followed, men like Ray Chapman and Ken Hackathorn. In the mid-1970s, a coterie of those who believed in the concept came from all over the world to meet at Ray's school, Chapman Academy, in Columbia, Missouri. Known as the Columbia Conference, that conclave marked the birth of IPSC, the International Practical Shooting Confederation. In time, a specific governing body for the sport in the U.S. would evolve, the United States Practical Shooting Association (USPSA).

From golf to automobile racing, it is human nature to evolve equipment which will give the competitor an edge in winning the game. This equipment will not always be practical for the original use from which the sport built around it evolved. Just as an Indy race car bears little relation to a vehicle for everyday transportation, some of the "race guns" that evolved to win IPSC were too unwieldy and impractical for even a police officer's uniform holster, let alone an armed citizen's concealed carry rig.

Disappointed by this evolution, some disaffected leaders of the sport broke away and created new organizations, hoping to return to Cooper's original concept of simulated gunfighting with practical combat handguns. One such evolution, in 1996, was IDPA. Another, slightly earlier, was the creation of the Single Stack Classic, led by pistolsmith Dick Heinie. For the Single Stack, rules would be those of IPSC, but the holster had to be concealable and not worn ahead of the hip, and the same was true of magazine pouches. (Guns and ammo would not have to be actually concealed in every stage, however.) The match would be devoted to 1911 pistols of any make, but with only single-stack magazines. Moreover, there would be no recoil compensators or optical sights, the bulky add-ons that had led to "space guns" dominating the sport in the first place.

The result was one of the most popular matches in the country. USPSA's management was seeing the handwriting on the wall. Not only did they add categories of competition for stock guns, ranging from Limited Ten (no comps or optics, no more than ten rounds in the magazine) and Production, but circa 2006 USPSA adopted the Single Stack Classic into its repertoire of matches, making it the USPSA Single Stack National Championship.

Come back with me for a little bit, and take a look at the shakedown cruise of the Single Stack.

Single Stack Classic2

In the gray morning drizzle of Thursday, May 4, 1995, Ken Cramberg stood with his back to three IPSC targets. At the signal he spun toward them, clearing his Colt National Match .45

auto from under the mandatory jacket, and we watched as he punched a .452-inch diameter hole through the A-zone of the leftmost of three targets in an *El Presidente* array 10 yards distant.

The rest of Ken's run was smoothly executed, but we who watched him knew we'd seen an historic moment. Cranberg had just fired the first shot of the first 1911 Single Stack Classic in Milan, Illinois.

The brainchild of pistolsmith and long-time IPSC competitor Dick Heinie, the Classic was ramrodded by Bob Houzenga, a career cop and perennially high-ranked competitor in the sport.

Springfield Armory was the lead sponsor, joined by Colt. Sponsoring stages were Caspian Arms, Competition Electronics, Ed Brown Products, Hellweg, JP Enterprises, K.C. Hilites, Rack Systems, and Smith & Alexander.

A growing number of action handgunners are learning that, sometimes, the timely thing is to go back in time. In this case, the concept was a return to "original IPSC," the first five or six years or so before the equipment race began in earnest. The rules were simple. You could use:

• A 1911 pattern pistol, with single stack magazines of the length standardized by the gun factory,

  • A barrel no longer than five inches,

  • No recoil compensator,

  • No optical sights, and

  • The holster must be behind the edge of the hip (International Concealed Carry Rule).

"Russell Cluver, the Illinois IPSC Section Coordinator, and I," says Heinie, "had been listening to new shooters complain about high capacity guns, even in current Limited Class, which leaves the standard 1911 at a great disadvantage in most courses.

"We knew the same guys were going to win, but it puts people on a more level playing field. People would enjoy it more this way, we thought. And I think the match proved us right."

Four 10mms and at least one .40 S&W and one .38 Super were used; all the rest were .45 autos, according to Heinie, who shot a 10mm along with Walt Rauch, Arnt Mhyre, and Ray Hirst.

Rob Leatham used a .40 S&W (with ammunition) loaded to 10mm length by seating the bullets out farther, allowing the use of 10mm magazines, which some believe function better in a 1911 than the stubby .40 S&W loaded to standard OAL (over-all length). Presumably, .40 S&W brass for practice is much more plentiful than 10mm, making this expedient worth the effort.

Most of the pistols were full Government Model length with five-inch barrels. However, more than a few 4¼-inch Commanders were in the field, and at least one determined old boy on my squad shot his carry gun, a neat little street-tuned Colt Officers, and shot it very well indeed.

Compliance Factor

There were no trick sights. No sneaky weasel tricks. There were more than a few pistols with trigger jobs that brought them down to pull weights that were suited better to meets than streets, but was it not Jeff Cooper himself who said of duty 1911 triggers, "Three pounds, crisp, is the word"?

Holsters were another matter. It was the only thing anyone whined about. The rule had been that the rig must ride no farther forward than the edge of the hip, and when people started asking, "Where's that?" it was clarified to read no farther forward than the seam on one's pants.

There was still whining, but the moaners were few in number. Houzenga and Heinie have been warned that next year, at least one shooter may show up wearing pants with seams located at the front trouser leg crease.

Holster choice seemed to break down into thirds. One well-represented contingent wore their street leather – inside-the-waistband holsters and the Milt Sparks Yaqui Slide or equivalent. A smaller number went with the speed rigs of the past – the Hackathorn Special that Sparks popularized, or Bianchi's Chapman Hi-Ride.

The third category wore 1995-class match gear – Riley Gilmore's slick plastic puppy designed for raceguns, and the same Safariland and Ernie Hill stuff you'd see in IPSC Limited.

The Team Safariland contingent had an experimental new race holster that they dutifully wore in the mandated position, behind the ileac crest of the pelvis.

The trick holsters were perhaps the one discordant note in the whole "back to basics theme" of the 1911 Single Stack Classic. Houzenga and Heinie and company are wondering what to do about it for 1996.

My own suggestion would be to stay with the "classic" format and require an inside-the-waistband holster. Let's see the gamesmen trick that one out.

Helluva Course

Houzenga has shot well in many IPSC Nationals, and routinely wins the Chapman Academy's annual Missouri Police Practical Pistol State Championships, the only such match in the country to my knowledge that is fired with the officer's departmental duty gun and leather, with each event replicating known gunfights instead of merely a "stage of fire."

He knows how to build challenging scenarios, and in the Single Stack Classic, I think he outdid himself. It was one of the most challenging events I've shot in more than 40 national and international matches I've entered.

Consider the second stage, what used to be called "schoolhouse exercises" in the early days of IPSC, titled here "Double Duty Standards III." Thirty-six rounds were fired in a total of 33 seconds, which wouldn't have been bad at all except for the breakdown.

Try six rounds in six seconds, from the leather, standing…at 50 yards. The single toughest stage of a PPC course, by contrast, is six shots under the same circumstances in 12 seconds at 25 yards; at the Classic, we had half the time at twice the distance.

Or, from 15 yards, five seconds to draw, hit each of three targets twice, including the transfer to weak-hand-only which does all the shooting. Or, from the same distance in the same five second space, draw and fire one on each, reload, and one more on each of the three IPSC Brussels targets.

I've shot the Bianchi Cup 10 times, and let me tell you, this one made the Practical Event at the Cup seem like NRA slow fire. And remember – it's done with a five-inch Government Model.

"Possible" on this was 180 points. Smart money was that it wouldn't be "cleaned," and anyone who scored over 170 points would win the stage. As I was coming off the line, someone yelled, "Mas, did you break 170?"

"Only in power factor," I replied.

Geezer Factor

You'd think guys who'd been shooting this sort of stage when Robbie Leatham was too young to chase cheerleaders – me and Ken Hackathorn, for instance – might've had an edge. Naaah.

Ken and I tied for 15th place on this one. Ted Bonnet won it – with a 154 out of 180 possible. I have to say it was the toughest such practical pistol stage I've shot in my life, and that ain't the age talking, kids, it's the mileage. The "best of the best," Bonnet had scored only 85.56 percent of "possible."

Consider also the fiendish last stage, "Snooze and You Lose." It looked simple enough: shoot a steel target that triggered a gravity turner when it fell, and then shoot the turning target; do a mandatory reload; and do it again on the second set.

The semi-surprise match bulletin didn't say how long we'd have to engage the turner, but since six hits were called for, we assumed it would be at least a two-second exposure.

Wrong, 1911-breath. We all got a "walk-through" in which the exposure time of the gravity turners was demonstrated. I figured I'd just do the mental count thing – "one thousand and one" equals about one second for me – so I'd know how to pace myself.

With only a slight hint of a Cheshire cat grin under his blond mustache, Bob Houzenga tipped over the first Pepper Popper to trigger the first turner. The Brussels spun. "One-thou-san…"

The target was gone.

He tripped the next. "One thou…"

Gone.

It was the first time I can recall that my jaw dropped while observing the walk through of a match.

Smokin' Run

I thought at first that I'd done okay. The sweet-trigger stainless Colt Government, tuned with Dick Heinie's Ultimate Defense Package, hammered four Black Hills 230 grain hardballs into the first turner, which I estimated to have been exposed barely more than half a second, and three into the next, which couldn't have exceeded half a second total exposure.

I felt pretty good about that – until Robbie Leatham smoked the thing in less than 6½ seconds, with six hits on each of the gravity turners, and losing only two points in hit value.

There were a total of 10 stages in the Single Stack Classic. An *El Presidente* was done true to the old rules, with the three targets the full distance apart – and from concealment. This may be the quintessential "IPSC Course of Old," along with the Cooper Assault Course.

Arnt Myhre edged Leatham on this one with 58 points out of 60 possible, using 6.78 seconds to react, turn, draw from concealment, shoot each of the three targets twice, reload, and do it again.

In third place was Merle Edington, whom I consider to be the man who established the U.S. Army as a force to be reckoned with in practical shooting, with 59 points scored in 7.42 seconds. Colt provided their excellent sportsman's jackets for the mandatory concealment in this stage, to "keep everyone equal." (Kept us warm and dry, too.)

Passenger 45

In "Passenger 45," you started seated and reading a magazine when the signal came to pivot out of your seat, take mandatory cover, and engage four "terrorists" a considerable distance behind you in a laboriously constructed airliner simulation.

A planeload of hostage targets ducked (partially) after you dropped the first one. Leatham captured this one with a brilliant 4.48 second run.

"Courtroom Defense II" was a crowd scenario in which your pistol and the mag(s) you'd need for the mandatory reload were in a closed attaché case on a desk in front of you. Arnt Myhre romped this one in 6.99 seconds, taking eight targets in an environment rich in "no-shoot" zones, and nailing six shoot targets at least twice.

"Don't Stop 'Til They Drop" put the shooter against six big poppers, six little ones, and a stop plate. No tactics, just shoot fast-straight-hard. Leatham won it in just over 7.5 seconds.

Tactical Thinking

"Embassy Incident" required the most tactical thinking as you moved between cover points, and, in the most crucial moment, faced a "truck that had you in the headlights." You had to shoot out the headlights (Bianchi plates) which set the opposing targets in motion for you to engage. Bonnet won this one too, edging out Leatham and Edington.

"Tri-Plex" was very well designed, forcing the shooter to engage from multiple positions at multiple angles behind all heights of cover. Jack Barnes, an ace in Open IPSC but unclassified in Limited, blew the big kids away, capturing this stage a third of a point ahead of Leatham.

"Wall of Shame" messed with your head. As you moved down a catwalk, you didn't just have to take the shoot targets out from behind the no-shoots, you had to shoot through wooden lath laid like bars across the shooting ports.

You knew consciously you could just shoot through them since they were wood, but something told you to move 'til you had a clear shot between them – and the clock was running the whole time. Bonnet won this event, followed closely by Merle Edington.

Officer Down

"Officer Down" was my personal favorite, because it demanded multiple skills and was true to the tournament's concept of, "It's the shooter, not the gun."

The scenario was the rescue of a wounded cop. You had to move through three positions, taking down a total of 10 targets. By the time you reached end game, you had to secure your own 1911, pick up a Mil-Spec Springfield Armory .45 on the ground by the uniformed dummy of the officer, reload it from slide lock with a magazine of hardball that you snatched from the pouch on the officer's duty belt, and take down the last four Pepper poppers. Leatham took this one like Grant took Richmond, almost five percent ahead of second place Arnt Myhre.

Helluva Match

Only the experienced competition shooter knows the difference between "Helluva Course" and "Helluva Match." The course is the challenge, the "shooting problem" itself. The match is the totality of hospitality, fairness, sportsmanship and camaraderie that makes or breaks the entire experience.

I shot on the first day with the hard-working, uncomplaining legion of Range Officers who made it work the rest of the time. We had the only bad weather. For the registered shooters, the gun gods smiled and decreed perfect climate.

There were no complaints, no protests, no beefs. At the end of the first day of scheduled shooting, things were running ahead of time-table, and by the time it was over – with the awards ceremony completed at the time it had been slated to start – Houzenga's splendid crew made the thing operate like the movement of a Patek Phillipe wristwatch.

That may be a poor analogy. Unlike that Rolls Royce of Swiss watches, the 1911 Single Stack Classic actually ran faster than it was supposed to, leaving 88 supremely satisfied competitors.

Rich Prize Table
You heard about this match, and you didn't come? "Oh, ye of little faith…"

Eighty-eight shooters vied in what first the sponsors and now the contestants feel was not over-confidently titled the first annual Single Stack Classic. None went home empty-handed.

No fewer than eight superbly customized Springfield Armory, Colt, Caspian and Baer 1911 pistols were awarded to the winners. Dick Heinie, a heavy hitter in the Pistolsmiths Guild, had called in a whole lot of chips to make this happen.

The winners, and the prizes, were:
• Match Winner: Rob Leatham (Larry Vickers custom pistol)
• 1st Grand Master: Arnt Myhre (Richard Heinie custom pistol)
• 1st Master: Doug Boykin (Jim Garthwaite custom pistol)
• 1st "A": Marvin Fair, Jr. (Bill Wilson custom pistol)
• 1st "B": John Gangl (Les Baer custom pistol)
• 1st "C": Mark Collazos (Dave Stagg custom pistol)
• 1st "D": Larry Pearson (Kim Ahrends custom pistol)
• 1st Unclassified: Jack Barnes (Mark Krebs custom pistol)

This game isn't winner take all. Note that one $2,000+ prize gun was taken by a score that was only 42.15 percent of Leatham's winning tally. Note that Merle Edington's powerful third place overall finish didn't win him a custom gun at all. Big dogs run with big dogs here, a fact not lost on Heinie and Houzenga who realize that little guys are the backbone of the sport.

What It All Means
We all wondered how we'd do if the playing field was leveled and we all had the same type of gun. The 1911 Single Stack Classic showed us two things about that, two things we had long suspected would be true.

First, the same people would win. Second, those of us who shot against them would feel a whole lot better about it nonetheless.

One of the great things about participating in events like the Bianchi Cup, Second Chance, the IPSC Nationals and, now, the 1911 Single Stack Classic, is the great people you meet. None of today's big name shooters have the egos you'd expect of a superstar. Ours is the most egalitarian of sports.

In a society that enjoys its sports vicariously on TV, we handgunners can shoot in the very same match as superstars like Leatham, Edington, Bonnet, et al. Not in a "pro-am" thing, not in a "we'll let you tag along if you give us money" thing, but in an "if you beat Leatham you're the champion and we'll damn well give you the chance to do it" thing.

This, in the last analysis, may be what so terrifies lightweight yuppie elitists when they look at shooters, their values, and the so-called "Gun Culture."

It's a place to learn things about yourself. I borrowed Dick Heinie's own Ultimate Defense Package Colt .45. This $2200 pistol (that you have to wait five years to have built on your own base gun) worked splendidly with the flawlessly functioning, match-grade Black Hills 230 gr. .45 hardball I fired through it.

Other "Carry Gun" Events

Heinie and company were a bit ahead of IDPA chronologically, but neither group was the first to work to bring "combat shooting" sports (which soon came to be called "practical shooting" instead) away from specialized guns that were suited for winning matches and not much else, and back to the sort of firearms people actually carried.

In the mid-1970s, Richard Davis created the sport of bowling pin shooting: "plinking for grownups," if you will, only instead of knocking tin cans off the back fence with a .22, you were blasting heavy tenpins three feet back off a big, rugged table, and whoever "cleared the table fastest" won. The whole "space gun" thing with auto pistols had started there, with master gunsmith (and former WWII sniper and national bulls-eye pistol champion) Jim Clark, Senior, creating the first 1911 "pin gun" for John Shaw of Tennessee. Richard was the founder of Second Chance Body Armor, and the inventor of the soft, concealable "bullet-proof vest." Ironically, the man who "bullet-proofed America's police" was never a cop himself: Rich was an armed citizen whose inspiration to create his brainchild was a shootout he won against a trio of armed robbers, in which he was wounded twice himself. What he wanted to promote was an event that tested skill with the real-world handguns that armed citizens and cops carried daily.

Accordingly, he soon divided his prize-rich annual Second Chance Match into a "space gun" division where recoil compensators and red-dot electronic sights were allowed, and a "stock gun" division in which they weren't. Like competed against like.

The National Rifle Association had long since included a side event for off duty guns with short barrels in their PPC events for police. From the beginning, IDPA provided for a BUG category. BUG stood for Back-Up Guns, the sort of short-barrel pistols and revolvers that a serious user might carry as a second gun, and that many in the interests of concealment would carry as their primary weapon in the real world.

A core tenet of "combat shooting" is that the more time one has shooting under pressure *with the gun one actually carries*, the better one will be with it. A streetwise ex-cop and current police trainer named Lance Biddle understood that better than most. He also understood that a whole lot of the armed citizens he trains now, and the cops he trained then and now, carried little five-shot revolvers or subcompact semiautomatic pistols on their own time. Yet, he noticed, they'd carry big ol' service pistols to shoot concealed carry matches.

Lance decided to do something about that. Here's the competition he created to test good people's skill with those little guns they wore every day to protect themselves and others.

Lessons From The Backup Gun Championships3

How do the various small handguns fare against each other in realistic combat competition? An ex-cop/current police trainer decided to find out, and a unique and instructive shooting match was born.

If you've competed in the National Championships of IDPA you've probably met Lance Biddle. He would have been running one of the stages you shot. As IDPA's Florida State Director, Biddle has been an ambassador for this reality-based handgun sport. As a match director and safety officer alike, he's a stern taskmaster, but a fair one when he arbitrates the rules. (Whoever said "It's easier to ask forgiveness than permission" has never shot a match under the watchful eye of Lance Biddle.)

That attitude comes from 22½ years as a street cop in a busy municipality adjacent to Columbus, Ohio. When Biddle designs a CoF (Course of Fire), he builds in street reality. A while back, cognizant of the fact that in his Florida stomping grounds even off-duty cops often carry small "pocket guns" instead of the full-size competition-grade handguns that often show up in regular IDPA matches, he decided to create an unofficial state championship for the truly small handguns that IDPA calls BUGs, or Back-Up Guns. He was inspired by Mack Rudisill, an IDPA regular who always competes with his daily carry J-frame snub and Speed Strips. Because you'll find a little bit of a smart-ass in anybody who's done police work as long as Lance and has psychologically survived, he jokingly called it the National Championships, and then the World Championships, of the BUG. When another smart-ass with a badge suggested he extend it to the rest of the known galaxy, Lance planted his tongue firmly in his cheek and titled it the BUG Championship of the Universe.

I heard about his second such match, and hit it in 2010 at The Gun Shop in Leesburg, Florida. Owner Gordon Schorer's wonderfully eclectic gun shop encompasses a state of the art indoor range where he and Biddle host regular IDPA matches, bowling pin shoots, and of course, the now-annual BUG event. Naturally, Pocket Pistols 2011 was there for this year's event, as well.